THE SOUND
OF THEATRE

A History

by
DAVID COLLISON

First published in Great Britain in 2008 by

PLASA Limited
Redoubt House
1 Edward Road
Eastbourne BN23 8AS

Email: books@plasa.org
www.plasa.org

ISBN 978-0-9557035-1-5

**This book is dedicated to Jack Mann,
one of the great pioneers of Sound Design.**

With special thanks to my wife, Alison, who was responsible
for much of the historical research for this book and
a great deal of painstaking editing.

With gratitude to Antony Horder who worked alongside me
during the early years when we were trying to convince
people that Sound Design was a good thing.

CHAPTERS

This board, you may say, is a tree, this muslin is a wall and that
spotlight the tropical sunlight – and the public will imagine it.
But a dog's bark must sound like a bark, and a train like a train!
THROCKMORTON'S 'CATALOG OF THE THEATRE' – NEW YORK 1937

INTRODUCTION

This book is an attempt to tell a history of the development of sound in the theatre from the days when sound effects had to be created by mechanical means, right up to the invention of digital audio technology. I have deliberately not called it The History of Theatre Sound because it is impossible to include all the contributions made by so many people in so many different countries during the whole of human history.

Live and mechanical effects have been employed in the theatre for many centuries. From the Ancient Greek theatre where gods created storms and hurled thunderbolts on a regular basis, through the era of the mediaeval mystery plays where all the sounds and fury of hell were conjured up, to the legendary theatrical spectacles of the 18th and 19th centuries, sound has always played a crucial part. Even during the 1950s and 1960s, every decent theatre prop room in Europe and America still contained thunder sheets, glass crashes, bird whistles, clock chimes, door slams, door bells and telephone bells. These would often be used for the occasional effect, partly to avoid the expense of hiring disc playing equipment and loudspeakers, and partly because many of these noises sounded more convincing than recordings played on the standard of equipment available at the time. To my mind, many of them still do!

Although references are made in the early chapters of the book to some of the major innovations from around the world, when we come to the development of amplified sound in the theatre, I have concentrated mainly on the United States and Great Britain and much of the story necessarily revolves around London and New York. On the mainland of Great Britain, 90% of the population lives well within 400 miles of the capital. This is part of the reason why London has always been the centre of influence in the British theatre and boasts the largest concentration of theatres in the world. There are more than forty major commercial theatres within central London, plus numerous others within Greater London. In addition, there are countless arts centres and fringe theatres which, in New York, would be called "Off-Broadway". Even though the United States is the size of some twenty Great Britains, one city, New York, has been the hub of American theatre sound since the 1930s. This was when Broadway took advantage of the explosion of audio technology in the Los Angeles area with the development of the 'talkies'.

The auditory experience had been an important part of theatre for many centuries and the question arose when researching this book: *Why has so little been written on the subject?* Countless volumes claiming to explain the history of Greek theatre, French theatre, theatre in the 17th century, etc., include no reference at all to sound, sound effects, noises off, or acoustics. Even "thunder" is missing from the index sections of most.

Perhaps even more extraordinary is the lack of information on sound in most books about technical theatre published during the 20th century. There were two specialist books written by stage managers in 1936: "Noises Off" by Frank Napier, which is mostly about the art of creating live effects backstage, and Peter Bax includes similar information in his book "Stage Management". Apart from these two volumes, there is very little mention of sound in general publications about technical theatre. For example, there were two important books by eminent British theatre practitioners published in 1949 purporting to be guides for anyone planning to build or equip a theatre: "Essentials of Stage Planning" by Stanley Bell, Norman Marshall and Richard Southern, and "Stage Planning and Equipment" by Percy Corry of Strand Electric. Although both books discuss theatre lighting in great detail, the first has no mention of sound or communications whatsoever (except for a general backstage illustration that happens to include a thunder sheet, a wind machine and a disc playing unit, none of which are captioned). Percy Corry's book has just one short paragraph: *For stage performances it is desirable to have provision for sound effects; the use of such effects has grown considerably since the development of mechanical reproduction. A double turntable with pickups, microphone, amplifier and speaker or speakers are desirable. If not actually provided in the initial stages, an electrical supply point should be placed near the stage manager's corner for the purpose.* In this book, devoted to theatre equipment, sound is covered by the recommendation of a plug socket!

Even in the USA as late as the 1970s, sound was not being taken very seriously in technical publications, as can be seen in the "Guide to the Planning and Construction of Proscenium and Open Stage Theatres" published for The American Theatre Planning Board Inc. in 1969. This discussed different configurations of stage and auditorium and highlighted technical facilities such as scenery handling and flying systems, with detailed specifications for lighting installations. What did they say about sound? The entire subject was covered in less than two hundred words by seven short bullet points, starting with the thought that sound reinforcement systems should be "considered" in auditoriums having an unusually large seating capacity. Other items to be considered were loudspeakers for sound effects, microphone and loudspeaker outlets around the stage, and low-voltage circuits for bells and buzzers. No further details or guidelines were given.

The theatrical experience, apart perhaps from mime or dumb shows, is a combination of visual *and* auditory experiences in equal parts. It therefore seems bizarre that books written about technical theatre by respected theatre practitioners should go into enormous detail describing scenery, lighting, and visual effects, and completely gloss over such an important element of the story. Perhaps it is the intangible and transitory nature of sound that causes 'noises off' to be perceived as less important than the visual effects which tend to remain imprinted on the mind.

Having said that, the research for this book did manage to uncover a few learned books and papers on the subject, and I am indebted to the academics and theatre practitioners we contacted for their invaluable knowledge and advice.

*****

My involvement with sound began by accident with my first stage management job. I did not set out to be a soundman. In fact, there was no such thing in those days. I just wanted to work backstage in a theatre. It was purely by chance that I became involved in an extraordinary transition from thunder sheets and bird whistles through various forms of disc and tape recording to computers and digital samplers. During my career of nearly forty years in the 'West End' theatre (London's equivalent to New York's Broadway), incredible advances took place in all forms of theatre technology, including a remarkable revolution in sound.

For me, it all started in 1954 at the Arts Theatre Club in Great Newport Street, London. This was a small theatre which at the time had a reputation for mounting high quality and sometimes avant-garde productions. Being a 'club' theatre meant that members were privileged to see plays that were not subject to the strict censorship of theatrical performances which was the law at the time in Britain. Certain topics, such as homosexuality were completely taboo, and any language thought to be too strong would receive the blue pencil treatment from the Lord Chamberlain's office.

The start of my career was traumatic. I had secured a job at the Arts Theatre through a combination of chance contacts and persistence. Working behind the scenes had always been a goal, but I had no idea what it entailed. I imagined an easy going, unstructured type of existence; spending a few hours with fun activities like making props or watching rehearsals, and turning up in the evenings to do exciting things backstage with a bunch of like-minded enthusiasts.

The reality came as a shock. The hours were extremely long and the work was taken very seriously. To survive, I would have to prove myself to a small team of dedicated professionals, some of whom were not entirely happy to welcome such a greenhorn.

The theatre crew consisted of a stage director (now called a stage manager), a chief electrician, plus two stage management teams each with a stage manager (now titled deputy stage manager) and two assistants. Each production ran for three or four weeks with one of the teams responsible for running the show. During the days, the other team would

The author aged 17 arrives in London.

be rehearsing the next production and, at nights, would become assistant electricians, propmen, flymen or scene shifters. During the change-over period at the end of a run, the entire staff would take down the scenery, load it all into a lorry to be unloaded in the workshop half a mile away, then load up the new scenery and set it up on the stage. As there was a matinee and evening performance on a Sunday, we had already completed a day's work before starting the change-over. We would often work through with little or no break until after the technical rehearsal on Monday night. Sometimes this meandered on into the next morning, and one had little time to recover before the opening that night.

It was largely because of the charisma and enthusiasm of the stage director, Robert (Bob) Batey, that we all worked so cheerfully for extraordinarily long hours on very meagre pay. It was an exhausting existence but, for a beginner, where could you find a better way of learning your craft?

Having never set foot backstage in my life and being only seventeen years of age, it has always mystified me what prompted Bob to take me on. Admittedly, I was the junior assistant stage manager – the lowest of the low – and the pay was only £5.00 per week, but there were plenty of experienced people in the profession who would have jumped at the chance to work in this prestigious little theatre. The artistic director received a mere £7.00 per week and even the actors, some of them big names, worked for subsistence salaries for the four or five weeks they were involved in rehearsals and performances.

The first morning when I presented myself for work, I was greeted by Mr. Batey, whom I had been pestering for a job for the past six months. "Welcome aboard, Davey", said Bob, grasping me firmly by the hand. (He is the only person ever to have called me 'Davey' and got away with it.) "You are going to be taking over the panatrope from Lynn. She has started another job but has agreed to work shows for us until you have learned the ropes. Meanwhile, I would like you to help Mike, our electrician, to cut colour. You will find him on the switchboard down those stairs at the side of the stage." Already, I was lost. What on earth was a 'panatrope' and how did one take it over? How could one possibly cut 'colour'? And why was there a telephone switchboard on the side of the stage?

I located a small dark-haired young man clad in white overalls. He was crouching beside a large contraption bristling with wheels and handles, which turned out to be the switchboard that controlled the stage lighting. Mike was uncommunicative and would obviously rather be left alone, but he grudgingly allowed me to help him cut the 'Cinemoid', or 'gels', for the different sizes of lighting frames. I was nervous and he was sullenly hostile. I could not have imagined that a few months later we would be sharing a flat.

At the end of the day's rehearsal on stage, I was introduced to the stage management team and asked to assist with preparing for the evening performance. "Could you strike that chair", said the stage manager. I looked blankly at him. Did he really want me to hit a chair? "Its <u>dead</u>", he explained patiently. Well, obviously. I was at a loss. Then, with a sigh, another member of the team grabbed the chair and stowed it off-stage. I was not doing very well.

Just before show time, Lynn arrived and asked me if I was happy to be taking over the panatrope. I assured her that I was looking forward to it very much. Invited to follow her up a ladder on to a small platform down stage off right, I was confronted with the contraption which was going to change my life; a large metal coffin with two 78 r.p.m. turntables and pick-up arms equipped with groove-locating devices.

On a table to one side was a rack with some twenty gramophone records. These were lacquer recordings especially cut for the show with two or three different tracks of music and effects on one side of each disc.

The production of SAINT JOAN was halfway through a four week run. That evening, I watched in awe as Lynn changed the discs, cued them up and, reacting to a cuelight from the stage manager, dropped the pick-up and turned up the volume. Sometimes she had to change a record whilst another was playing and then add a new sound on top of the one that was running. I wondered if I would be capable of emulating such dexterity.

The plan was for me to tackle some of the easier cues at the next performance. So, the following day, I managed to practice for a while when the rehearsal on stage broke for lunch. That night, for the first time in my life, I operated sound equipment with a live audience. It was under close supervision, of course, and there were no disasters. I was very pleased with myself. During the next few performances, I was to take over more and more cues until, on the fifth night, I would be handling the entire show.

The third show came and went with me nervously, yet successfully, tackling some of the trickier sequences. But the next night, Lynn was not in the theatre half an hour before the show as usual and – horror – had still not arrived when it was nearly time for curtain up. Bob Batey said that I had better go up on to the 'pan platform' and be ready to start the show.

Moments before curtain up when all the actors were assembled on stage, Lynn came clambering breathlessly up the ladder just as the warning cuelight came on for the curtain up music. My relief was short lived, however. She stood for a while, swaying slightly, peering with incomprehension at the cuelight. Then, shrugging her shoulders and waving vaguely at the panatrope, she slumped down on to a chair, announcing thickly: "You do it. I'm drunk."

This was truly my baptism of fire. Suddenly, I experienced that sick feeling in the pit of my stomach that was to become so familiar over many years of first nights. I was petrified that I would select the wrong disc and during some very quiet and dramatic scene on stage, instead of a gentle wind, the sound of cathedral bells would come crashing out. Or I would have the front-of-house loudspeakers turned on instead of one of the backstage speakers. Or the volume would be up when I dropped the pick-up and the audience would hear a loud 'crack' as the stylus skidded into the groove.

The 'stand-by' cuelight had been on for some seconds. No more time to think. The 'go' light lit up and we were off. I filled the auditorium with sound. Somehow, I got through the show with no major disasters and was congratulated by Lynn, now seriously hung-over, and by the stage manager and, most importantly, by Bob Batey who knew exactly what had been going on. Suddenly, I was one of the team.

When the run of SAINT JOAN drew to an end, I was asked to repeat my performance on the panatrope for the next production, André Gide's THE IMMORALIST. This was to be directed by the theatre's new artistic director, the 24 year old Peter Hall, who liked to experiment with music and sound effects in his productions. This was his first job in London, having made a name for himself directing plays at the Oxford Playhouse.

Although I managed to work with lighting, props and flying scenery on subsequent productions, which is what I really wanted to do, Peter Hall kept asking for me to return to the 'pan platform'. He would say things like: "Sound is an important and integral part of my next production and I really need someone I can rely on". It seemed that I had a natural aptitude for dropping the needle into the groove at the correct moment and he was determined to exploit this talent. He was very persuasive and had the knack of making you feel vital to the production. He appeared to welcome suggestions even from such a junior member of the team – which, of course, was very flattering. Soon, I was accompanying him to the local sound company to help select the effects.

After leaving the Arts Theatre two years later, I worked for Peter Hall as a sound operator in some of the big commercial theatres in the West End and, subsequently, as a freelance sound designer at the Shakespeare Memorial Theatre, Stratford-upon-Avon where, at the age of 27, he became the artistic director and went on to create the Royal Shakespeare Company. Later, he became artistic director of the National Theatre of Great Britain when it opened in 1976. He was subsequently knighted in 1977.

In those early days of operating the equipment and then becoming a sound designer, I became acquainted with the two leading innovators of recorded sound and amplification in the London theatre, Jack Bishop and R.G. Jones, both of whom started in the 1930s. I was also fortunate enough to know Bill Walton who founded a company in the 1950s called Stagesound, which moved the industry into a new era. Like me, none of these gentlemen started with any formal training in electronics. What they all had in common was an inquiring mind and a love of the theatre.

As described later in the book, I joined Richard Pilbrow's fledgling company, Theatre Projects, and went on to design the sound for more than fifty West End musicals. The sound company within the Theatre Projects Group, with a recording studio complex and an equipment rental business, grew to become the UK's leading theatre sound operation. I was involved with a talented new breed of audio artists and technicians, some of whom went on to set up or join rival companies. As is inevitable when young enthusiasts start new ventures and introduce new technology, one of these companies eventually succeeded us as market leader.

Because I was lucky enough to work on many Broadway musicals transferring to London, I was able to meet some of America's finest sound designers. Researching this book has given me the excuse and the enormous pleasure of renewing my acquaintance with these colleagues. An added bonus was being introduced to the people who now run the major theatre sound companies in New York.

It is because I have first-hand knowledge of the personalities who changed the face of theatre sound during a remarkable period of technical development, that I wanted to write this story.

It is a large subject and I apologise in advance to the many people and their important achievements I have inevitably omitted. I do, however, look forward to receiving outraged letters and emails and if there should be a second edition of this book, perhaps I will be able to include some of these omissions.

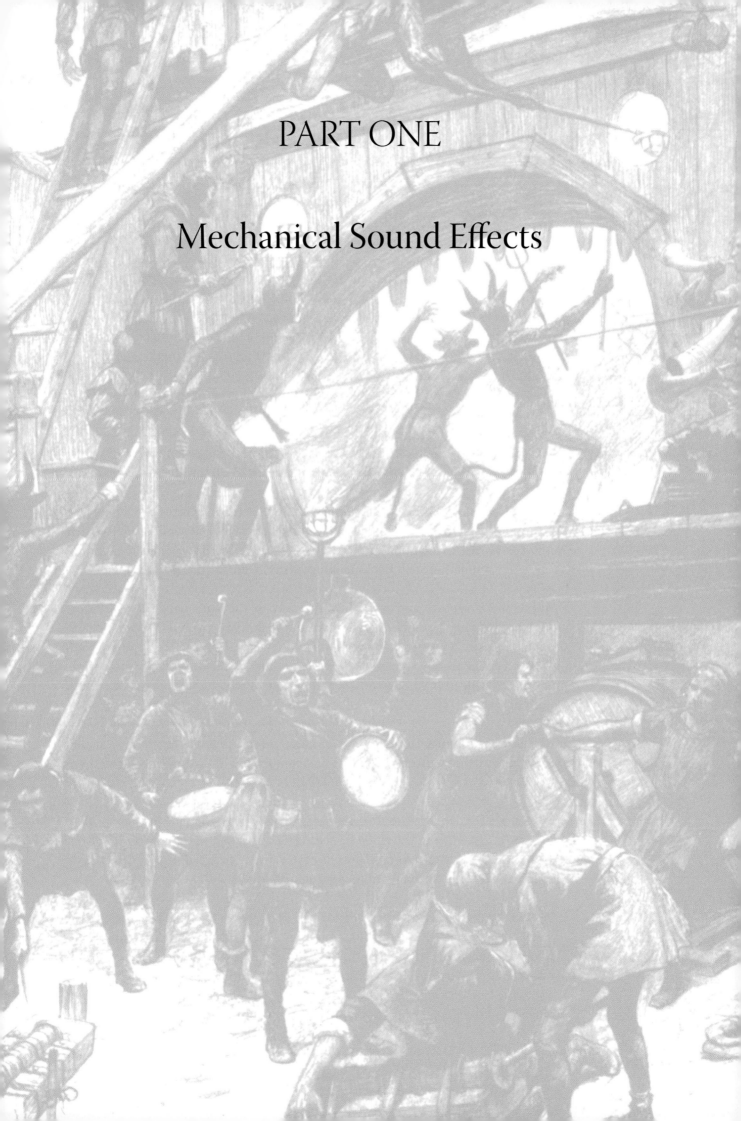

PART ONE

Mechanical Sound Effects

1   THE ANCIENT GREEKS AND ROMANS

The first great theatrical age in the history of Western civilization began in Greece, notably Athens, during the 4th and 5th centuries BC. It evolved from a long tradition of poetry declaimed by poets and from male choruses singing stories. What we think of as "drama" occurred when these two strands were brought together. Heroic and tragic stories were related by one actor together with a chorus who sang and danced in unison. It is possible that a man called Thespis, the first recorded "actor", introduced this huge innovation, which is why actors today are called 'Thespians'. For these performances, both the actor and the chorus wore masks.

Comic plays were added to the tragedies, and both took place alongside religious rites at festivals to the god Dionysus. Prizes were awarded for the best plays.

The next great innovation occurred when a second actor was introduced, possibly by the poet Aeschylus (525-456 BC). A third actor was brought in by either Aeschylus or his contemporary, Sophocles. Sometimes, especially in comedy, a fourth actor together with non-speaking 'extras' were used.[13]

In the Greek tragedies and comedies, the fury of the gods called for thunder, storms and earthquakes. The Greeks had the technology to build sophisticated outdoor theatres, and we know they found ways to replicate at least a few sound effects. They also used stage machinery, including wheeled platforms on which prearranged tableaux could be shown, and a crane by which the god could descend from heaven.[7]

In the Roman Empire, theatrical performances were highly regarded with the greatest plays being written during the 2nd century BC. These were performed on temporary stages in Rome or in existing Greek theatres.

From the 1st century BC, the Romans began to build permanent theatres which were very different from those in Greece. They were built on flat ground, not on hillsides, and had vast surrounding walls of masonry, often elaborately decorated. Small theatres could be enclosed rectangular buildings with a roof.

By the end of the 1st century BC, tragedy had gone out of fashion. The last known tragedy was staged in 29 BC, but comedies continued to be performed and 'pantomime' became extremely popular. This type of entertainment involved a masked dancer performing in dumbshow accompanied by a singing chorus. Pantomime lasted as long as the Roman Empire in the West, and it was still being performed in the East during the Byzantine period (3rd – 15th centuries AD).[13]

Acoustics

It is believed that Pythagoras (circa 580-500 bc) was the first person to seriously research sound and acoustics, and it was between his period and that of Aristotle (384-322 bc) that the problems of creation and transmission of sound were reduced to generally accepted theories.

One of Aristotle's significant pronouncements was that sound waves do not behave in the same way as light, since they are not confined to straight lines. He also began to understand the importance of reflection and absorption, noting that the chorus in a theatre produced less sound if the floor was made of a mixture of sand, chaff and straw rather than being of hard flat sand. This realization prompted him to recommend using dry and smoothly plastered wood for a proscenium.[1]

In the 1st century bc, the Roman architect Vitruvius produced his huge work "De Architectura". This included detailed instructions for the successful building of theatres, with particular attention given to acoustics. Crediting the Greek sources he used for his work, including Agatharcus, Aristoxenes, Democritus and Anaxagoras, he says that the "ancients" learnt how to build the stepped seating in a theatre so that the sounds issuing from the stage could be heard in a clear and agreeable manner by the whole audience.

Vitruvius explains that sound waves spread outwards like the ripples on still water after a stone is cast in – an analogy which is still widely used in text books today – but whereas the circles in water only spread horizontally, sound waves extend in all directions. He then takes this principle to expound upon his theories of acoustics, many of which form the basis of modern theatre acoustic design.

He talks of unwanted reflections, stating that:
- *A line drawn from the lowest to the highest seat should touch the tops of all the seats, as any protrusions will throw back the voice and cause disturbances.*

- *The 'dissonant places' are those in which the voice, rising first upwards, is obstructed by some hard bodies above and in its return downwards, checks the ascent of its following sounds.*

- *The 'resonant places' are those in which the voice, striking against some hard body, is echoed in the last syllables so that they appear doubled.*

- *The 'circumsonant places' are those where the voice, wandering round, is at last retained in the centre, where it is dissipated, and, the final syllables being lost, the meaning of the words is not distinguished.*

He then describes what he calls the 'consonant places' where voice clarity and amplification can be aided by reflections:
- *the 'consonant places' are those in which the voice, aided by something below (reflections from the stage floor?), falls on the ear with great distinctness of words. Hence, if due care be taken in the choice of the situation, the effect of the voice will be improved, and the utility of the theatre increased.*

Could actors be heard in a Greek theatre?

WE KNOW THAT THE Greeks and Romans were thinking about acoustics, but experts seem to disagree about whether some form of amplification was used. The Dutch author and lecturer Benjamin Hunningher, writing in 1954, comments that because the theatre in Athens was so large, it is difficult to see how the actors could have made themselves heard without some form of assistance.

Hunningher tells us that in the time of Sophocles (495-406 BC) the theatre in Athens had 78 rows of seats, and held 14-17,000 people. In the middle of the theatre, it was nearly 73 metres (240ft) from the first row of seats to the top row. To the left of the actors, it was 26 metres (84ft) from first to last row, and to the right of the actors, 32 metres (105ft) from first to last row. From the first row of seats to the performing actor would be another 9 – 11 metres (30-35ft).

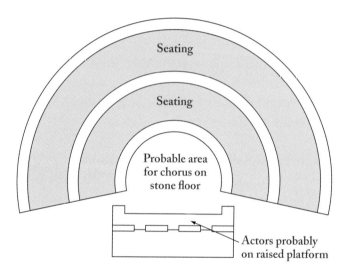

Plan of a typical
Greek theatre.

These figures can be compared to the Paris and Vienna opera houses, where it is 28 metres (93ft) from curtain line to the furthest seat, and at Bayreuth it is 30 metres (100ft). Even if the top few rows of seats were not built until the time of Sophocles, as some experts claim, in the earlier time of Aeschylus the front to back row measurement would still be an enormous 55 metres (180ft).[1]

Distances to back row of seats
Athens – outdoor theatre   180ft   55m (Aeschylus period)
                               240ft   73m (Sophocles period)
Paris and Vienna Opera   93ft   28m
Bayreuth Festspielhaus   100ft   30m

Hunningher carried out some acoustic tests in the Athens theatre (as it was in 1954) in different weather conditions. He concluded that if the audience was already familiar with the words, then they could hear and understand them at 135ft.[1] Like modern opera, there was a great deal of repetition in Greek plays. Important phrases were repeated, probably so that they could be directed at different parts of the auditorium. On the other hand, if the audience was unfamiliar with the play, Hunninger says that the distance for intelligibility was reduced to 110ft.

The theatre in Epidaurus holds the same number of people, but the auditorium is wider so the distance from the front to the back row is under 150ft. Even so, this still seems to be too far for the human voice to be heard clearly, unaided.

Once plays with dialogue became important, Greek theatres had a back wall to the acting area, preferably made of wood, and at least as tall as the actors. When an actor speaks, the sound waves go back as well as forward; so the backward waves hitting the wall would have bounced forward to form one large wave that carried much farther than would be the case without the help of the back wall.

By the 5th century BC, the requirements for realism led the back wall, initially there for acoustic purposes, to be used as an indication of the place of action; the 'skene' (as it was called) therefore became the fore-runner of our modern idea of 'scenery'.

Both Pythagoras and the Roman architect Vitruvius mention the resounding qualities of hollow spaces behind wooden walls. 'Skene' in Greek translates as 'tent', 'hut', or 'booth', so the wooden wall seems to have become a more complicated construction. Some sources suggest that it was used as a changing area for actors.

Hunningher discounts the theory that the stone floor of the stage would have helped the acoustics for the actors, pointing out that the chorus was in front of the actors, thus soaking up the sound waves bouncing off the stone floor. Although he could find no archaeological evidence, he believes that there could well have been a wooden platform for the actors to raise them above the chorus. Performing on a solid timber stage could have improved audibility as well as visibility.

He also believes that the paraskenia (projecting wings) were added about 450 BC to improve audibility. They were built as three-dimensional structures, which would have enclosed the acting area like a shell.

Masks – help or hindrance for audibility?

THE MASKS WORN BY actors at this period, were like helmets with gaps at the mouths, and could have done nothing to assist audibility. Comic masks sometimes had small funnels at the mouth, but these would have caused a directional effect, making intelligibility more difficult for most of the audience. The reason for wearing masks was so that the actors could play a variety of parts. They were not for sound.

To be a professional actor at that time, one would have needed enormous vocal power, stamina and flexibility; power to be heard at great distances, stamina because the actors performed four plays during one day, and flexibility because they not only had to play both men and women, but they also had to be able to sing. The use of only three or four actors per play may have continued because of the scarcity of performers with the necessary skills and dedication. Like opera singers today, they were highly trained and had to keep their voices in top condition. There is a story about Hermon, a comic actor and contemporary of

Aristophanes (448-380 BC), who was so busy doing his vocal exercises that he arrived late at the theatre and missed his performance completely because the previous plays had been hissed off by the audience.

In 1996, Sir Peter Hall's production of Sophocles' OEDIPUS PLAYS premiered in the ancient theatre of Epidaurus before its run at the National Theatre in London. The director decided that since the actors wore full masks, they would need amplification in order to be heard throughout the vast auditorium. The sound designer, Paul Groothuis, quickly discovered that microphones within the masks sounded unnaturally 'boomy', so he made holes in the tips of the noses and mounted them in there. The distributed loudspeaker system, one row at the front of the auditorium and a second row half way back, provided a good low level coverage of sound. Naturally, some purists were outraged at the very idea of amplification, but there were many comments from audience members saying that it was the first time they had been able to hear all the words.

Conjecture on Ancient Greek amplifiers

ACCORDING TO VITRUVIUS, the Greeks also discovered how to amplify the voice. Beginning with the statement that: *"harmony is an obscure and difficult musical science"*, he gives a detailed and (to me at least) impenetrable description of the different sounds produced by the human voice and musical instruments.

He then explains how to build "amplifiers". This is a theory also mentioned by Aristotle. Bronze vases are placed between the auditorium seats designed to resonate at predetermined frequencies depending upon their size. He gives detailed instructions for the number of vases, and their position for different sizes of theatre. Sizes of vases are to be worked out using mathematics. He says:

"...brazen vases are to be made...depending on the size of the theatre. Between the seats of the theatre, cavities having been prepared, they are disposed therein in musical order, but so as not to touch the wall in any part, but to have a clear space round them and over their top; they are fixed in an inverted position, and on the side towards the scene are supported by wedges not less than half a foot high; and openings are left towards the cavities on the lower beds of the steps, each two feet long and half a foot wide. By the adoption of this plan, the voice which issues from the scene, expanding as from a centre, and striking against the cavity of each vase, will sound with increased clearness and harmony, from its unison with one or other of them. Hence he who carefully attends to these rules, to the nature of the voice, and to the taste of the audience, will easily learn the method of designing theatres with the greatest perfection." [14]

If you could not afford bronze, Vitruvius says that pottery would be a viable alternative: *"Many clever architects who have built theatres in small cities, from the want of other, have made use of earthen vessels, yielding the proper tones, and have introduced them with considerable advantage."* These rules were for theatres being built of solid material such as marble, stone or rubble. However: *"all public theatres which are constructed of wood, have many floors, which are necessarily*

*conductors of sound. This... may be illustrated by... the practice of those that sing
to the harp, who when they wish to produce a loud effect, turn themselves to the
doors of the scene, by the aid of which their voice is thrown out."*

Sadly, Benjamin Hunningher in "Acoustics and Acting in the Theatre of Dionysus
Eleuthereus" says that Vitruvius's bronze vessels – or even traces of them – have
never been found in the ruins of Greek or Roman theatres. He feels that Vitruvius
was repeating the theories of the Greek philosopher and musical theorist
Aristoxenes and, although incredibly detailed and scientifically correct in many
ways, there seems to be no evidence that they were ever put into practice.

The use of natural amplifiers should not be discounted, however, as they have been
incorporated into buildings in many parts of the world. They can be seen in Islamic
architecture and in mediaeval churches both in Serbia and Switzerland. In Serbian
Orthodox churches, ceramic acoustic resonators have been found built into vaults,
walls and floors. They look like large domestic jars with a hole punched in their
bases. In the Russian Orthodox Church, the priest is out of sight behind a heavy
solid screen for much of the service and, before the days of microphones, he would
not have been heard without some acoustical assistance. Two recent studies of
some churches, however, found that the resonating jars did not provide any
discernible improvement to the acoustics.[17] This conclusion is not proof that the
concept does not work in other buildings, however. After all, they have been a
feature in many public buildings for hundreds of years. In modern times, similar
devices called Helmholtz resonators are used in buildings, particularly small
recording studios, to adjust the acoustics. An example of how they work can be
demonstrated by blowing across a bottle to produce a tone. Bigger or smaller
bottles will produce different tones. Similarly, the resonant frequency of a Helmholtz
resonator – basically, a container with an opening – will depend upon its volume.

Sound effects in Greek theatre

ACCORDING TO OLIVER TAPLIN, Professor of Classical Languages and Literature
at Oxford University, the only surviving source which specifically mentions a
sound effect from the Ancient Greek period is in a study of language called the
Onomasticon, compiled by Julius Pollux, a Greek scholar of the 2nd century AD.
He mentions a machine called a 'Bronteion' used in the Greek theatre to produce
thunder: *"The thunder maker: underneath the stage in the background, sacks of
hide inflated with air and filled with small round stones are brought against plates
of brass."*[15]

If they felt that thunder was worth imitating, it seems likely that other sound
effects would have been attempted. Professor Taplin confirms that there is
evidence of actors being able to imitate the noise of animals – and hinges!

We have found only one reference to making the sound of wind for storms in the
ancient period; *"...wind machines, consisting of long, thin pieces of wood of different
widths, with holes of varying shapes bored through them and whirled around the
head by means of a thong, were known to the ancients."* [2]

We can find no evidence to back up this statement, but the use of such a simple and effective device does not seem unlikely.

Sound effects in Roman theatre

ACCORDING TO VITRUVIUS, "sudden claps of thunder" accompanied the appearance of a god or on the turning of sections of the back wall to alter the décor.[14] Although he does not go into detail, it does indicate that thunder effects were used in the Roman theatre. There is more information on Vitruvius's comments on stage spectacles in Chapter Three of this book, as his influence on Renaissance theatre was immense.

In the 1st century AD, Heron of Alexandria seems to have invented, or at least accurately recorded, a thunder-machine. Heron, also called Hero, wrote extensively on mathematics and machines, and is credited with many inventions, including the first steam engine. Among a huge number of descriptions of automata, including many powered by water, he gives details of two mechanical theatres, both of which required thunder crashes. His technique for making thunder may have been invented much earlier. Heron himself states that the thunder for his mechanical theatre which plays out the story of Nauplius is an improved version of a device designed by his predecessor, Philo of Byzantium (born about 280 BC).[16] Ctesibus (or Ctesibius) is also credited as having designed an automated theatre in 200 BC, which might have included a method of making thunder.[15]

Our research has not been able to find a reliable source to prove that a full-size version of Heron's thunder-machine was ever built and used in the live theatre, although it would appear to be perfectly practical. Several sources say that his thunder-machine had a chute made of metal. S J Scherrer, writing in the "Journal of Biblical Literature" states that the chute was made of skins. He translates Heron's words thus: *"...when a sound is required, a reservoir containing weights is let go, so that falling down upon a prepared hide, which, as we have said, is dried and arranged like a kettledrum, they give the sound".*

Heron's design for a thunder machine for his automated theatre. The cord on the right released the bronze balls at the top. The balls fell through the baffles onto a stretched skin at the bottom. *This sketch is taken from a 14th century Greek manuscript as redrawn by Robert S Brumbaugh in "Ancient Greek Gadgets and Machines", 1966.*

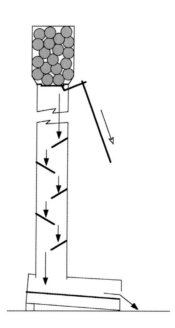

A replica of Heron's machine has been made at Smith College's Department of History of Science in Massachusetts in 2000. The replica uses metal throughout rather than skins. Although it is only one and a half feet tall, and uses ball bearings, it apparently makes an extraordinarily loud and convincing noise!

There are two references to a device resembling what later became known as the 'thunder-run'. This idea then disappears, as far as our research has revealed, until the 1600s. Saint Hippolytus of Rome, an early Christian scholar who died in 235 AD, talks about sorcerers artificially producing thunder by rolling stones down wooden planks on to plates of brass. This appears in Hippolytus's "Refutation of All Heresies". This is not, of course, a reference to thunder being used in the theatre, but as a theatrical device for pagan religious use. However, it is another indication that this method of producing thunder had been invented.[15]

Diderot's Encyclopedie (published in France between 1751 and 1772) says:
"Artificial Thunder was known as 'Claudiana tonitrua' when it was heard in the Roman Theatre said Festus (Roman historian), because Claudius Pulcher thought to imitate the sound of bursts of thunder by rolling many rounded stones down an assembly of planks set on a slope, instead of the previous imperfect and feeble method of imitation which consisted of making the noise with nails and small stones by shaking them vigorously in a bronze basin."

We can find no evidence or descriptions of effects other than thunder being used in the Roman theatre, although, like the Greeks, the actors might well have created sounds vocally.

A range of musical sounds might well have been incorporated into Roman spectacles. For example, there was a pipe organ known by the Greeks as 'Hydraulikon' and by the Romans as 'Hydraulus'. The invention of this instrument is credited to an Egyptian who lived around 250 BC. A similar device was certainly employed around 500 AD by a deviser of spectacles. Theodoric the Great wrote about him: *"He makes waters surge up from the depths and cascade down again; flames run evenly around; organs thunder forth strange sounds; and he fills the pipes with exotic blasts of air, which makes them utter a melodious sound."*[3] The Oxford Companion to Music states that a terracotta model of the instrument was dug up in Carthage in 1885, and the remains of an actual specimen (dated 228 AD) were excavated at a Roman site near Budapest in 1931. Apparently, the resemblance to a modern organ is startling. It had a row of pipes and a keyboard with each key operating a perforated slider to open and close the pipe. A continuous supply of air was provided by an ingenious system involving water pressure; hence the name Hydraulikon. According to old records the instrument was so powerful that the sound could carry for sixty miles and players were compelled to plug their ears!

2 MEDIAEVAL THEATRE

From the break up of the Roman Empire until the end of the Dark Ages, there is little evidence of any kind of drama in Western Europe, although one imagines that stories were still being acted out during this period. In the Byzantine Empire, pantomimes from the Roman era were still being performed.

As the Greek theatre had flourished at the festivals of the god Dionysus, mediaeval drama emerged from the worship of the Christian God. The earliest liturgical drama for which texts survive is from the mid to late 10th century. Later, plays depicting religious stories were staged to mark important dates in the Church's calendar, along with morality plays and secular, comic pieces.[13]

The very earliest mention of a sound effect we have found from our sources is in a 13th century play called ADAM, wherein there is a depiction of hell that requires an *"infernal din".*[4] Quite how this was to be achieved, there is no indication.

In England, these religious plays were either civic-controlled events or a combined product of city and church. The financing came largely from the craft guilds and the actors were paid. Biblical plays could be divided into a series of pageants, using separate wagons for performances at a number of sites within a city or town. However, more common was the use of fixed location staging – sometimes a circular acting area with a series of scaffolds around the edge.[5] These religious plays sometimes had 'interludes' where comic secular pieces were performed, similar to French farces.[13]

Drama was immensely popular in France from the 11th century. Some stage directions still survive from the 15th and 16th centuries, when solidly-built timber stages (even for outdoor performances) were used to accommodate elaborate machinery and trap-doors. In Germany, Passion plays were performed on wooden stages erected in market places between the 12th and 17th centuries, and similar events were taking place in Italy. From 1460 to 1540 a Passion play was staged annually at the Coliseum in Rome.[5] At Velletri, a stage was built in stone in the early 16th century, set against the city walls. The city's Passion play was performed there until 1563.

Poland, Scandinavia, the Low Countries, Hungary, Croatia and Bohemia also have a history of religious plays in this period. In Spain, dramas were performed inside churches, and processions, tableaux and later plays were performed outside. There were also private theatrical performances in wealthy households in Spain, and maybe in other countries too.[13]

In all these countries, large sums were spent on creating magnificent special effects – elaborate scenery, miraculous appearances, deaths, earthquakes, flying scenes, lighting effects, explosions and so on. The greatest sound effects were needed for scenes involving Hell, but thunder was also needed for God giving the

Commandments, the appearance of Angels and on many other occasions. Music, both sung and played, was also used extensively. [5]

There is first-hand evidence that thunder effects were being used throughout Europe during the 1400s and 1500s. In 14th century France, there is reference to thunder produced by *"stones rolled about in a tub".* An English cycle play called Doomsday, produced in York, used a similar device for an earthquake.[4]

The use of drums and stones in reverberant containers shows a direct link with the theatre of the Ancient Greeks; the main difference being the addition of explosions created with gunpowder. The following examples are from "The Staging of Religious Drama in Europe in the Later Middle Ages" edited by Peter Meredith and John E Tailby:

Pre-1420: Prades Assumption (Catalan) has the following instructions:
"Lucifer and the other devils are to take an anvil and hammers to make a loud noise when the time comes"
"...when the angel returns to Paradise, there is to be a noise with explosions."

1439: For a production performed inside a Church in Florence:
"there comes a volley of shots imitating Heaven's thunder"

1542: For a religious play at the Church of Athis-Sur-Orge, there is a contract with a painter to provide:
"the cannons and flaming fireworks necessary for the devil-scene."

1580: Religious play at Modune:
"they shall make a great blaze of fire and noise every time the devils take some dead to Hell, every day."
"They shall fire cannons and bombards when Gog and Magog greet Antichrist."
"They shall supply the large cannon and falconets with necessary petards to make earthquakes"
(a petard is a translation of the French word "Bosse", which was a bottle filled with powder which broke on landing and exploded when ignited by an attached slow match.)

1583 – Lucerne: A list of people involved in the production contains:
2 x Thunderers.
4 x Musketeers
4 x Hornblowers
(also smoke makers)

An extract from payments for the same production:
ITEM: For a new thunder barrel and for renovating the barrel of the old thunder barrel
ITEM: For 12lbs of powder for the guns and the thunder

1501: Mons Passion Play had a thunder machine. The people operating the thunder machine had a written cue sheet, and a list of the equipment involved in the thunder machine is given in the accounts for payments:
ITEM: Two large vellum skins used for a cask of fir wood and a skin of parchment used to cover a cauldron: all this for Hell.

ITEM: Two large flat bronze basins
ITEM: A pound of brass used for joining together two copper basins
ITEM: A pivot of iron and 4 pieces of iron and 4 eyelets to turn on it and two
handles 16 fasteners to attach them to two great vats.

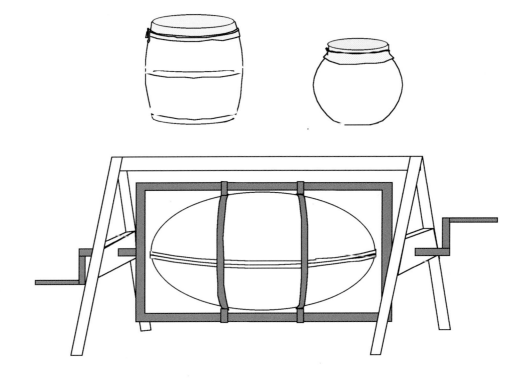

Thunder drums made
from a wooden cask
covered with vellum
skins and a cauldron
cover with a skin of
parchment.

Conjectural design
for a thunder
machine with two
large copper basins
joined together and
filled with rocks
and turned within a
metal frame.

Max Culver, in "A History of Theatre Sound Effects Devices", quotes a slightly differently version of this thunder machine: *"...four pivots of iron, each having four iron bands and four rings to turn two handles, sixteen staples to attach them to two large copper tubs, for making thunder in Hell, weighing 24 pounds, at 2 shillings per pound; 48 shillings."*

In the same Mons Passion play, there is also mention of a 'thunder sheet'. This is the earliest reference found of making thunder by shaking a suspended sheet of thin metal, a device used in the British theatre until well into the 1950s. An excerpt from the Mons records reads: *"to Pierart Viscave, tinker, for the installation of two big sheets of bronze for the aforesaid mystery, place in Hell to make thunder, as been paid: 32 shillings"* [4]

Music, both instrumental and sung, played an important part in many mediaeval plays, to create atmosphere and to cover a break in the action. Many plays took place outdoors and, presumably, the musicians and singers were placed around the playing area so they could be heard. There are records of horns and trumpets coming from beneath the scenery, thunderers being in the attic of a house, and musketeers listed as being all round in attics.[4]

These mediaeval religious plays had reached their peak by the late 1400s and declined during the following century. In Paris, the acting of religious plays was forbidden in 1548. In England, the Reformation brought them to an end by 1588. Similarly, they ceased in European countries in areas that became Protestant.

Religious plays had their longest life-span in Spain where, after a late flowering, they were finally forbidden in 1765.[7]

This Victorian illustration of creating the effects backstage for a 15th century mystery play should be treated with caution, but it does indicate what might have gone on.

3   ELIZABETHAN AND JACOBEAN THEATRE

The renaissance and birth of modern theatre

"The Renaissance" describes a time of radical change in European culture during the 15th and 16th centuries, when the achievements of Ancient Greece and Rome were rediscovered. During this period, beginning in Italy, Greek and Roman theatre was of intense interest and many ideas were adopted.

The writings of the Roman architect Vitruvius were known in manuscript form from the early 1400s in Italy, and were published in Rome during the 1480s.

Based upon the works of Vitruvius, the Italians designed a new kind of theatre; a rectangular building with a roof, with a semi-circle of seats facing a flat-fronted stage area, complete with a proscenium arch and scenery. The first permanent modern theatre (as far as we know) was built in Ferrara under Ducal patronage at the very end of the 1400s.

It is because of the beauty of the theatre architecture and the stage settings, and also the development of opera and ballet, that Italy deserves her reputation as the cradle of modern theatre.[7] Several methods of creating the sound of thunder and wind seem to have originated in Italy, as will be discussed later in this chapter.

Theatre in England

This development of the indoor theatre by the Italians and the organized *commedia dell'arte* companies of professional actors who performed throughout Europe, paved the way for the first of many permanent theatres to be built in London. As far as we know, these were all open-air courtyard buildings. The first one, simply known as "The Theatre", opened in 1576, soon to be followed by the Curtain, the Rose, the Swan, the Globe, the Fortune, and the Hope. The most famous of these was the Globe, built in 1599, where most of Shakespeare's plays were produced. The Globe was destroyed by fire in 1612, but it was rebuilt the following year and remained in operation until 1644, when it was demolished.

Theatrical performances became very popular in England during the 1500s and, apart from public theatres, various types of live entertainment were being staged elsewhere; pageants and masques were produced to celebrate great events, and universities and schools performed classical Roman plays to help the students become more familiar with Latin. Some of these productions were played at the court of Queen Elizabeth I. In 1566, for instance, the Queen saw several productions in the hall at Christ Church college during a visit to Oxford. Some of these Roman plays featured thunder, and two needed the effect of a pack of hounds – presumably an assembly of barking actors!

Plays and masques were frequently staged for the Queen at court, and as the court often went "on tour", temporary stages were erected in the halls of the grand houses visited. There is a reference to the use of a thunder-effect in the Office of the Revels accounts record for 1571-2: *"Iohn Izarde for mony to him due for his device in counterfeting Thunder and Lightning in the playe of Narcisses."* [2]

By the early 1600s, the court masques incorporated elaborate scenery and stage machines. These were not for consumption by the general public, but they were important in the development of the English theatre, particularly the spectacles produced by Inigo Jones from 1605 to 1613, the words for several of which were written by Ben Jonson. [7]

Groups of actors toured the country to put on plays for the general public, and some of these troupes must have been of a significant size. This can be seen from the 1589 inventory of properties from Philip Henslowe, an important actor/ manager. The list gives an indication that he was touring scene cloths and painted signs, three dimensional scenic pieces, weaponry and armour, and numerous props including false limbs, masks, heads and wings. Although actors often wore their own clothes, there were specialist wardrobe items such as hats, crowns and animal costumes. There must have been ten or twelve musicians as the list of instruments included three trumpets, drum, chime of bells, treble viol, bass viol, a bandora, a cittern, two rackets, three timbrells and a sackbutt. [9]

Around the early 1600s, small private indoor theatres were being set up where performances were not affected by the weather. The audience for these theatres tended to be better educated, demanding a more subtle style of plot and dialogue, and more elaborate staging and effects. [7]

Were sound effects used in England?

THERE ARE PLENTY OF references to music and effects in Shakespeare's plays. Brock, in "A Study of the Use of Stage Sound in Elizabethan Drama" says that audiences would have expected a large number of sound effects – and required much more realism than what they actually saw upon the stage in terms of scenery. That the audiences expected sound effects is confirmed by an apology for the lack of them in the prologue to THE TWO MERRY MILKMAIDS, a play by one of Shakespeare's contemporaries:

> *This Day we entreat All that are hither come, To expect no noyse or Guns, Trumpet, no Drum, Nor Sword and Targuet; but to heare Sence and Words, Fitting the matter, that the Scene affords. So that the Stage being reform'd, and free From the lowd Clamors it was wont to bee, Turmoye'd with Battailes; you I hope will cease Your dayly Tumults, and with us wish Peace...*

Brock surmises that there were many more sound effects in the original productions of plays than those actually given as stage directions in the printed copies we now have. The original stage directions have been lost because they were edited out for the printed versions of the plays (which were often considered to be the dialogue only), or simply left out by the printer through carelessness. It is also likely that the number of stage sounds increased during the Elizabethan period, as the theatre became more professional.

Where did the sounds come from?

IN THE GLOBE AND similar courtyard theatres, there were several areas where the noise-makers could operate. Vocalised effects and smaller sounds like hoof beats and bird song were probably created behind curtained doors leading on to the stage from the 'tiring house'. It is sensible to assume that sounds specified as "from within" would have come from these areas at stage level.

A typical Elizabethan courtyard theatre.

The tiring house was a structure at the back of the stage with three levels. The first was a raised inner stage often used for intimate scenes, the second was a central balcony for the actors, and the third level consisted of a central gallery where the musicians, when not needed on the stage, would play curtained off from the public. At either side of the musicians gallery, there were large curtained off spaces used for dressing rooms and for storage.

Some experts think that the drums and other equipment for thunder, the chambers (cannon) and machinery for lowering pieces of scenery would have been in these storage areas at the top of the tiring house. There is general agreement that the great bell was located here, close to the roof, and rung by using a long rope as in churches and other public buildings.[8]

W J Lawrence (author of "Pre-Restoration Stage Studies") says: *"through the apertures (of the turret) stage ordnance were let off, a custom that led to the destructive fire at Shakespeare's Globe. Here thunder was simulated by "roll'd bullet" and "tempestuous drum", and here was situated the windlass or other rude machinery whereby...the substantial deity-bearing cloud was lowered."* [8]

There was a large understage area beneath the whole of the inner and outer stages, accessed by trap-doors in the outer stage and by a "grave trap" in the inner stage. Inevitably, this area was used for noise making – as is confirmed by the stage direction in Shakespeare's ANTHONY AND CLEOPATRA: *"Music of the hautboys is under the stage"*

In the private enclosed theatres that started to appear in the early 1600s, the large tiring house did not exist. The sound effects department would therefore be operating behind, below and around the stage much as it does today. Masques and other entertainments for the Court, mounted on temporary stages in halls, would presumably have had a similar arrangement, although we cannot be sure how elaborate were the constructions.

When were sounds used?

BROCK, IN "A Study of the Use of Sound Effects in the Elizabethan Drama", suggests that off-stage sounds were used much as they are to this day. For example:

To establish the scene and create atmosphere
Several plays open with thunder and lightning indicating a storm. Alternatively, bird-song creates a feeling of being calm and denotes the outdoors. Cock-crows or bells indicate time. Music can engender a festive or sombre mood. Huge events such as battles, riots and celebrations can be more effective if created by noises off-stage, and left to the imagination of the audience.

To reproduce physical happenings
Realistic sounds indicated by the script, such as pistol shots, clocks striking, references to hearing horses hooves, trumpet calls or alarm bells.

Symbolic effect
Sounds that an audience would recognize as symbols for events; thunder for a supernatural happening, drums for a marching army, horns for hunting, fanfares to indicate arrivals, defeats, victories, etc. The influence of mediaeval drama is still around during this period and many plays called for sounds to evoke gods, spirits, devils and ghosts.

To create drama
To help create a climax or a 'lift' to a big scene – e.g. for spectacular processions (when musicians could join the actors on stage to create a bigger and more impressive crowd scene). Crowd scenes could be made to seem bigger by the addition of off-stage noise. Toasts are often accompanied by much rolling of drums, playing of trumpets and setting off of guns. Magnificent speeches are

ended with fanfares and guns – for instance, *"Cry God for Harry! England and Saint George!"* from Shakespeare's Henry V, followed by the stage direction: *"Alarum, and the chambers go off."* (chambers = cannon)

Scene links

To indicate that time and place remain constant, the same sound can be played from one scene through to the next (e.g. the storm scenes in Shakespeare's King Lear). On the other hand, changing the sound between scenes can indicate a new location and, indeed, a new mood.

To start and finish a play

Appropriate music, or even sound effects, to denote the beginning and end of a performance can be especially useful in theatres without curtains.

Were there sound technicians?

Many sounds were made by the musicians, but other effects must have been created by stage hands. There is a reference to *"hirelings"* being used. This is confirmed by a description of making thunder and lightning while discussing a production of Dr Faustus (1647) which refers to a *"twelve pennie hireling"* who is to operate the lightning effect – implying that extra back-stage staff were hired in as necessary.[2]

Description of English sound effects: 1580–1642

The following list of sound effects in plays from this period comes mainly from "A Dictionary of Stage Directions in English Drama 1580-1642" by Alan C Dessen. Items from other sources are indicated. This sample of effects amply demonstrates that the backstage sound effects team and the musicians were kept pretty busy.

Alarum or alarm (see also bell and chime)

An alarum according to Rider's Latin Dictionarie of 1640, is: *"... a sound or peale of trumpets or bells to call men together or to go to warre,..."*

As well as an off-stage trumpet or bell, it could be a drum noise. The alarum is often accompanied by 'excursions'; a running on to the stage by soldiers to indicate a battle or skirmish.

The alarm can also herald a more general presence of danger or disorder, and in this case, a bell might be used. Following Duncan's murder in Shakespeare's Macbeth, Macduff says: *"Ring the alarum bell."* And when the alarm has been sounded following a street brawl, Othello cries: *"Silence that dreadful bell!"*.

There is an amusing anecdote concerning an alarum, from Thomas Heywood's "An Apology for Actors" 1612 (reprinted for the Shakespeare Society in 1841) as follows: *"...certaine Spaniards were landed the same night, unsuspected and undiscovered, with intent to take in the towne, spoyle, and burne it, when suddenly, even upon their entrance, the players (ignorant as the towne'smen of any such attempt) presenting a battle on the stage, with their drum and trumpets strooke up a lowde alarme: which the enemy hearing, and fearing they were discovered, amazedly retired..."*

Stage directions during battles are usually for commands played on musical instruments, most often by drums and trumpets. These specific sounds would be recognized by the average Elizabethan theatre-goer:

Flourish – A musical fanfare. In battle scenes, this is nearly always used to indicate either the start of the action or a victory. It is also used for the entrance or exit of a noble person, coronations, proclamations, toasts, arrival of players, and for general rejoicing.

Sennet – A colourful musical prelude to indicate the appearance of a ruler, a commanding general or for a special state ceremony. A ruler can have his own special sennet – or signature tune.

Charge – A call to advance and assault. This can be a solo drum, or drum and trumpet, or drum, trumpet and fife.

March – Accompanies an army on the move, or a formal procession. This is a drum signal, but can also be played on the trumpet, fife or sackbut. "Dead marches" often feature in tragedies to accompany a funeral procession. Different types of marches could be played to indicate in which country the action was taking place; e.g. a Danish march requires a kettledrum.

Skirmish – Drum signal to deploy troops.

Retreat – A trumpet call used as a signal to withdraw or disengage.

Parley – Trumpet call indicating a truce or summons to talk between enemy forces.

Tucket – Trumpet call as an order to march, or for the arrival of heralds, messengers or persons of minor rank.

Levet – A wake-up call played on a trumpet.

Battle noise and metallic crashes and clatters

To create the sound of a battle, there would be a collection of swords, pikes, cudgels, and various items of ironmongery for people backstage to crash and clatter as appropriate to add to general shouts and cries.

Other metallic sounds are specified, such as: *"Here within they must beate with their hammers."* to denote a blacksmith's shop in the play LORD CROMWELL. Or, in a madhouse scene in THE PILGRIM, there is a requirement to *"Shake Irons within"*. Another *"noise within"* appears in THREE ENGLISH BROTHERS to denote the pulling up of an anchor chain. [2]

The script for SPANISH CURATE by Fletcher & Massinger (1622) warns the backstage crew to have *"pewter ready for noise".* Then, when the words "the ladles, dishes, kettles, how they fly all" are spoken, the script calls for *"a great noise within".*

The stage crew would also have means of creating door slams and the sound of bolts and latches as for: *"A noise is heard as if the gates were broken"* in CONSPIRACY by Killigrew (1635) or *"On a sudden is a kind of Noise like a Wind, the doors clattering, the Tombstone flies open"* in SECOND MAIDEN's TRAGEDY by Middleton (1611).

Bells (see also alarum and chime)

The great bell at the top of the tiring house would sound alarms, indicate church tower clocks, and herald ceremonies. Hand bells would have been used for gate and door bells, town criers, etc. A set of chimes would be in the musicians' arsenal to denote a peal of church bells, and to indicate supernatural events.

Birds

Specific birds named in stage directions include raven, crow, cock, nightingale, and cuckoo. Larks are mentioned in several plays, but are not specifically called for in stage directions.[2]

The earliest account of bird sounds in a performance appears in the records of a miracle play performed at Coventry in 1573, for which a man received fourpence for imitating the cock that shamed Peter after his three denials (in the New Testament story). Evidence of bird noises used in other countries is scarce, except for nightingale song. For example, at the Hotel be Bourgogne in Paris, 7 out of 71 productions called for a nightingale during the period 1622-1635.[4]

In 1581, ARRAIGNMENT OF PARIS by Benbow mentions *"an artificial charm of birds being heard within"*. John Bate in "The Mysteryes of Nature and Art" (published 1635), describes actually hearing a man using a "Sparrow Call" to produce different bird noises, and a brilliant bird imitator who could *"imitate with his mouth the whistling of a Blackbird, a Nightingall and Lark, yea almost any small Bird, as exquisitely almost as the very Birds themselves; and all is by the cunning holding the artificiall blade of an Onyon in his mouth."*

In 1634 a public pageant preceded a performance of Shirley's THE TRIUMPH OF PEACE, and Sir Bulstrode Whitelock records: *"After the Beggars' antimasque, came men on horseback playing upon pipes, whistles and instruments sounding notes like those of birds of all sorts, and in excellent consort, and were followed by the antimasque of Birds".* [4]

Whistles and mechanical devices are indicated in many stage directions. For example, the play PILGRIM by Fletcher in 1621, calls for *"Music afar off. Pot birds".* These "Pot birds", required to create a forest effect, may be alluding to the creation of warbling sounds by blowing into a bowl of water through a pipe. Possibly, they had already invented what are now called 'bird warblers'; the whistle that has a receptacle filled with water through which one blows and the bubbles make a warbling sound. These could still be seen in many theatre prop rooms when I started in the theatre in the 1950s. Even today, they remain part of an orchestral percussionist's armoury for use in novelty compositions.

There is a description of a mechanical device for imitating birds in Thomas Nashe's "The Unfortunate Traveller" (the earliest English adventure novel, written in 1594): *"...chirping birdes, whose throated beeing conduit pipt with squared narrowe shels, and charged siring-wise with searching sweet water, driven in by a little wheele... made a spirting sound, such as chirping is in bubling upwards through the rough crannies of their closed bills."* [2]

Although he was not writing for the theatre, John Bate in "The Mysteryes of Nature and Art" (1635) gives detailed instructions of how to manufacture various whistles and blowing instruments to imitate the *"voices, calles, cryes... of a cooko, a peacock, a bitern, a leuat* (leveret?), *a stag, a quaile, a small bird, a hare, a drake, a hedgehog, a plover, a puppie and a foxe.* He even had larger instruments for mimicking the sounds of *"the Hogge, Cow, and Lyon".* These were designed for use *"in sundry and severall parts of the Garden, the more antique and ridiculous, the more pleasant and delightfull".* There is no evidence that any of these were used in the theatre, but his book does prove that noise-making devices were around at the time.

Chimes (see also alarum and bells)
Small bells arranged by size, suspended on a bar and played with a hammer were often used to accompany supernatural events. Using bells to indicate the supernatural continued into, and throughout, the 18th century.

Echo
There are several instances of an echo effect achieved by an off-stage voice repeating the last word or words of the actor onstage. For example, in THE DUCHESS OF MALFI by Webster (1614), Antonia's last words are echoed to emphasize the death of the Duchess. Several other plays, including HOG HATH LOST HIS PEARL by Robert Tailor (1613), have the off-stage voice repeat part of the actor's words in order to seemingly answer his questions, while in ANYTHING FOR A QUIET LIFE by Middleton & Webster (1621) the echo effect is employed to make the onstage voice seem louder.

Guns and Cannon
The off-stage sounds of hand guns, pistols or cannon being fired were often specified, as in *"A pistol shot within"* from LOVERS PROGRESS by Fletcher (1623), *"A flourish of trumpets and two pieces go off."* and *"A Peal of Ordnance are shot off."* both from Shakespeare's HAMLET.

A *peal* refers to the discharge of guns or cannon, usually as an expression of joy.

Ordnance was the general term for guns and cannons of all kinds and a *Piece* was any piece of artillery used to fire a shot. A *Chamber* was a small cannon used for explosive effects. The word "Chamber" did not refer to a military weapon of the period, but was a term used in theatres and firework displays, as seen in the stage directions for the play, CONTENTION: *"Alarmes within, and the chambers be discharged, like as it were a fight at sea".* "Chambers" were without long barrels or carriages, and were loaded with blank charges and fired on signal.

A description of how to use *chambers* and make *saussisons* (explosive charges) is given in "Mysteries of Nature and Art" by John Bate (1635). Although John Bate is talking here about making fireworks for pageants and large outdoor events, the theatrical versions were probably similar.

Chambers

Take a Rocket case of what size you shall thinke fitting, according unto the report you would have it give; choake one end of it close, and put it into a Former without a broach, then fill it one inch and a half or more (as you think fit) with whole gunpowder; then drive a bottom of leather hard into it, this bottom of leather must be pierced with a small hole in the middle, with a hot iron, or else it will be apt to close againe. Fill then the other part of the coffin with a slow composition, up to the top, then take it out and binde 6, or 7, times about it a strong packthred in that place where the bottom of leather is, and it is made; you may binde divers of these on a row or frame rayle or such like, and put fire to their open ends, and they will burne slowly until they come to the bottom of leather, and then each will give a report or blow one after another orderly, as you gave fire unto them.

Saussisons

Saucissons are of two sorts, eyther to be placed upon a frame, or such like, and to bee discharged with a trayne of gunpowder, or else to be discharged out of the mortar piece. The standing saucisson is thus made; you must roll paper or canvas, nine or ten times upon a roller and choake the one end of it; fill it then with whole gunpowder, and then choake the other end also, then cover all the Saucisson with cord, and glew it over; then pierce one end of it, and prime it with a quill filled with gun powder dust; place it upon a frame having a hole for the quill to passe thorow; then fire it by a traine of gunpowder layd under the frame, it will give a report like Canon.

Saussisons are sometimes called *saussisous*; the two words seem to refer to the same thing. Max Culver in "A History of Sound Effects Devices" says that the *Saussisous* was later called a *mitrailleuse* or *tringle*.

Culver also points out that firing guns in the theatre did, of course, cause accidents. Burbage's men must have been using them when the Globe theatre burnt down; a contemporary report states that the blaze *"fell out by a peal of chambers... the tampin or stopple of one of them lighting in the thatch that covered the house, burn'd it down to the ground."*

Ben Jonson, in a poem referring to the same event, says there were two chambers:

> *But, O those Reeds! Thy mere disdaine of them,*
> *Made thee beget that cruell Strategem,*
> *(Which, some are pleas'd to stile but they madde pranke)*
> *Against the Globe, the Glory of the Banke.*
> *Which, though it were the Fort of the whole Parish,*
> *Flanck'd with a Ditch, and forc'd out of a Marish,*
> *I saw with two poore Chambers taken in,*

And raz'd e're thought could urge, This might have bin!
See the worlds Ruines! Nothing but the piles
Left! And wit since to cover it with Tiles.

Horses
"A trampling of horses" is required in Insatiate Countess by Marston &
Barkstead (1607).

Although the sound of horses' hooves is often required, we can find no evidence
of how this was achieved. It was such a common effect that stagehands or musicians
must have devised their own methods – possibly using hollow blocks of wood.

Carriage wheels are needed in A New Way to Pay Old Debts. Perhaps a real
carriage wheel was placed behind the stage.[2]

Hunt
"A cry of hounds within" is required in Every Man out of His Humour by Ben
Jonson (1599), and in Shakespeare's Titus Andronicus: *"enter Titus Andronicus*
and his three sons making a noise with hounds and horns."

The noise of a hunt could, of course, be achieved with horns and the shouts of the
hunters, with the baying of hounds created by dog imitators – although it is
possible that trained dogs were used in some instances.

In a performance of Palomon And Arcyte given for Queen Elizabeth I in the
hall of Christ Church College, Oxford in 1566, the yelping of hounds was heard
outside the windows (i.e. off-stage). This was so good that some of the audience
believed that the hunt was real: *"...a cry of hounds in the Quadrant, upon the train*
of a fox in the hunting of Theseus, with which the young scholars, who stood in the
windows, were so much taken, (supposing it was real), that they cried out, "Now,
now! – there, there! – He's caught, he's caught!" All of which the Queen merrily
beholding, said, "O, excellent those boys, in very troth, are ready to leap out of the
windows, to follow the hounds." [4]

In 1583, the Queen's court saw a performance of Dido which obviously featured
some spectacular effects, including a hunt: *"a goodlie sight of hunters with full crie*
of a kennel of houndes, Mercurie and Iris descending and ascending from and to an
high place, the tempest wherein it hailed small comfects, rained rose water, and
snew an artificial kind of snew, all strange, marvellous, and abundant." [6]

Music
As well as playing all kinds of music during the plays, the musicians provided the
flourishes and fanfares, often taking part in processions on the stage. They were
also responsible for a number of sound effects as previously mentioned. Favourite
instruments included:

> *Percussion* – Timbrel (shallow and open on one side), tabor (small, light drum
> which can be played with one hand), naker (a kind of kettledrum which
> apparently indicated royalty) and a chime of bells.

Brass – Trumpet (two types – straight with a flaring bell, and bent round like a modern bugle), horn, cornet, sackbut (with a long trombone-like slide).

Woodwind – Hautboy (oboe), recorder, fife, pipe, flute.

Strings – Viol (six-stringed instrument played with a bow) and lute.

In the play ENGLISH MOOR by Brome (1637), something called a Sowgelder's horn is required before the line: *"What hideous noise is this?"*. The Sowgelder's horn is mentioned in at least two other plays and was presumably an instrument capable of making a most unpleasant sound.

Noise
The word "noise" is used in many stage directions and is usually some kind of off-stage commotion, be it a crowd or a band of musicians. The script normally specifies the type of noise.

Pyrotechnics (also see Guns and Cannon)
Pyrotechnics were linked to supernatural events. For example, in SILVER AGE by Heywood (1611): *"The Devils appear at every corner of the stage with several fireworks...fireworks all over the house".*

Thunder
The sound of thunder was used a great deal as a dramatic device, not only for storms, but to indicate supernatural forces at work and, sometimes, to mask the sound of machinery. The various methods of creating thunder had changed little from mediaeval times; i.e. banging drums, and rolling heavy stones around in wooden containers or metal basins. However, we can find no mention of the thunder sheet – a large piece of flat suspended metal which is shaken – which is strange because it is a simple and effective device which we know was used in a Passion Play in Mons back in 1501.

In Italy, where they had entirely enclosed theatres, cannon balls were rolled above the ceiling of the auditorium. There are also several descriptions of the *thunder-run*, a device which was to become very popular in the 1700s in England. But even this was not a new idea. As mentioned in the chapter on the Romans, rolling large stones down a wooden ramp or metal chute, dates back to the 1st century BC.

Drum and Rolled Bullet
There is a description of making thunder in "The First Booke of Architecture" by Sebastian Serlio (translated into English in 1611): *"You must make thunder in this manner: commonly all Scenes are made at the end of a great Hall, whereas usually there is a Chamber above it, wherein you must roule a great Bullet of a Cannon or of Some other great Ordinance, and then counterfeit Thunder."*

The mention of a great hall with a chamber above means that he was referring to the Italian enclosed theatres. The open-air courtyard theatres in England had no ceiling over the main auditorium and the space above the stage (the top level of the tiring house) was somewhat cramped for rolling cannon balls around.

The stage direction from Crete Wonder: *"...drumes make thunder in the tiring house..."* was probably more practical.

This is born out by another quote from 1647: *"...the tragedies of Doctour Faustus in which Tempest shall be seen shag-haired Trivills, runne roaring with squibs in their mouths, while drummes make thunder in the tiring house, and the twelue pennie hirelings make artificial lights in her heauens."* [2]

But a way seems to have been found to roll the bullets in a courtyard theatre, as evidenced in the prologue to Ben Jonson's Every Man in his Humour (1616):[8]
> *Where neither Chorus wafts you ore the seas;*
> *No creaking throne comes downe, the boyes to please;*
> *Nor nimble squibbe is seene, to make afear'd*
> *The gentlewomen; nor roul'd bullet heard*
> *To say it thunders; nor tempestuous drumme*
> *Rumbles to tell you when the storme doth come.*

The stage direction in a play performed for Queen Elizabeth I in a hall in Oxford, calling for *"subterranean thunder"* makes one wonder if the back-stage drum might have been augmented by cannon balls being rolled around *under* the stage platform.

Thunder box or bowl
A variation of the rolled bullet method calls for *"a concave wooden affair containing iron balls and either rocked on the floor or rotated by hand in a horizontal plane."*[4] This harks back to the use of stones in barrels and copper basins employed in mediaeval religious plays. Indeed, there is reference to metal bowls being used much later, in 1733.

Thunder-run
The earliest mention of a thunder-run since Roman times (large balls rolled along a trough) seems to be by the Italian Sebastian Serlio, in "The First Booke of Architecture" translated into English in 1611, although his description is rather vague.

Nicola Sabbattini provides full instructions for a thunder-run in "Practica de Fabricar Scene, e Machine ne' Teatri" published in 1638: *"This effect is very easy to produce for it requires only a channel made of ordinary boards long enough to give duration to the thunder desired. Once having made the channel, it must be firmly placed above the heavens, and within it some steps ½ a foot high must be made according to the directions below; when we want to imitate thunder, a man, placed for that purpose must take two or three iron or stone balls, about thirty pounds in weight, and must release them into the channel, one after the other, according to the judgment of the director. Care must be taken that the channel must not be placed horizontally, but slightly inclined, The larger the channel may be, the more natural the thunder may seem."*

This would seem to be a development of the existing Italian method of rolling weights around above the ceiling of the auditorium, but in a more controlled fashion and with the addition of steps to allow the balls to drop as they rolled along. The heavy balls dropping would add a "boom" to the rumbling sound, probably causing the audience to feel the effect through the vibrations of the building.

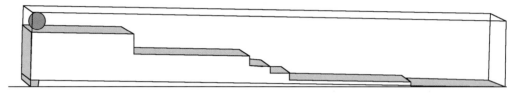

Sabattini also describes an interesting way of creating a lightning effect. I doubt whether today's health and safety authorities would be altogether happy with a stagehand perched on a scaffold with what seems to be an early version of a flash-box in his hand: *"There must be a man placed behind the Scene or Scaffold in a high place with a boxe in his hand, the cover whereof must be full with holes, and in the middle of that place there shall be a burning candle placed, the boxe must be filled with powder of vernis or sulphire, and casting his hand with the box upwards the powder flying in the candle whill show as if it were lightning. But touching the beames of this lightning you must draw a piece of wire over the Scene, which must hang downwards, whereon you must put a squib covered over with pure gold or shining sattin which you will; and while the Bullit is rouling, you must shoote of some piece of Ordinance, and with the same giving fire to the squibs, it will worke the effect which is desired."* [6]

In the same book, Sabbattini outlines ways of distracting an audience at the moment when a scene change is taking place, in order to make the transformation as magical as possible! He suggests planting someone at the back of the room to attract attention to himself by disorderly behaviour, or there could be a pretence that part of the spectators' seats have collapsed. A further suggestion is that drums may be beaten and instruments sounded. He indicates that this last method is generally to be preferred, since the first two sometimes cause undesirable alarm among the spectators. [6]

England's Inigo Jones and Germany's Joseph Furttenbach the Elder both played important roles in disseminating Italian stage practices throughout Europe. In "Mannhaffter Kunstspiegel" (1663), Furttenbach describes the practical use of an Italian thunder-run which does not seem to have any steps: *"On the upper floor a runway is made of dry boards, 4 feet wide and the length of the entire building. The boards are not nailed down fast, and side walls one and a half feet high are built so that the stone balls do not roll out of the runway. Two men are stationed at each end of the runway and twelve stone balls about eight-pound size are placed ready for the thunder. When the signal is given by the bell for the sound of the thunderstorm to begin, a man gently rolls one ball upwards the entire length to give the low sound of the beginning. Then a ball is rolled gently downwards. When the storm is to grow stronger, one man throws a ball violently onto the boards, and a man from the other end starts one violently so that there are two heavy strokes like powerful claps of thunder just over the audience. Then more are added until all twelve balls are in action."* [4]

Whistles

Whistles would not normally be a problem, but a Seaman's pipe to create a seafaring whistle (now known as a Bosun's call) was apparently an expensive item. Rather than owning one, there is evidence that these were hired for specific productions. There are two entries in the "Revels Accounts" of 1573/4 and 1574/5 referring to: *"A Whissell of Syluer for A ship Master hiered"* and *"The hyer of a Marryners whissell"*.

Wind

There is little evidence of any machine or device for creating the sound of wind during the Elizabethan period in England. Wind is mentioned in a number of plays and there are numerous storm scenes. There is one specific stage instruction in Second Maiden's Tragedy by Middleton, 1611: *"On a sudden is a kind of Noise like a Wind..."* It must be assumed that if the producers of plays went to such lengths to produce the sound of thunder, there will have been some method for augmenting this with wind noise.

One can conjecture that musical instruments like drums, cymbals and whistles were used, or they might possibly have been familiar with a method of producing a whirring and whistling effect by attaching the ends of thin pieces of wood to a cord and whirling it round one's head. This method is first described by Sabbattini in "Practica de Fabricar Scene e Machine ne' Theatri" in 1638. Joseph Furttenbach witnessed this in the Italian theatre, and was using the technique in his German productions by 1663 when he wrote: *"Several thin rulers or pieces of veneer two feet long, three inches wide and no thicker than a knife blade have a small hole the size of a quill at one end where a cord one and three quarters feet long is tied. Someone takes the cord in his hand and swings the ruler with all his might. When many rulers are whirling, they roar like a hurricane"*. But sound alone was not sufficient to achieve Furttenbach's theatrical effect: *"At the same time great bellows may send a wind out through hidden bored holes so that a strong wind actually blows on the audience. This whistling wind with the thunder and lightning, especially if the lights are darkened, will seem like a natural storm."* [4]

The end of an era in England

After the age of Shakespeare, English play-writing suffered a decline as no playwrights emerged with the stature of Shakespeare or Jonson except, perhaps, for John Webster (The White Devils and The Duchess of Malfi). Opera was becoming popular on the Continent by the middle of the 1600s, and the very first operas in England appeared in the 1650s, in private performances. Then, when the English Civil War began in 1642, theatres closed and acting was forbidden. London was officially without a theatre until 1660.

4 THE RESTORATION IN BRITAIN AND THE BIRTH OF AMERICAN THEATRE

Birth of the American theatre

AMERICAN THEATRE ORIGINATED with actors visiting Virginia from England, and it continued to develop along English lines. The first theatres were built in Williamsburg (1716), New York (1732) and Charleston (1736), although none of these theatres survived for more than a few years. By 1750 companies were performing in both New York and Philadelphia; many other colonies at this period being too puritan in outlook to favour play-acting.[18]

By the end of the 18th century, religious beliefs had relaxed, and acting companies, either resident or touring, could be found in all the major towns along the east coast. The Chestnut Street Theatre opened in Philadelphia in 1794, based upon the design of the Theatre Royal in Bath, England.[7]

From the beginning of the 1800s, a succession of well-known actors from England arrived in the US, and many chose to stay. The American star system began, and they became the founders of theatrical dynasties.[18]

The oldest continuously operating theatre in America is the Walnut Street Theatre in Philadelphia, which opened in 1809. Theatres were also operating in New York at the Park Street Theatre, in Charleston at the Charleston Theatre, and in Boston at the Federal Street Theatre.[19]

Gas lighting was introduced at the Chestnut Street Theatre, Philadelphia, in 1816. This was the first American theatre to have this innovation. It was not until the following year that the Lyceum in London became the first theatre in England to be lit entirely by gas, followed a month later by the Theatre Royal, Drury Lane.[20] The Chestnut Street Theatre was destroyed by arsonists just four years later, in 1820.

As the city of New York grew, it became the centre of theatrical life, leaving Philadelphia behind. Many new theatres were built: the Anthony Street Theatre (1813), The Chatham Garden Theatre (1824), the Lafayette and the Bowery Theatres (1826), The Opera House (1833) which became The National Theatre in 1836, The Franklin Theatre (1835) and The Broadway Theatre (1847). By this time around half a million people lived in Manhattan.

In 1869, New York had twenty-one theatres, most of which were clustered around Broadway.[19]

As people moved west, theatre followed; the first permanent playhouses were build in St Louis in 1837, Chicago in 1847 and San Francisco in 1853.[18]

In 1881, the Savoy theatre in London opened with an electrical lighting installation. The electrical revolution quickly spread across America and by the end of the century, most theatres in America were lit by electricity.[20]

A new style of theatre involving large numbers of local people emerged during the early 20th century. This was known as Community Theatre. By 1930 there were over one thousand non-commercial theatres, which included both community and college theatres.[19]

The proscenium theatre in England

KING CHARLES II WAS restored to the throne in 1660 at the end of the Civil War and theatres began to flourish once more. The king had been in exile on the Continent for many years and had become accustomed to watching plays with actresses, painted scenery and stage machinery in theatres with proscenium arches and curtains. It is not surprising that he encouraged their adoption in the new public theatres in London, which were roofed, and had a proscenium arch with a window opening into a music room above it. However, a memory of the Elizabethan courtyard theatre remained in the form of a forestage in front of the proscenium, and an apron stage jutting out into the auditorium. In front of the proscenium arch, doors opened onto each side of the forestage. Another important innovation occurred in theatre design in 1730 when the orchestra moved to a well in front of the stage – the orchestra pit.[7]

Many playhouses were built in the provinces, based on the design of these London theatres. Only three now remain in a recognizable state; the Theatres Royal at Bristol, Margate and Richmond in Yorkshire.[7]

Charles II controlled the re-established London theatre by issuing Letters Patent, initially to two men, Davenant and Killigrew in 1662. This gave them a monopoly over serious spoken drama within the city of Westminster. However, people used a variety of ruses to get round the Patents system and drama was soon appearing in non-Patent theatres. They circumvented the Patents system by introducing singing and dancing interludes into spoken dramas. This brought about the distinction between 'legitimate' and 'illigitimate' theatre – expressions still in use today.

In 1737, Prime Minister Robert Walpole, concerned about growing political satire in the theatre, introduced the Licensing Act, which tried to strengthen the old Patent system. Managers of 'unlicensed' theatres and places of entertainment added yet more subterfuges in order to perform spoken dramas, such as putting on concerts with 'free' plays in the intervals, or charging for tea and providing 'free' plays.

The Act did have one major and lasting effect on English drama; it stated that all scripts had to be submitted to the Lord Chamberlain for approval before any performance was permitted. He could order words or whole scenes to be altered or deleted, or the entire play could be forbidden. This law was only repealed in 1968.

In the print by Hogarth (circa 1738) called "Strolling Actresses in a Barn", the 'Act against Strolling Players' (a section of the Licensing Act) lies on the crown in the foreground, under the baby's bowl of gruel. The playbill on the bed announces that this *'Company of Comedians from the Theatres at London'* is embarking on *'the last time of Acting before ye Act commences'*. It is also interesting to note that the lady in the rose-coloured dress on the right is leaning her book against a salt cellar containing a rolling-pin which was apparently used for making 'thump-and-rattle' noises. On the table in front of the box is a tinder box and Jupiter's 'thunderbolt'. Next to the flower-wreathed arch against the left hand wall, are two of the great rollers used to simulate the motion of the waves, and to the right of these hang a large drum and a trumpet.

"Strolling Actresses in
a Barn" by
William Hogarth.
*Picture courtesy
Antony Horder*

Audiences seemed particularly attracted to theatrical productions with stage machinery, special effects, dances and songs. There was a lack of well-written 'straight' plays in Great Britain, partly because of the new censorship. Many theatres turned to spectacle and the people flocked to the new, larger theatres where amazing scenic effects were possible and financially viable.

The Queen's Theatre, designed by Vanbrugh, opened in 1705 and became the home of opera in London. Its great size created acoustic problems. During the

18th century, many experiments were made in theatres to try to improve audibility and visibility for all.

Both comedy and tragedy were stretched to include some spectacular elements if at all possible. If not, then short spectacles, dances and songs were given between the Acts. This thirst for stage effects annoyed Edward Howard, who wrote in "Six Days Adventure" in 1671: *"...and though the ear be the principal sense to receive satisfaction from the Stage, yet we find, that of seeing has not seldome a greater predominancy, whilst scenes, habits, dances, or perhaps an Actress take more with Spectators, than the best Dramatick Wit, or contrivance of the Age..."*

Another reference to stage effects appeared in the Spectator, April 1711: *"Among the several artifices which are put in practice by the poets to fill the minds of an audience with terror, the first place is due to thunder and lightning, which are often made use of at the descending of a god, or the rising of a ghost, at the vanishing of a devil, or at the death of a tyrant. I have known a bell introduced into several tragedies with good effect: and have seen the whole assembly in a very great alarm all the while it has been ringing. But there is nothing which delights and terrifies our English theater so much as a ghost, especially when he appears in a bloody shirt. A specter has very often saved a play..."* [6]

The Spectator points out, however, that spectacle is no substitute for a good script: *"The tailor and the painter often contribute to the success of a tragedy more than the poet. Scenes affect ordinary minds as much as speeches; and our actors are very sensible that a well-dressed play has sometimes brought them as full audiences as a well-written one....But however the show and outside of the tragedy may work upon the vulgar, the more understanding part of the audience immediately see through it, and despise it."* [6]

The greatest actor of the day, and the actor whose impact was greater than any other before or since, was David Garrick. He was actor-manager at the Theatre Royal, Drury Lane from 1747-1776 and was responsible for many changes in theatre design. For example, members of the audience were no longer permitted to sit on the stage and, in 1765, he introduced hidden lighting. Candles with reflectors were placed in the wings and along the front of the stage (footlights), replacing the chandeliers hanging over the stage. [20]

Around 1771, David Garrick employed Philippe Jacques de Loutherbourg, a successful painter and member of the French Royal Academy, as his scene director. Audiences wondered at the beauty of his splendid cut-outs and romantic scenery, and were amazed by his fires, storms, volcanoes and cloud effects, whose dramatic success relied heavily on sound. De Loutherbourg became internationally renowned for his sensational stage effects while continuing his successful career as a landscape painter.

Storm scenes

THE SOUNDS OF WIND, rain and thunder were an important element in the stage spectacular. Many of the tried and tested techniques from previous eras were employed and improved upon.

For thunder, the rolled bullet in a wooden or metal container, as previously described, seems to have become known as the *Mustard Bowl* method. There are several references dating from the early 1700s. One assumes the name came about because of the similarity between bowls used to grind mustard and the bowls used to roll bullets around for creating thunder. Alexander Pope in 'The Dunciad' (1729) wrote:

> *'Tis yours to shake the soul*
> *With thunder rumbling from the mustard-bowl.*
> *With horns and trumpets now to madness swell,*
> *Now sink in sorrows with a tolling Bell.*

A further reference to this method of thunder-making appears in THE STAGE-MUTINEERS or A PLAY-HOUSE TO BE LETT (1733):

> *Farewell the shrill-oak'd Trump, and slacken'd Drum...*
> *And, o ye Iron Bowls! Whose massy Balls*
> *The Thundering Jove's great clamours counterfeit.*

There is an account in William Dunlap's book, "The Life of George Frederick Cooke" (1815) of Cooke's boyhood encounter with a thunder barrel. It appears that Cooke was hiding in a barrel backstage during a performance of MACBETH, when he suddenly found himself fastened in with two twenty-four-pound cannon balls and being rolled across the floor.[8] Presumably, the sound of the thunder was somewhat muffled that night and might well have included some high-pitched yelping noises.

De Loutherbourg's miniature spectacle

THE THUNDER-SHEET AND the wind-machine finally seem to have been used in England towards the end of the 1700s. The thunder-sheet was used by David Garrick's scene director, Philippe Jaques de Loutherbourg, in an entertainment he devised which took the form of an automated theatrical spectacle in miniature. With the unwieldy name of "Eidophusikon", it had three-dimensional sets and models, a moving panorama and fantastic lighting and sound effects. The Eidophusikon was so successful that, in 1782, it was presented at the Exhibition Rooms in the Strand, London, for a second season. The public was promised: *"The elegant and highly favoured SPECTACLE... In the course of which will be introduced the celebrated Scene of THE STORM & SHIPWRECK. To conclude with the Grand Scene from Milton with the usual accompaniments."* Apparently, the Grand Scene involved Satan with his troops on the edge of the Fiery Lake and the raising of pandemonium – which *"filled the audience with horror".*

A contemporary account by William H Pyne claims that mariners who experienced De Loutherbourg's storm at sea declared it *"amounted to reality".* Going on to describe the storm, he wrote: *"The thunder was no less natural, and infinitely grand; a spacious sheet of thin copper was suspended by a chain, which, shaken by one of the lower corners, produced the distant rumbling, seemingly below the horizon, and as the clouds rolled on, approached nearer and nearer, increasing peal by peal, until, following rapidly the lightining's zig-zag flash, which was admirably vivid and sudden, it burst in a tremendous crash immediately over-head."* [4]

Here we have mention of the thunder sheet, but there was also a thunder barrel or similar device: *"The sounds which accompanied the wondrous picture struck the astonished ear of the spectator as no less preternatural; for, to add a more awful character to peals of thunder, and the accompaniments of all the hollow machinery that hurled balls and stones with indescribable rumbling and noise, an expert assistant swept his thumb over the surface of the tambourine, which produce a variety of groans, that struck the imagination as issuing from infernal spirits."* [4]

William Pyne also mentions De Loutherbourg's wind machines. These would appear to be a similar idea to the wind machines often mentioned in the 1800s, whereby silk or canvas stretched tightly over a revolving wooden slatted drum creates a moaning or screaming sound depending upon the speed of the drum and tightness of the canvas. Pyne describes: *"two machines, of a circular form, covered with tightly strained silk, which pressed against each other by a swift motion, gave out a hollow whistling sound, in perfect imitation of loud gusts of wind."* Also used were: *"large silken balls, passed hastily over the surface of the great tambourine"* [4]

The Eidophusikon also had a wave machine, a rain and a hail machine, similar to those which became common in the 1800s:
"The rush of waves was effected by a large octagonal box, made of paste-board, with internal shelves, and charged with small shells, peas, and light balls, which, as the machine wheeled upon its axis, were hurled in heaps with every turn...For the rain, a long four-sided tube was charged with small seed, which, according to the degree of its motion, from a horizontal to a vertical position, forces the atoms in a pattering stream to the bottom, when it was turned to repeat the operation. The hail was expressed by a similar tube, on a large scale, with pasteboard shelves, projecting on inclined planes, and charged with little beads; so that, sliding from shelf to shelf, fast or slow, as the tube was suddenly or gently raised, the imitation was perfect." [4]

Whether De Loutherbourg actually invented any of these machines, or merely brought them to England, is not clear. However, he had a reputation for constantly surprising theatre audiences by inventing bigger and better effects and one can assume that Garrick would have used them at Drury Lane. One can also be sure that his ideas were copied by other theatre practitioners in England.

Stealing one's thunder

ALTHOUGH VARIOUS FORMS OF the *thunder-run* had been used in Italy since the early 1600s, and the idea was known in England and Germany, it seems probable that the first practical version was not constructed in England until 1709, the occasion when the famous phrase, "Stealing One's Thunder" originated.

The phrase is attributed to critic and playwright John Dennis (1657-1734), whose play, APPIUS AND VIRGINIA, opened on February 5th 1709 at the Theatre Royal, Drury Lane. It closed after only four or five nights to be replaced by MACBETH, staged by a different company. During the first performance of MACBETH Dennis recognized the sound of his thunder-run which, to give him his due, had probably cost him a lot of money to install. Not unreasonably in the circumstances, this thoroughly upset him and he stood up and remonstrated. According to which account you believe, he cried out:

> "*S'death! That is **my** Thunder.*"
> Alexander Pope, 1729

(this is the oldest account, written a mere 20 years after the event)

> *Damn them! They will not let my play run, but they steal my thunder!*
> Handy-book of Literary Curiosities.

> *See how the rascals use me! They will not let my play run, and*
> *yet they steal my thunder!*
> Biographia Britannica

The thunder-run was taken up by other theatres, as seen in a report by Addison in the Spectator (1714): *"I was there last Winter at the first Rehearsal of the new Thunder, which is more deep and sonorous than any hitherto made use of."*

There is a list of properties and scenery from London's Theatre Royal, Covent Garden in 1743 which includes *"86 thunder balls, the thunder bell and line."* [4] The thunder bell and line were there to cue the thunder by ringing the bell, a common practice at the time. In "Memoirs of the Life of John Philip Kemble" by James Boaden (1825), a thunder bell and a curtain bell were listed in the inventory of properties for the Theatre Royal, Crow Street in 1776. [8]

The Theatre Royal Bristol had a thunder-run, the remains of which can be seen today. Theatre historian Richard Southern described it as being double *"running the total width and back"* over the audience. It is uncertain whether it was installed when the theatre was built in 1766, or added later.

Not all thunder-runs were above the auditorium, some were constructed at the side or the back of the stage. In 1749, the Dresden Opera House in Germany had a zig-zag run at the back of the stage. [4]

The Drottningholm Palace Theatre, or Drottningholms Slottsteater, located at Drottningholm Palace in Stockholm, Sweden, was completed in 1766. After King

Gustaf III was assassinated in 1792, the theatre was closed up and virtually forgotten. At the beginning of the 1920s, the court theatre – complete with working stage machinery and many original sets and costumes – was "rediscovered" and restored.

The stage machinery included a device for making thunder mounted above the forestage. This is a long box, pivoted at the centre, which can be lifted by pulleys at one end to send the stones inside rumbling to the other end. The principle is similar to the pivoted boxes filled with dried peas or lead shot popular for making a rain effect during the 1800s.

Drottningholm Palace Theatre in Sweden, built 1766, has a pivoted thunder box above the forestage which can still be seen. There is also a wind machine.

In Russia, according to Max Culver in "A History of Theatre Sound Effects Devices" a machine used in serf theatres during the late 1700s and early 1800s produced thunder from beneath the stage. These private theatres were owned by rich Counts

Thunder Machine
Ostankino Palace
Theatre, Moscow,
circa 1795.

who kept serfs as actors, scene builders, etc. To create the thunder, two wheels with an uneven "cog-like" appearance were attached to a central shaft. By turning a handle, the two wheels circled the shaft, creating a rumbling sound on the wooden floor. An example can be seen at the theatre within the Ostankino Palace, former summer residence of the Counts Sheremetev, originally situated several miles to the north of Moscow, but now within the city. The theatre was built around 1792 -1795 and all the original stage machinery is still in working order. Today, the theatre is used as a concert hall.

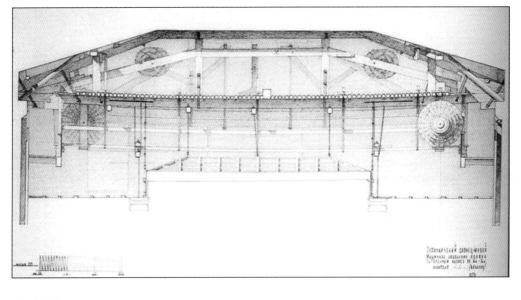

It is difficult to understand this drawing of the basement at the Ostankino Palace Theatre, but the thunder machine is apparently located beneath the auditorium floor in front of the proscenium.

Rumble cart from the Theatre Royal, Drury Lane, London *donated to the Theatre Museum, London.*

The rumble cart, also known as a thunder cart (or *Le chariot du tonnerre* in France) was a sturdy wooden box mounted on four octagonal wheels. When the box is filled with stones or other heavy weights and hauled across the stage floor, the juddering of the uneven wheels causes the floor itself to vibrate and rumble. In some instances, to create an effect of thunder overhead, it was trundled across the ceiling of the forestage or auditorium.

The thunder cart was in use as far back as the 1600s in Italy according to George Moynet in "Trucs et Decors – La Machinerie Theatrale". He was writing in 1893, however, some two hundred years later, and it is not clear upon what he based his facts. Thunder carts do not seem to have come into their own until the 1800s.

We do know that at least one French theatre had a form of rumble cart in 1761, as one is mentioned during a description of the Paris Opera by Jean-Jacques Rousseau in his novel, "Julie, ou La Nouvelle Heloise": *"a heavy cart, rolled over (the proscenium) arch...not the least agreeable instrument heard at our opera."*[10] It is interesting to note that the cart seems to have been rolled above the proscenium arch, rather than behind the scenery at stage level.

Guns and explosions

APPARENTLY DE LOUTHERBOURG invented a mechanical drum to achieve explosive effects. William Pyne gives a first-hand description of the sound of a distress signal at sea: *"He caused a large skin to be dressed into parchment, which was fastened by screws to a circular frame, forming a vast tambourine; to this was attached a compact sponge that went upon a whalebone spring; which, struck with violence, gave the effect of a near explosion; a more gentle blow, that of a far-off gun; and the reverberation of the sponge produced a marvellous imitation of the echo from cloud to cloud, dying away into silence."* [4]

However, theatres were still using pyrotechnics for the sound of explosions and gunfire. Small cannons were fired during THE BATTLE OF BUNKER'S HILL at the Haymarket Theatre Boston in 1797. A letter from the producer, named Burk, explained to another theatre how the melodrama's battle scene should be carried out: *"The Americans fire – the English fire – six or seven of your men should be taught to fall – the fire should be frequent for some minutes...small cannon should be fired during the battle, which continued with us for twelve or fifteen minutes".*

Perhaps the producers of the day were too fond of startling their audiences with loud bangs. In his play, THE CRITIC (1799), Sheridan parodies the over-use of sound effects:

> *Puff:*   *But take care, my dear Dangle! The morning-gun is going to fire. (Cannon fires)*
>
> *Dangle:* *Well, that will have a fine effect!*
>
> *Puff:*   *I think so, and helps to realize the scene. (Cannon fires twice) What the plague!* **Three** *morning guns! There never is but one! – Aye, this is always the way at the theatre: give these fellows a good thing, and they never know when to have done with it.*

5 FINAL DAYS OF EFFECTS MACHINES

Melodramas and music-halls

IN 1802, A TALE OF MYSTERY (originally in French) opened at the Theatre Royal, Covent Garden (later to become the Royal Opera House) and was the first play to be called a "Melodrama". This was a genre of rapid action where virtue always finally triumphed over vice. It featured elaborate settings, stage effects and music. Melodramas had been delighting the uncritical new audiences that crowded the popular theatres in France, and soon became equally popular in England. Both Covent Garden and Drury Lane theatres succumbed to this mania for dramatic stories and spectacle and there was no lack of fire, floods and earthquakes, with many productions incorporating real animals – dogs, horses, even elephants.[7]

The Theatres Act of 1834 removed the monopoly for the official production of "straight" plays that had been enjoyed by Drury Lane and Covent Garden theatres since 1737 (although the Lord Chamberlain's power of censorship remained in place until 1968). Other London theatres such as the Lyceum, Olympic and the Princess's could now produce drama. There followed a spate of theatre building to accommodate a rapidly expanding audience. Gas lighting began as early as 1817, allowing new scenic effects. Theatre during the 1800s was more popular in England than before or since.

The style of entertainment known as music-hall in Great Britain, and vaudeville in America, began in the 1850s and soon formed a major part of popular theatre, providing permanent employment for all kinds of acts – singers, comedians, dancers, jugglers, magicians, etc. – who constantly travelled from town to town. Some of the leading music-hall performers became great stars.

Melodramas, pantomimes and spectacles, where text usually came a poor second to scenery and effects, remained popular until the end of the 1800s when the histrionic performance style perpetrated by actor-managers such as Sir Henry Irving and Sir Herbert Beerbolm Tree gradually went out of fashion. Until then, the public flocked to experience the spectacles relying on big impressive sound effects, often using ideas and devices from the previous century.

Thunder

THUNDER WAS ALWAYS THE favourite and new machines, or variations on the old, were invented. The 'thunder-run' was still the loudest and most impressive device, and they were installed in many of the larger old theatres and included in new buildings into the early 1900s. The Théatre-Francais in Paris had a thunder-run added prior to 1832, which, according to Georges Moynet, was used with *"thrilling realism"*.[11]

Many large theatres were being built using stone and metal, and the effect of cannon balls rumbling above a wooden ceiling across the auditorium was no longer an option. Most of the later thunder-runs followed a zig-zag design, running down a wall at the side or rear of the stage.

According to Max Culver in "A History of Theatre Sound Effects Devices", the London Lyceum's thunder-run, constructed in 1886, used six inch, eight inch and nine inch cannon balls which dropped eight feet from hoppers into a one inch thick boiler plate, and then rolled down a chute.[4] The Royal English Opera House (now the Palace Theatre) opened in 1891 with a thunder-run, and Her Majesty's Theatre also included one when it was re-built – for the fourth time – in 1897 (two were demolished by fire and one knocked down).

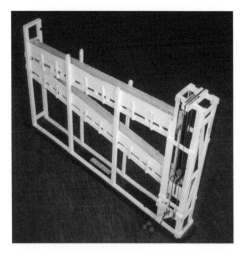

Model of a zig-zag thunder-run showing the pulley-operated lift to transport the cannon balls to the top of the tower. *Theatre Museum, London*

Two New York theatres had thunder-runs in the early 1900s. One of these was used for Henry Irving's tour of FAUST in 1901. Ellen Terry was Irving's leading lady, and apparently she was concerned about the effect being sufficiently dramatic. The property man therefore put 50 pound cannon balls into the thunder-run instead of the usual 30 or 40 pound balls. During the final performance, some of these 50 pound balls are said to have left the track and crashed to the floor outside Ellen Terry's dressing room.[4]

Zig-zag Thunder-run on wall of the stage house in the Thalian Hall, North Carolina, built 1858. *Thalian Hall Center for the Performing Arts, Inc.*

Between 1897 and 1913, the New York Metropolitan Opera House installed a thunder-run which had electric motors to operate doors to shut off sections of the trough. Thus, the volume and duration of the thunder could be altered. The zig-zag trough extended from the roof to the sub-cellar, and used small iron balls.[4]

In Germany, they developed what was known as the "rabbit hutch" method of holding and releasing the cannon balls. At the top of the thunder-run, and at right angles to it, were a number of shelves each holding several cannon balls. The shelves were sloping into the trough of the run, but were held back by doors. Thus, the timing of the peals of thunder could be controlled by opening the doors on cue. Moreover, different sizes and quantities of cannon balls could be pre-loaded in the rabbit hutches to produce a variation in the sound quality. The Bayreuth Festspielhaus was still using its "rabbit hutch" thunder-run in 1929.[4]

The French version, called the "Tremie", was summed up by George Moynet in 1893: *"Its general direction is oblique, slanting, and it changes direction at right angles. If at the centre bullets of iron are released into this hopper, they roll on the first oblique slope with a rumble which increases. At the first change in direction, there is a drop accompanied by a resounding shock, then the cannon ball takes a more rapid course on a new slope, until the next jump; finally it encounters the last which takes it to the floor of the stage, covered with steel plate which produced the final crash. The fall lasts scarcely several seconds."* [4]

"Rumble carts", as described in the previous chapter, continued to be used extensively during the 1800s in England and on the Continent, either instead of thunder-runs or to augment them. We know that the Dresden Opera House had a six-wheeled version. They were very versatile and could be used for earthquakes and other general rumbling sounds. The type of noise and the amount of floor vibration generated could be varied by adjusting the weights in the cart and the speed of movement.

Towards the end of the 1800s, it seems that the cumbersome thunder carts and thunder-runs began to lose favour, to be replaced by thunder-sheets, thunder drums and "Venetian-blind" crash effects. In contrast to the show-stopping rumblings and crashes vibrating throughout the theatre which were such highlights of the melodramas and even operas of the age, these more controllable sounds were particularly required as the trend towards realism gathered pace.

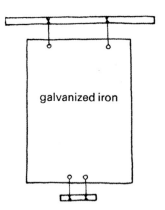

Thunder-sheet.

Another reason for the growing popularity of thunder sheets and drums was because they were relatively small and portable and therefore ideal for touring companies. Thunder-runs were bulky and costly constructions requiring a lot of manpower to operate and, of course, were only installed in some of the larger theatres.

Thunder-sheets were widely used in America and, in 1893, George Moynet stated that the thunder-sheet was the standard device for producing thunder in France: *"The average size for a large theatre is two meters (78 inches) high and eighty centimeters (32 inches) wide. The sheet is suspended from the top by metal supports, chain or angle-brackets, and is shaken sharply by hand, at the corner or by a handle."* [4]

Drums and sheets were also versatile in that they could be "played". A thunder drum can be hit hard to produce a sonorous boom or, with two sticks, the skilled operator can make it rumble. Similarly, a single vigorous shake of a thunder sheet results in a metallic crack of thunder and continuous smaller exertions will make the sound of it rolling away. In the hands of well rehearsed operator, the two instruments creating the high cracks and the low booms would produce a very convincing sound.

The construction of a typical thunder drum was a large square frame over which moistened cowhide was tightly stretched. It was then heated to dry and tighten the hide. The frames varied in size from around 3 foot (1 metre) square to 6 foot (2 metres) square.

A French thunder-drum was described by Georges Moynet in 1893: *"This is a kettle drum whose diameter is little larger than that of ordinary drums, but whose length is singularly increased by as much as two meters. This drum, covered by two well-stretched donkey skins, is laid out horizontally on some supports. The musician uses a large, well-padded drumstick not unlike those used for kettledrums."* At the Theatre de Chatelet in Paris, thunder-drums were used beneath the stage in 1912 for a volcanic eruption. By 1902, the "thunder-box", a large square frame covered with rawhide, was seen in German opera houses. At the Bayreuth Festspielhaus, four men operated four massive thunder-drums called "Glockenklavier" for Wagner's operas. One German thunder-drum used heavy balls which rested on top of the drum and bounced as the drum was struck. [4]

In America, Lincoln J Carter, a producer of "sensational melodramas" claimed that he had invented a new device for creating thunder for his production of THE TORNADO (1913), which he called the bull-drum: *"This consisted of a steel cylinder about three times the size of the largest bass drum. Heavy rawhides were spread tightly over the ends, resembling very much a huge drum."* [4]

There is reference to electrically operated thunder-drums in the early 1900s with motors activating the drum beaters. In the New York Metropolitan Opera House, for example, two thunder machines high in the flies were operated by electricity in 1913: *"a large drum, with beaters worked by electricity, and a series of octagonal wheels revolving over wooden sounding board"* [4]

In Ronald Harwood's book "Sir Donald Wolfit" he tells how the last of the great British actor-managers was never satisfied that the storm scene in KING LEAR was loud enough. This, despite the fact that he employed a wind machine, a rain machine, two timpani, a large empty water tank beaten with a padded stick, a thunder sheet, and a sound effects record. Wolfit started acting in 1920 and toured his own company around Britain from 1937 to 1953.

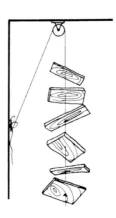

Venetian-blind
crash effect.

The Venetian-blind crash effect was for the sudden loud noise of a thunder clap, to startle the audience. It was also useful for other crash effects, and is described by Jean-Pierre Moynet as being in use in France before 1873. Basically, it consisted of planks of wood suspended above the stage which, when released, fell to the stage with a satisfying clatter. The rope threaded through a hole in each plank was knotted to keep the planks apart. Varying the sizes and types of timber would produce a different sound and sometimes pieces of iron were included to add to the effect.

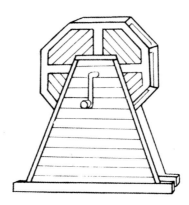

Avalanche
Machine.

Variations on the old thunder barrel design, also known by now as the 'avalanche machine', appeared as late as 1926. Apparently, the famous actress, Dame Edith Evans presented a machine to the Old Vic Theatre in London for the play DELILA in which she starred. Frank Napier, stage director at the Old Vic, recalls the machine in his book "Noises Off". He describes what became known as the "Edith": *"It consists of a large cast-iron stand, upon which an octagonal drum rotates. The drum measures some three feet six inches across by one foot six inches thick. The sides are of wood and the barrel of sheet-iron. The sides are joined together with stout pieces of wood screwed on outside the sheet-iron to give added strength. It is fed with cannon balls through a trapdoor in one side, which, when the drum is turned by hand, rush round and make a splendid crashing, rumbling, grinding noise.*[12] An avalanche machine could be filled with a variety of materials – metal, bricks, glass, stones – to produce all kinds of different rumbles and crashes.

Wind

WE KNOW THAT Philippe Jacques De Loutherbourg had invented a machine to create the sound of wind for his "Eidophusikon" spectacle by 1782. The contemporary account says that it used drums with stretched silk rubbing together to create a whistling sound. This is not dissimilar from the wind machines familiar in many theatres up to the 1950s, based on a sturdy frame supporting a hand-cranked revolving wooden cylinder with raised slats along its length. The silk was stretched over the cylinder so that when the cylinder revolved, the raised slats rubbed against the silk to produce a swishing sound. The faster the machine was cranked, the higher in pitch became the sound. Some machines had the fabric fixed at one end and either weighted at the other end, or kept taut by springs. More sophisticated machines had a method of varying the tautness by means of a foot pedal or a handle in order to increase and decrease the depth of sound. Silk appears to have been favoured for the early machines, but this was replaced in many later versions by canvas which is much more durable.

The Germans had an electrically operated wind machine at the Deutsche Theatre, Munich in 1897, and the Dresden Hoftheater had two wind-machines by 1902 – a small portable machine for locating the wind in a specific place around the stage, and a four-man machine located under the stage. Both machines used linen.[4]

Wind Machine
*donated by the
Theatre Royal, Drury
Lane to the Theatre
Museum, London.*

Rain

THE SOUNDS OF RAIN, hail, waves and surf were created in a number of ways, mostly involving small objects such as pebbles or dried peas swirling round in some container, such as a large wire sieve or wooden tray.

The 'rain box' or 'rain tube' took the form of a long wooden box, sometimes several metres in length, which could be tilted to set pebbles or dried peas pattering from one end to the other. We know De Loutherbourg was using this device in the 1780s. Inside the box, timber or metal ledges were fixed at intervals for the pebbles to bounce off. Some versions were pivoted so that they could be inverted once the pebbles had reached the bottom. The operator would stand at one end of the box and simply lift it or drop it to make the pebbles roll gently back and fro. Two rain boxes could be used to maintain a more continuous rainfall. The rain box was also very effective for creating the sound of surf.

Right
The author with
a replica of a
rain box.
Theatre Museum,
London

Far right
Rain box at
His Majesty's
Theatre, London.
Photo: Billy Rose
Theatre Division,
The New York
Public Library

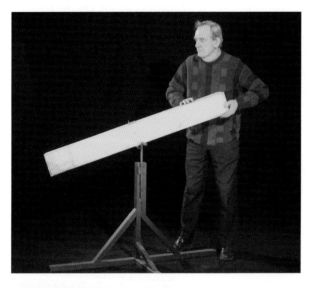

Russian Rain box
Ostankino Palace
Theatre, Moscow,
circa 1795.

A Russian rain machine in the Ostankino Palace Theatre, Moscow, dates from around 1795. It consists of a long vertical box with strips of bended metal fixed to the walls. Dried peas or shot trickling from above make 'plinking' noises as they bounce from one strip of metal to the next.

There were many ways of using small objects to simulate rain or surf; one of the most popular being the rain drum. As an assistant stage manager in 1955, I was actually given the task of swirling dried peas around on the surface of a large drum, suspended under the stage to create a most effective surf effect. All the sounds in this Christmas show, LISTEN TO THE WIND, set in Victorian times, were deliberately stylized. We even used a thunder sheet for the storm scene – and what an excellent effect that was!

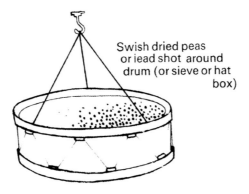

Swish dried peas
or lead shot around
drum (or sieve or hat
box)

Rain or
surf drum.

For the same production, we made a rain tray as described by our stage director who had seen them used in the 1930s. This was a wooden tray about 30-inches (76cm) square with twenty or thirty 2-inch (5cm) nails knocked into the surface. Dried peas gently swirled around in the tray made a swishing sound combined with a very satisfactory 'plinking' of peas bouncing off the nails. A heavier rain sound can be achieved by lining the base of the tray with tin and using lead shot or marbles.

Yet another variation on the same theme was the 'rain cylinder' or 'rain drum' in use during the 1880s in France, Britain and the USA and frequently used well into the 1930s. This was another rotating barrel to be filled with pebbles, lead shot, dried peas, etc., depending upon whether light rain, heavy rain, hail or surf was required. Some cylinders were solid and had strips of wood fixed inside to collect and let fall some of the peas as the drum revolves. Others, as the example from the Theatre Royal, Drury Lane, had wire mesh to catch the peas and make a more metallic sound.

Far left
The author with a rain drum donated by the Theatre Royal, Drury Lane to the Theatre Museum, London.

Left
Rain drum hanging above the stage. Thalian Hall, North Carolina (built 1858). *Thalian Hall Center for the Performing Arts, Inc.*

Some of the later rain cylinders were powered by electric motors. The Deutshe Theatre in Munich had one in 1897, and the Birmingham Repertory Theatre in England had one in 1925. Even as late as 1938, Century Lighting Inc. in New York had a rain cylinder in their catalogue.[4]

In the mid 1950s, director Peter Hall saw the Moscow Arts Theatre performing a play in London that featured an impressive storm. Apparently, this production had first been mounted in the 1930s, and had not been changed or updated in any way, even to the extent that cannon balls were rolled around the stage floor to create thunder and the rain was simulated by two ancient machines. It so happened that Peter Hall was about to direct Peter Sellers in a play called BROUHAHA at the Aldwych theatre in London, which required the star to create a storm in front of the audience. Consequently, we had copies made of the two machines.

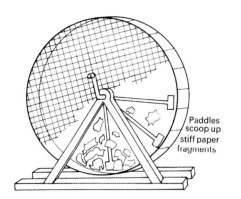
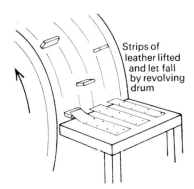

Right
Gentle rain
machine.

Far right
Splatter rain
machine.

The first machine was a fixed drum with wire netting sides and a handle to turn wooden paddles. Inside the drum were torn up pieces of stiff paper or card. When the paddles were turned, they swished through the paper with some of it scooped up and dropped back through the revolving mechanism. The sound it made was very much like a gentle rain.

The other machine had a revolving wooden drum with a small platform near one end to which were tacked three strips of leather. As the drum revolved, randomly spaced pieces of wood stuck to the drum lifted and released the strips of leather. The leather slapping on to the platform made a very convincing heavy rain sound and, of course, the faster the drum was wound the heavier the rain sounded.

These machines sounded so good that I attempted to record them for my sound effects library, but I was unable to capture the essence of these physical sounds. The disappointing noise was merely paper rustling and leather slapping. It made one realize that some of these old machines played in a live theatrical context were probably more dynamic and realistic than the best of modern sound systems using recordings of the real thing.

This was confirmed by another example of trying to record a live effect. During the 1960s, I was sound designer for a play starring Trevor Howard called TWO STARS FOR COMFORT, during the course of which there was a downpour of rain. The lighting designer, Richard Pilbrow, suggested that real water should be sprayed from a perforated pipe suspended above the stage into a canvas trough (hidden by a scenic ground-row). The idea being that he could side-light the dropping water and this would be seen sparkling through the door and window in the back of the set. Unfortunately, the window had to be filled with gauze (scrim) which obscured a view of the rain. Although it did look very good indeed through the door, when the play was rehearsed on the set, it became obvious that the door would be kept closed during a rain storm. Consequently, the door was only opened briefly when the characters entered, and the rain was never really seen at all. The removal of this visual effect was only discussed briefly because the 'sound' was so totally convincing. After all, it was real water droplets hitting canvas and then, as the trough filled slightly, hitting canvas and water as though there were puddles being generated. At the time, I ran the Theatre Projects Group sound company and our effects library began to receive requests for the "marvelous rain effect" we had supplied for TWO STARS FOR COMFORT. So we took our equipment to the theatre and made several recordings from different perspectives. None of them sounded at all convincing!

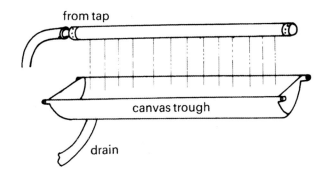

Rain Trough.

In "Stage Noises and Effects" (1958)[12], the author, Michael Green, declares that a hose leading to a pipe perforated with holes, which pour water onto a sheet of corrugated metal is superior to any recorded sound effect. So this use of real water was not new, and similar experiments must have been tried ever since mains water became available – and maybe before.

Storms

AN ADVERTISEMENT circa 1930 from the American company, Cleon Throckmorton Inc., states that they would build to order any effect – rain, lightning, hoof-beats, snow-cradles, waterfalls – whatever you need. And they declared that *"every theatre should have its thunder and wind apparatus."* The full-sized professional thunder sheet cost $7.00 and the 14-inch drum wind machine cost $15.00.

An article in the Boston Herald dated April 1903 gives a wonderfully graphic account of a storm sequence experienced at the Tremont Theatre in Mrs Fiske's production of MARY OF MAGDALA. It begins with two deafening crashes *"that seem to rend the air, and then a loud rumble that fades away as from it rise the roar of wind and the pour of rain. A flash, brilliant, dazzling, lights the stage...."* etc. The reporter is then allowed backstage to see how all this is achieved. From one of the galleries overlooking the stage, he first describes the thunder-run: *"What appears to be an impoverished bowling alley occupies most of the space. Above it is a compartment filled with big iron balls, and directly below on the alley is a heavy, double steel plate. Alongside the alley is a trough, slanted on an opposite incline. Next to these stands an iron cylinder with a hole in its top. Further along are a couple of churn-like objects, a huge thing that would resemble a drum if it was not square, and a great sheet of iron, suspended from the ceiling and with handles at its lower end."* The stage crew stand by: *"Six men surround the bowling alley, two at each end of the alley proper and two at the long trough that runs alongside it. Other men station themselves at the various appliances. He who stops before the iron cylinder picks up a shotgun and loads it. Then he rams the muzzle into the cylinder."* The storm begins: *"A red lamp on the wall, unlighted till now, flashes. It is the signal for the storm. For a moment you do not know what has happened. You see the flash of the red light, and your senses are numbed by the noise. All the machinery of the storm is set in motion at once. The gun is fired, and the resonance of the shot makes you jump. The cannon balls drop from their box and thunder down the alley. There, two men catch and throw them into the other alley, where they run back to be picked up by other men and replaced in the box for another round. The man at the sheet iron is working it frantically, and the dull boom of the drum rumbles ominously. At the wind and rain machines, men are grinding as if their lives depended on it – and probably their jobs do. The light flashes again, and this time it means silence for a moment."* There are several sequences with pauses for the actors to speak, until the storm ceases: *"The last peal of thunder sounds; the cannon balls are laid away, and the storm brewers wipe their brows and rest."*

Backstage at the Broadhurst Theatre. The sound effects department for TEN LITTLE INDIANS. *New York Herald, 27 August 1944*

The producers preferred to pay a crew of effects men rather than put up with the thin "scratchy sound" produced by disc recordings. To the left of the picture, an empty box is to be dropped for a heavy falling object. In front of this is a rain cylinder filled with dried peas. In the foreground a sieve is being swirled to give the sound of surf while, to the right, the wind machine is cranked. The man as the back has an outboard motor mounted on a barrel of water to give the effect of an approaching motor boat. Hanging on the wall, the square object is a thunder drum. Also seen is a hose pipe leading to the rain over the doorway on the set.

In 1916, Arthur Krows' book "Equipment for Stage Production" shows a hand-cranked *"wind siren"* with a megaphone attachment *"so that the sound may be directed toward any given part of the stage".* An electrically operated version was patented in 1924. In the same year, another machine was patented which used an electric motor to drive a kind of fan which had thin perforated blades to make a wind sound.[4] Theatres constructed their own versions with two lengths of bamboo fixed to the shaft of an electric motor. By 1938, the American company, Century Lighting, Inc., were marketing an electric wind siren.

Crashes, gunshots, explosions

VARIOUS FORMS OF THE "Clatter machine" or "Crash machine" seem to have been around since the mid 1800s and probably before. These were used for comic effects, such as someone falling or objects being dropped or smashed off-stage, or for any occasion where sudden sharp sounds were required. They were even used for rapid gunfire, perhaps for firing squads or later, for machine guns. The principle of the clatter machine was the same as the ratchet-rattle used by orchestral percussionists. An upright frame had several slats of stiff timber fixed at the top. Beneath the frame, a revolving drum with protruding paddles would lift and release the slats causing them to slap back on to the frame with a loud crack. To increase the volume, some machines had the slats in pairs with the rear ones fixed to the frame and the front ones free to slap back. To vary the sound, other machines had the slats resounding on a surface of canvas padded with horsehair. The example in the Victorian painting of a backstage scene, "Her First Bouquet", shows two rows of slats with the revolving drum in the middle. Above the clatter machine is a thunder drum and above that seems to be a thunder sheet.

HER FIRST BOUQUET
by Charles Green –
1868
Clatter machine
backstage with "bass
tambour" (drum)
and thunder sheet
hanging above it.
*Photo: Chris Beetles
Gallery Limited*

It was quite common to use real guns and explosives for the extremely popular battle scenes during the 1800s and early 1900s. The guns often fired blanks, but sometimes an explosive charge would be held in place with wads of paper or hair rammed down the barrel so that the audience could see an actual projectile. Some theatres preferred leather for the wadding as it was less likely to catch alight and set the scenery on fire, but there were, of course, many accidents.

On the right, the author with a clatter machine and on the far right a variation with slats hitting a canvas-covered horsehair cushion. This sounds very much like a burst of rifle fire. *Machines donated by the Theatre Royal Drury Lane to the Theatre Museum, London.*

In 1846, the Garrick Theatre in London caught fire *"owing to some wadding lodging in the flies after the performance of the BATTLE OF WATERLOO".* In the early 1870s, an American actor was killed in a Washington theatre when *"too heavy wadding entered his head from the gun of a horrified comrade"* Moynet noted in 1875 that *"extras in battle scenes quite often wounded each other, although they were supposed to be firing into the air. Loaded firearms were handed out to the actors and extras, and the ramrod used to load them would be chained to the wall, lest it was forgotten in the excitement."* [4]

By 1870, Jean-Pierre Moynet said that the French were using a device called a 'tringle' with 30 or 40 pistol barrels loaded with gunpowder to create a fusillade. This is a more modern version of a row of 'saussisons' or 'chambers' used at least as far back as the 1500's (see Chapter 4). The touch-holes of the barrels were linked by a slow or faster burning fuse as the effect required. In the USA, they developed a slightly safer version of the tringle using firing pins and a safety bar to prevent accidental firing. [4]

A blank cartridge fired into a milk churn or a barrel partly filled with water will greatly amplify the sound, and was effective for simulating an explosion. Towards the end of the 1800s, explosive charges were being ignited electrically and this led to the safer use of the "bomb tank". This is a large metal tank (for example a domestic cold water storage tank) with a metal mesh covering, from which a large firework is suspended. The metal tank not only prevents accidents, but it reverberates to enhance the explosion. Bombs, or 'maroons', could be obtained in the UK from theatre lighting hire companies and are still available today.

A pistol shot with a blank cartridge in a real gun is usually more effective than a recording. It has immediacy and impact and the sound reverberates naturally within the acoustics of the theatre, whereas a recording will carry with it a different set of acoustics. Gunshots were also simulated by such simple methods as hitting the seat of a leather chair with a bamboo cane or, indeed, wielding the slap-stick (see page 60).

There was an occasion when, as an assistant stage manager, the starting pistol I was using for an off-stage effect refused to fire. The stage manager, who was more quick-witted and experienced than I, grabbed a short length of wooden batten – which had fortuitously been left near the prompt corner – and thwacked it on to the stage floor. There had only been a short delay and, surprisingly, no members of the cast mentioned it.

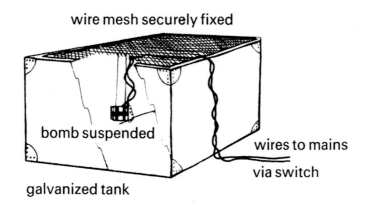

Bomb tank

Bells

MANY TYPES OF BELLS are constantly required in theatrical performances for churches, clocks large and small, doors, telephones, etc. One of the most famous examples was in the production of THE BELLS, produced in 1871 at the Lyceum theatre in London. This melodrama used the sound of ghostly sleigh bells to remind the lead character about the murder he had committed, and it made Henry Irving a star overnight. He later became the first English actor to be knighted.

Although hand bells and chimes were normally used, there are instances of huge bells hanging backstage operated by ropes. One extreme example was given by Godfrey Turner in his book, "First Nights of My Young Days" (1887), where he writes that the great English actor, Edmund Kean, introduced a pageant between the third and fourth acts of Richard II during which *"the peal of church bells was, I believe, the first ever heard within a playhouse walls."* [8] A huge bell was common, of course, in the courtyard theatres of Elizabethan times.

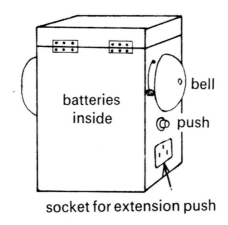

Bell box.

Recordings of church bells were used as soon as the technology became available, but smaller bells and buzzers are among the few sounds which are often performed "live" today. As an assistant stage manager in 1956, I recall lurking in the wings with a small bell and hitting it with a six-inch nail at the dramatic moment when the little bracket clock had to strike. We also used the real thing for doorbells, often activated by the actors. For electric doorbells and non-electronic telephones, although recordings are widely used, the 'bell box' is still in use. The box, containing batteries, normally has two different sounding bells, or a bell and a buzzer, fixed to either side. Each bell has a push button and an alternative socket for an extension lead, so that the unit could be operated remotely by the stage manager.

Animals

BEFORE THE ADVENT OF good quality recording and playback systems, theatre technicians continued to be inventive in the ways they used everyday objects to mimic sounds. Water-whistles remained a favourite for warbling birds, although different bird sounds (and cheeping crickets) were also created with reed whistles and penny whistles.

Dogs, cats and larger animals growling or roaring were mostly made by actors or stage crew. In "Noises Off" (1936), Frank Napier has a chapter on mimicking animal sounds, and gives the useful advice that in order to obtain the correct sound, the intending mimic *"should pay a visit to the beast or bird in question".* Sometimes large megaphones were employed to amplify or distort vocal sounds. The megaphone was also a good device for making ghostly voices or effects. Another amplifying tool was a metal bucket into which the mimic would moo or roar.

As evidence that animal imitators were taken seriously in the American theatre, James R Pitman, prompter for the Boston Museum Company, was credited in 1869 as: *"An adept at simulating the barking of dogs and the crying of babies".* And, in 1874, in an article for a magazine entitled "Secret Regions of the Stage" Olive Logan commented that: *"nothing resembles the braying of a donkey as the voice of a man who has made it his special study".*[4]

According to Edgar E. Willis writing in the American "Journal of Broadcasting" (1956/57), there was a radio actor who became an expert at vocalizing animal sounds. During the rehearsal for a radio play in 1925 where the cast were meant to be shipwrecked on the Galapagos Islands, for fun he happened to imitate a seal barking. The director asked him to keep it in. Thus began the sound effects career of a man somewhat appropriately named – Bradley Barker. Other American broadcasters of the period specializing in animal sounds included Harry Swain, Donald Bain and Else Mae Gordon.

In the New York Herald Tribune, 30 January 1938, there is an article about Clarence Straight, who was *"one of the top practitioners of a singularly uncrowded profession. He devotes his life to the imitation of animal, bird and insect noises."* In the production OF MICE AND MEN at the Music Box theatre, he stood in front of a microphone in a specially constructed acoustic booth and created the atmospheric sounds of nature. *"As the curtain goes up on the Shalinas Valley in shimmering haze of early twilight, from the far distance seems to come the mournful baying of a coyote. Then wild dogs bark savagely. An owl hoots and the coyote bays again. The evening is alive with sound as George and Lennie, the tragic central figures of the play, come ambling into sight along the river bank. Throughout the entire first scene, Straight continues these animal sounds into the microphone, making each one with the effortless ease of a virtuoso. They are controlled by an operator below the stage and released through loudspeakers set at various strategic spots."* Apparently, Straight was an actor whose talent for animal mimicry was discovered when a horse whinny was required for a radio play. This led to a new career and even his own radio programme.

Percy Edwards was a very popular radio broadcaster in Britain from the 1940s to the 1970s. His act consisted of describing country scenes and making all the bird and animal noises. He was so brilliant that he had a second career mimicking animals for film soundtracks. It so happened that we had a recording of one of his cock crows in our library and it was a constant source of amusement when we played this, along with three or four real cocks crowing, to theatre directors. Inevitably, they would choose the Percy Edwards version because it sounded "more realistic". We would say nothing!

Creaks, squeaks, growls and roars

A MOST USEFUL DEVICE for a variety of sounds, depending upon how it is 'played', was constructed from a small barrel with both ends removed and one end replaced with a piece of plywood (or a drum skin for a higher pitched effect). A piece of string fixed firmly through the centre of the head and impregnated with resin is held taut with one hand; then, using the other hand, the string is pinched with a piece of leather and drawn along it. This produces a really good squeaking door or the creaking of ship's timbers, but by altering the tautness of the string and the amount of 'pinching' with the leather, it can also produce convincing roars and growls.

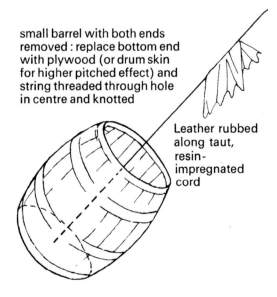

small barrel with both ends removed : replace bottom end with plywood (or drum skin for higher pitched effect) and string threaded through hole in centre and knotted

Leather rubbed along taut, resin-impregnated cord

Door/ship creak barrel.

The bull-roarer, as the name implies, makes a roaring sound which could be an animal or even a wind. This was normally a piece of timber with holes drilled in it attached to a piece of cord and whirled around the head of the operator. A similar effect can be achieved by whirling short lengths of hose pipe. This effect has been around for centuries, and may possibly go back to the Ancient Greeks.

Horses

WOODEN BLOCKS BANGED TOGETHER or on to various surfaces were still being used for horse's hooves, as were coconut shells. During the 1960s, I recorded coconut shells more than once for plays where the horse had to do something specific and the results were never queried by the directors.

In Germany, America and Britain, from 1887 to 1919, a few attempts were made to manufacture machines with wooden cups, real horseshoes on wooden blocks, or coconut shells being mechanically drummed on to interchangeable surfaces.[4] Some of these were patented, but history does not relate how successful they were.

Horse's hooves,
Alhambra Theatre
London.
*Photo: Billy Rose
Theatre Division,
The New York Public
Library for the
Performing Arts,
Astor, Lennox and
Tilden Foundations*

From the Strand Magazine a photograph shows an instrument with three wooden blocks on the end of arms pivoted at one end. The fixed centre arm has a guide in the form of an arc within which the outer arms can move. The operator can move the two outer arms rhythmically so that their blocks strike the centre block. The piece in the magazine states that this horses hooves effect *"is highly realistic"*.

Carriages

WE CANNOT FIND MUCH evidence of how they made the sound of carriage wheels although, as they were easily available, one can imagine a stage carpenter taking a pair of wheels and fixing them to a shaft to be pushed over a suitable service; e.g. gravel laid on the stage floor. Add the horses hooves and jingling of harness and there is your carriage. Alternatively, they might well have used an avalanche machine filled with gravel to make the wheel sound.

Trains

RAILWAYS AND SPECTACULAR train crashes often featured in melodramas and one of the ways of simulating the wheels clattering over the rails involved a revolving drum covered in metal, against which a metal wheel or roller was placed.

A ridge on the drum provided the rhythm of the train passing over the gaps in the rails. Added to this would be bells, whistles and the hissing of steam. A modified version of this machine also served for carriage wheels and other vehicles. A similar device can be constructed from a shallow wooden box sitting on metal castors. The box is made to rotate around a fixed central pivot so that the castors run on a metal plate or circular track on the floor. Different sounds can be created by varying the load placed in the box. Two or three gaps or bumps in the plate or track will add the rhythm of a train.

Max Culver in "A History of Theatre Sound Effects Devices"[4] cites a similar Russian contraption which had a metal surface upon which two heavy iron rollers could be made to rotate around a central shaft. The surface had the occasional 'bump' to create an uneven rumbling sound.

To create the 'chuffing' of a train, sometimes sheets of sandpaper were rubbed together, or on to some resonant surface. A stiff broom and a hand brush could also be rubbed on to a big drum. Another idea was to beat wire brushes against a long length of stove pipe.

The most famous train effect in the British theatre was created for Arnold Ridley's THE GHOST TRAIN. First produced in London in 1925 at the St Martins theatre where it received a muted response, it was transferred to the Garrick theatre early the following year to become an enormous success. The undoubted star of the show was the unseen train – which required a crew of ten stage hands. The train "appeared" three times by means of carefully orchestrated sequences using the following instruments:

1   tubular bell (E flat) with small padded mallet
1   garden roller pushed over bevel-edged struts screwed to stage,
    30 inches apart
1   18-gallon galvanized iron tank with large padded mallet
1   bass rope drum and pair of sticks
1   side drums with wire drum brush
1   side drum with medium padded mallet
1   thunder sheet
2   compressed air cylinder (obtainable from British Oxygen Company)
1   train whistle fitted to one of the cylinders
1   tin amplifier (megaphone) fitted to the other cylinder with counterweight to
    place in its mouth (to vary the steam hiss sound)
1   stationmaster's whistle (for mouth)
1   milk churn with lid
2   electric or hand-driven motors

Visual effects
2   spotlights focused on windows of the waiting room set
2   slides cut as carriage windows of train to move in front of spotlights
    (long strips of plywood cut with a series of square holes)

REALISM IN SOUND BEHIND THE SCENES: RAILWAY NOISES "OFF."

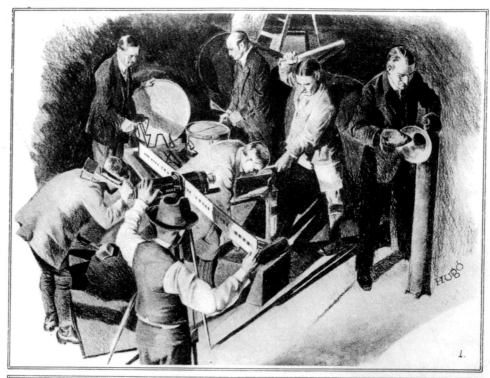

Creating the
effects for
THE GHOST TRAIN.
*Raymond Mander
and Joe Mitchenson
Collection*

PRODUCING SOUNDS OF A TRAIN: (1) A "BATTERY" OF DIN, INCLUDING A COMPRESSED - AIR CYLINDER (RIGHT) FOR HISSING STEAM ; (2) DRAWING A ROLLER OVER STICKS, AND (INSET) THE CAUSE OF THE "SOUND" THUS REPRESENTED.

The first sequence begins with the stage manager hitting the tubular bell twice – a warning bell signifying that a train is due. After a pause, the bass drum and large metal water tank begin to be drummed upon rhythmically with heavy padded mallets, at first gently, growing louder as the train approaches. Then two men start a pair of motors (exactly what these are is unclear) and another commences a rhythmic wire brushing on a small side drum. The intensity and texture of noise is increased by the rattling of a thunder sheet and the hiss of steam from a compressed air cylinder. As the train enters the station, a heavy garden roller is pulled across wooden struts fixed to the stage floor and the spotlights are switched on with the "window" cut-outs moving across the beams.

The tempo is decreased as the train comes to a stop and everything becomes silent except for the steam and the metallic clanking of a milk churn being repeatedly hit with its lid. When the train is due to leave, the stage manager blows a whistle which is answered with two sharp blasts on the train whistle attached to the second compressed air cylinder. The stage manager then begins to slowly beat the second side drum, the thunder sheet is given a shake, the motors are started, the water tank is beaten in time with the side drum, the bass drum is beaten quickly and continuously, and the garden roller starts to move. There is a puff of steam and the lighting technicians move their cut-out slides in front of the spotlights with gathering speed to give the effect of the train passing the waiting room windows. When the lights cut out, the well-rehearsed crew reduces the sound while increasing the tempo and the train fades away in a reverse sequence of the approach.

The train has two further appearance with slightly different stage directions for their operation, and these can be seen in French's acting edition of the play. I have been unable to discover what the "two electric or hand-driven motors" actually were. I kick myself now when I think that I designed the sound for a stage musical of the BBC television series DAD'S ARMY in which Arnold Ridley starred – and I never asked him about one of the most famous stage effects ever.

In 1982, THE GHOST TRAIN was produced at the Alhambra Theatre in Durban, South Africa. Prior to the production, the theatre's Head of Drama, John Moss, visited the author, Arnold Ridley, in England to discuss the play. He became fascinated by Arnold Ridley's description of how the audience reacted to the sound of the train and determined to attempt the original effect. Although a recording of a train was used, it was the physical vibration of the garden roller and drums, and the immediacy of the steam and whistles that made the hairs stand up on the backs of the audience's necks. John Moss wrote to me: *"Even though I had been involved in all the technical set-ups and knew exactly what was going on, I still felt that some bloody great steam train was makings its way across the stage!!"* John also related an interesting fact that emerged from his meeting with Arnold Ridley; apparently, it was the enormous success of the play that spawned the idea for the spooky ghost train ride we now take for granted in funfairs.

In contrast to the success of the Durban production, I saw an English touring company in 2004 in a version of the play that relied solely on recordings. It was disastrous. I felt sorry for the actors striving, and failing miserably, to convince the audience that they were terrified by a canned sound coming from a couple of loudspeakers. Oh dear!

The use of drums and water tanks brings to mind an incident involving JOURNEY'S END, the play by R.C.Sherriff set in the trenches during the First World War. It was some time during the 1970s when I was working one evening with my colleague, Tony Horder, in our recording studio. Tony answered the doorbell to find a worried-looking stage manager from the Cambridge theatre, just down the road. They were in the interval of a revival of JOURNEY'S END and their tape machine had packed up. This was a major problem as the climax of the play relies upon a massive barrage of gunfire and explosions. Tony grabbed one of the Revox tape decks from our dubbing room and we took it round to the theatre. Whilst he was plugging it into their system, I became aware of intense activity at the back of the set. An elderly gentleman was busy assembling a collection of dustbins, tea chests, brooms, hammers, stage-weights, etc. Upon enquiry, the stage manager explained that their propman had actually worked on the original production at the Apollo in 1928, before tape recorders were invented; and he was determined, single-handedly, to create the battle sounds as they did in the good old days. In some ways, I was rather sad that we had cheated him of his moment of glory.

Vehicle engines

FOR VEHICLE ENGINES IN the early part of the 20th century, sometimes electrically-driven sewing machines were used, placed in boxes to make them resonate. The added toot of a car horn would signal what the sound was meant to be. For airplanes and other engine sounds, motorized fans were adapted with the blades replaced by strips of leather, and a piece of wood was placed so that it was thwacked by the flailing leather. A variable speed fan would add to the realism. A variation had short leather thongs attached to the shaft of a motor (or an electric drill), with each thong having a metal or wooden ball fixed to the tip. The motor was set running next to a snare drum to create an airplane motor, or the same device could replicate a machine gun against a very tight drum head, a big engine against a bass drum, or a riveter with a compressed air cylinder.

Doors and other noises

A STANDARD PIECE OF kit in theatre prop rooms was a 'door slam'. This was usually a full-size door in a solid frame (sometimes on castors) with an assortment of catches and locks. More portable versions came in the form of large boxes with doors. The door slam was widely used well into the 1970s as most theatre loudspeaker systems could not reproduce the impact of the real thing.

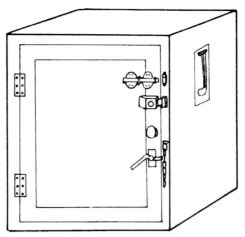

Door slam.

stout timber box with door
and bolt, latch, chain, handle,
knocker etc.

Another live effect which was far more convincing than early recordings was the 'glass crash'. This was a large box (often a tea chest) lined with a blanket and containing pieces of broken glass. On cue, a sheet of glass laid across the top of the box was smashed with a hammer. The initial crash is enhanced by the bits of broken pane falling on to the glass already in the box.

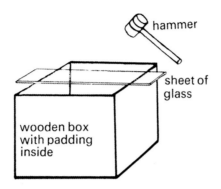

Glass crash.

A slightly different sound for a glass or crockery crash was created by having broken pieces in a container. These were suddenly tipped into a wooden box or a metal bucket – depending upon the sound required.

The maid screams as she falls down the stairs and drops the tray of crockery. Scene from LIFE WITH FATHER. *New York Herald Tribune, 31 December 1939*

For the sound of walking on gravel, e.g. a person walking up the drive, a simple wooden tray filled with gravel would do the trick. The actor or a stage manager walks on the spot doing 'feet acting', just as footsteps are dubbed into movie films today. For an army on the march, there are instances of large gravel trays for several pairs of feet.

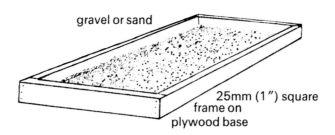

Gravel Tray.

Smaller items seen in many prop rooms include the 'cork popper' – a pop-gun made from a bicycle pump with a cork stuck in the end – and the slap-stick for simulating the crack of a whip.

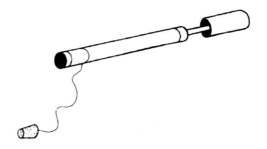

Cork popper using bicycle pump.

A slap-stick consists of two long pieces of flat wood held apart at one end by a small spacer so that when the instrument is knocked against a solid object the two pieces of wood make contact with a loud crack. An alternative version had no spacer, but one of the pieces of wood was hinged. Slap-stick became a term used to describe the physical comedy routines popular in the theatre during the late 1800s and, later, in the silent movies. The Oxford English Dictionary states that the word 'slap-stick' originates in the USA. However, similar devices were used in Commedia dell'arte performances, which began in Italy in the 1400s and flourished until the 1700s. The characters, identified by costumes and masks, were reminiscent of the Roman comic plays and led to the tradition of English pantomime in the 1800s. The Punch and Judy puppet show (originally called Punch and Joan) can also trace its roots to Commedia dell'arte characters. Mr. Punch often used a slap-stick during the performances.

On the right
Slap-stick

On the far right
Slap-stick built
into comic cudgel

Smack plywood whip against firm object

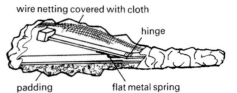

wire netting covered with cloth

hinge

padding

flat metal spring

Machines from the Theatre Royal, Drury Lane

THERE ARE SEVERAL PHOTOGRAPHS in this book of noise-making machines donated to the Theatre Museum in London by the Theatre Royal, Drury Lane around 1970. A prop room in the Theatre was to be cleared out for use as a technical equipment store for a newly formed company, Theatre Sound and Light Limited. The museum's curator was invited to Drury Lane by the general manager, George Hoare, and when he opened the door to the prop room, a treasure trove of ancient sound effects machines was revealed.

To find out more about these machines, I talked to Jennifer Hoare, George's widow, and she thought that they were all made in the 1930s for pantomime productions. This did not quite tally with the theatre's list of productions, as there were only three pantomimes during that period. If one went back to 1900, however, there were more than twenty pantomimes or spectacles for which these kind of sounds could have been required.

When I visited the Theatre Museum's store in May 2002, for me, the most wondrous machine was a colossal device for making giant's footsteps. Jennifer Hoare said that this was used in JACK AND THE BEANSTALK in 1935. This contraption takes two men turning a barrel with levers attached to lift, in turn, six solid timber beams 6 feet (2 metres) high. At the top of each piece of timber is a bolt to retain two large metal washers. Thus, when each beam is lifted and then dropped with a heavy thump on to the wooden base, it is followed by the 'chinking' of metal washers bouncing up and down. Somehow, that little touch just brings it to life.

Giant's footsteps machine donated by theTheatre Royal, Drury Lane to the Theatre Museum, London.

It looked as though the machine had gone through several stages of repair or modification. Some of the timbers seemed older (perhaps cannibalized) and whereas most of the joints are beautiful dovetails, metal screws had been used in a few places. Perhaps the machine actually dates back to a previous production of JACK AND THE BEANSTALK in 1899.

The collection from Drury Lane contains one enigma. This machine has a revolving wheel made of iron with a heavy metal weight resting on it. The scraping sound could resemble the mechanics of carriage wheels or, perhaps, some kind of lathe – were it not for the piece of wood fixed to the rim of the wheel. This lifts the weight on each rotation, briefly interrupting the scraping noise, then lets it fall with a metallic 'clank'. Could it be for a ship's engine or a factory machine or a comic car? Whatever its purpose, it demonstrates the ingenuity of stage carpenters to invent machines for any specific sound required.

'Mystery machine'
donated by the
Theatre Royal, Drury
Lane to the Theatre
Museum, London.

Theatre of ideas and realism

SPECTACULAR MELODRAMAS REQUIRED huge effects, around which the entire production could be planned; but a new kind of drama was emerging that called for more subtle sounds.

It is generally acknowledged that Henrik Ibsen was the founder of modern prose drama with plays such as BRAND (1866) and PEER GYNT (1867). August Strindberg, a fellow Swedish playwright, participated in this move towards realism on stage with, among others, THE FATHER (1887) and MISS JULIE (1888). Soon, playwrights throughout Europe were inspired to develop thought-provoking theatre with realistic situations and dialogue. George Bernard Shaw's first play, WIDOWER'S HOUSE, was produced in London in 1892 and ARMS AND THE MAN in 1894. Into the 20th century, Shaw was writing plays like PYGMALION (1913) and Anton Chekhov in Russia was producing UNCLE VANYA (1900), THE THREE SISTERS (1901) and THE CHERRY ORCHARD (1904).

With the theatre of realism came the use of atmospheric sound effects placed in the production to enhance or heighten the drama. Chekhov used animal and bird sounds to establish atmospheres and rural settings. He also specified sounds that were integral to the action, as in THE CHERRY ORCHARD where the distant chopping down of the orchard is crucial and has to be totally believable. The play also contains one of the most contentious effects ever specified by an author – that of the house's heart breaking "like a violin string snapping". Some translations describe it as "the sound of a rope breaking as if from the sky". This is a soundman's nightmare – as I can testify. Every director knows in his or her mind what it is, but they cannot explain it – and probably would not like it if they heard it.

In 1904, Vladimir Nemirovitch-Danchenko, a director at the Moscow Arts theatre, wrote endorsing the use of naturalistic sound effects in THE CHERRY ORCHARD: *"A pause is not something that is dead, but is an active intensification of experience, sometimes marked by sounds stressing the mood; the whistle of a factory or steamer siren, the warbling of a bird, the melancholy hoot of an owl, the passage of a carriage, the sound of music coming from a distance."* [4]

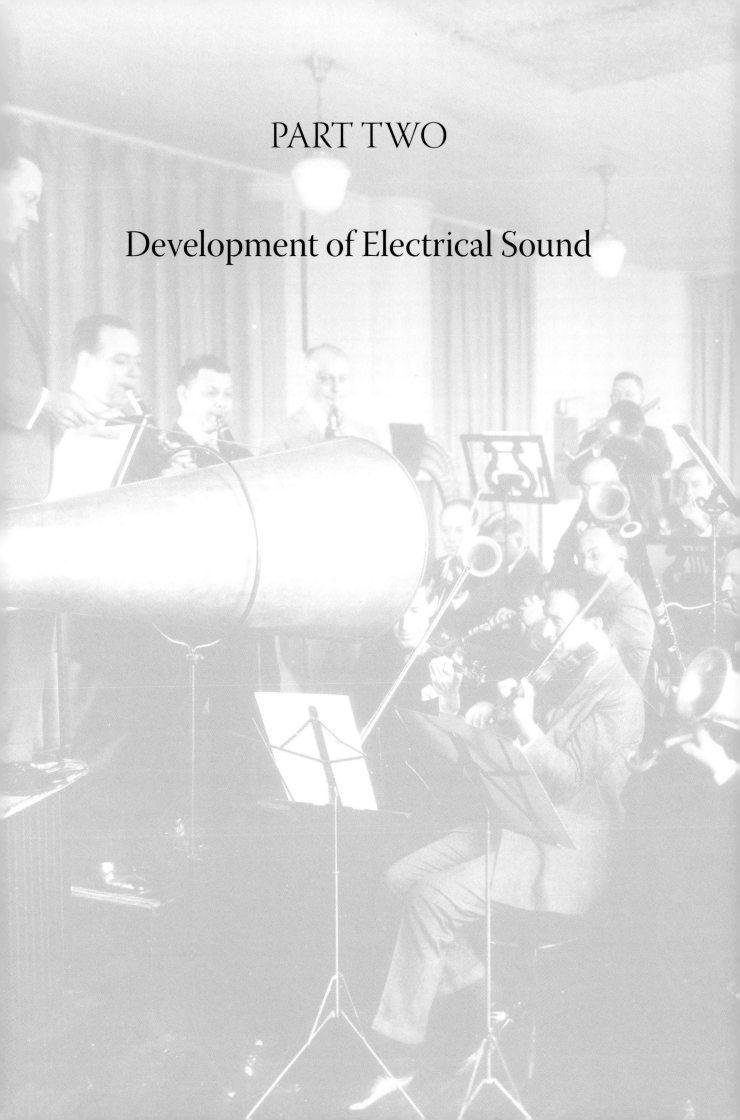

PART TWO

Development of Electrical Sound

6 CHRONOLOGY OF KEY INVENTIONS

The recording and reproduction of sound and the development of public address systems, talking pictures, and radio and television broadcasting all began with the invention of the telegraph. This breakthrough only became possible when people like Volta, Ampere, Oersted and Faraday developed electrical theory and demonstrated that current could flow along a wire. The telegraph simply consisted of breaking the current flowing between two telegraph instruments in a pre-decided manner. The signal pattern created could then be translated into words.[7]

The invention of wireless telegraphy, the telephone, and the sound recording machine, all happened within a remarkably short period of time. These technical achievements not only changed for ever how we communicate and how we listen to music, but they heralded a revolution in the use of sound in the theatre. The transition from live sound effects to the playback of recorded sound actually took its first faltering steps way back in the late 1800s. In 'Theatre in the Victorian Age', author Michael Booth mentions a baby's cry being played on a phonograph in a farce called THE JUDGE at a London theatre in 1890.

But it was really another forty years before 'electric' sound became widely available in the theatre. The development of the 'Talkies' during the 1920s and 1930s paved the way for sound in the live theatre. The ability to reproduce music and effects for the stage and to amplify the voice of the actor – it really all began there.

Live theatre has never had the resources to invest in major technical research projects, but it is very adept at seizing upon and adapting the latest innovations. From the days when the method of flying scenery was adopted from the hoisting of sails on ships, to the computer sound and lighting boards brought about by the invention of the 'chip', advances in technology have always been seized upon by theatre practitioners.

I thought it would be interesting to compile a chronology of the development of sound reproduction and transmission to see when various innovations became available for use by the enterprising theatre technician. There follows a summary of some of the major players and landmark events in the development of recorded sound, public address and radio broadcasting – starting in 1820 with early demonstrations of electricity.

1820   ***Danish physicist Christian Oersted discovered that an electric current creates a magnetic field.*** Pushing a compass under a live electric wire caused its needle to turn from pointing north, as if acted on by a larger magnet. Oersted discovered that an electric current creates a magnetic field. But could a magnetic field create electricity?[15]

1821   ***The world's first electric generator created by British inventor, Michael Faraday.*** Reversing Oersted's experiment, he found that a weak current would flow in a wire when it was revolving around a permanent magnet. In other words, a magnetic field caused or induced an electric current to flow in a nearby wire. Mechanical energy could now be converted to electrical energy.[15]

1837   ***The first workable telegraph invented by American Samuel Morse.*** The patent, applied for in 1838, was finally granted in 1848. Not a professional inventor, Morse had seen Faraday's recently published work on inductance, and was captivated by electrical experiments. His system used a key (a switch) to make or break the electrical circuit, a battery to produce power, a single line joining one telegraph station to another and an electromagnetic receiver or sounder that upon being turned on and off, produced a clicking noise. He completed the package by devising the Morse code system of dots and dashes. A quick key tap broke the circuit momentarily, transmitting a short pulse to a distant sounder, interpreted by an operator as a dot. A lengthier break produced a dash. Telegraphy became big business as it replaced messengers, the Pony Express, clipper ships and every other slow-paced means of communicating. The fact that service was limited to Western Union offices or large firms seemed hardly a problem. After all, instant communication over long distances was otherwise impossible.[15]

1841   ***Sir Charles Wheatstone invented a telegraph instrument which would print letters.*** This was a forerunner of the Teletype machine which came many years later. Wheatsone had previously designed the first economically successful electric telegraph line in England, installed along 13 miles of railway track between Paddington and West Drayton. He was also the first person to use the term "microphone" – a device for converting acoustic power into electric power that has essentially similar wave characteristics.[7]

1844   ***A telegraph line between Washington, D.C. and Baltimore.*** This employed Wheatstone's system for printing letters and numbers.

The Western Union Telegraph Company. With the growth and extension of electrical telegraph, all telegraph lines were amalgamated into the one company. Western Union became a highly influential corporation with a virtual monopoly on the electrical transmission of information in the United States. This included information flowing to the nation's newspapers as Western Union also controlled the Associated Press.[7]

1848   ***The first electrical long-distance telegraph line in Germany.*** The line ran for more than 500 kilometers from Berlin to Frankfurt/Main and was spearheaded by Werner von Siemens of the newly formed Siemens & Halske Telegraph Construction Company.[11]

1857 *The 'phonautograph' was invented by a French scientist, Leon Scott de Martinville.* The machine used a large horn that terminated in a thin membrane, or diaphragm, at the centre of which was fixed a hog's bristle. A 'graph' of the sound was traced by the bristle on to a lamp-blacked glass plate and later (1859) on to lamp-blacked white paper fixed to a revolving brass cylinder. The machine was designed to be used in teaching physics and was not able to reproduce sound.[20]

This wooden and plaster barrel horn Phonautograph design dates from July 1859.
Photo: Jean-Paul Agnard

1863 *The 'Telephon', forerunner of the telephone, built by German inventor, Philipp Reis.* Thirteen years before Alexander Graham Bell patented his telephone, Philipp Reis had a machine that was able to transmit and receive speech, albeit faintly.

1869 *Western Electric was founded.* The company was to become the largest electrical manufacturer in the United States; a major player in the manufacture and distribution of telephones and, later, of sound equipment for the film industry.

1874 *The German company, Siemens, starts work on the first transatlantic telegraph cable from Ireland to the U.S.*[11]

The principle of the 'dynamic' or 'moving-coil' transducer described by Ernst W. Siemens. This was a device for audible transmission which used a circular coil of wire in a magnetic field, supported so that it could move axially. He filed a patent in the USA for a "magneto-electric apparatus" for "obtaining the mechanical movement of an electrical coil from electrical currents transmitted through it". He did not build a working model. This was left to Alexander Graham Bell who used this technology for the telephone two years later.[10]

1876 *The microphone invented by Emile Berliner (1851-1929).* This was a device for converting sound waves into electrical voltages. A German who had emigrated to the United States at the age of nineteen, Berliner was largely a self-educated man but, like all inventors, he possessed a logical and enquiring mind.

The idea of what he called a 'loose contact' transmitter came to Berliner in a flash of inspiration when talking to a friend who ran a local telegraph station. The discovery that current going over the wire is increased when a firm contact is made with the Morse key, gave him the clue. That night, he rigged up an experiment – and it responded.

His first microphone used the head of a toy drum as a diaphragm. The delicate loose contact, a startling innovation in electrical science, was made with a steel dress button hanging by a fine metal thread so that it touched the point of a steel sewing needle which had been projected through the drum head from the back. When attached to a battery, this contact was found to act as both a transmitter and a receiver.

Many people working at the time on the principle of the microphone laid claim to the invention. On November 17 1891, however, the American patent office finally pronounced in Berliner's favour. Berliner can be said to have invented the microphone as his patent covered the principle of any variable contact used in the transmission of the sounds of a human voice; i.e. the principle upon which the microphone is based.[14]

The telephone patented by Alexander Graham Bell. Although there were other contenders, Bell is usually credited with the invention of the telephone. He filed a patent on February 14 1876, for his *"Improvement in Telegraphy"*; i.e. the speaking telephone. Only hours later, Elisha Gray arrived at the U.S. patent office to file a similar invention. Both men had independently designed a device that could transmit speech electrically. There are many historians who firmly believe that Gray, and not Bell, invented the telephone. Gray certainly thought so.[7]

Were it not for the fact that Alexander Graham Bell's grandfather had an ability as an actor, this modest Scotsman might never have developed an interest in the mechanics of speech that led him to become one of the most important pioneers of modern communications.

Originally a shoemaker in Scotland, Bell's grandfather had a talent that drew him towards the stage. Unfortunately, the acting profession was not thought suitable for a properly brought up young Scot in those days, so he became what was known as a 'reader'. In this more respectable guise, he would stand upon the stage and declaim passages from Shakespeare to discerning audiences.

His vocal prowess led him into the teaching of voice production, and he eventually moved to London where he opened a school of elocution. He was successful in not only assisting people in overcoming stammering and lisping problems, but also teaching cockney girls to talk like ladies and foreign gentlemen to speak well enough to fit into English society. Bell's school continued after his death and Bernard Shaw used it, many years later, as the model for his play PYGMALION.

The pioneering work in elocution was carried on by Bell's father who wrote textbooks on correct speech and invented a code of symbols called "Visual Speech" which became a reliable guide for training deaf people to speak intelligibly.

Alexander Graham Bell was born March 3, 1847 in Edinburgh. He grew up deeply involved in the study of speech and obviously had a good ear, as he was a talented musician. When both of his brothers died of tuberculosis and Alexander himself was threatened, the family moved to Brantford, Ohio. Here, Bell became a teacher specialising in the mechanics of speech and training deaf children to speak. He made two friends who were to play an important part in his life; Gardiner Hubbard was president of one of the schools where Bell happened to be teaching, and Thomas Sanders was the father of one of Bell's deaf pupils. [7]

By 1875, Bell had become interested in electricity and was experimenting with the possibility of sending several messages over a telegraph wire simultaneously. Hubbard and Sanders offered to support Bell in his experiments and it was agreed that they would form a company and share in whatever profits might accrue. [7]

Bell knew that the voice is carried to the ear through varying sound waves which vibrate the eardrum. These tiny movements are transmitted to the base of the cochlea which contains an incompressible fluid. The fluid then transmits these vibrations to all surfaces of the cochlea where numerous nerve endings react and transmit auditory sensations to the brain. It followed that sound waves from a voice must be capable of vibrating other sensitive surfaces. The question was, how could these vibrations be picked up and superimposed upon a current flowing along a wire – and then be picked up again at the other end?

Bell first experimented with similar metal organ reeds at each end of a wire. He reasoned that they might be made to vibrate sympathetically, like the strings of a piano, in response to a human voice. [7]

A young man named Thomas Watson had been assigned the job of building all the experimental equipment which Bell needed. One day in June 1875, Watson made the happy mistake of connecting one of the reeds too tightly. When he plucked at it to free it, another moment of scientific truth occured. That plucking twanged along the wire and was heard distinctly by Bell who happened to be holding another reed pressed tightly against his ear at the other end. [7]

Using his knowledge of the anatomy of the ear, he set up an experiment with a thin magnetic reed fastened to a small drumhead (acting as a diaphragm) with a battery powered electromagnet placed behind it. The idea was that the drumhead would vibrate to the sound of a voice, just like an eardrum, causing the reed to move backwards and forwards in response.

Then, as the reed moved towards the magnet and away, it would cause a current to flow in the coil around the magnet, first in one direction and then in another. A wire connected from the coil of the electromagnet to a similar device should cause the second electromagnet to reproduce the patterns of electrical current. This would make the second reed vibrate in sympathy causing the drumhead to create sound waves identical with the one at the sending end.[7]

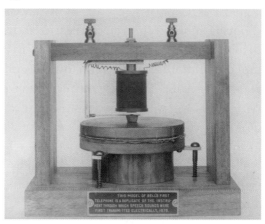

This model of Bell's first telephone is a duplicate of the instrument through which speech sounds were first transmitted electrically in 1875. *Library of Congress. Washington, D. C. 20540*

This was the theory. The first intelligible words were transmitted when Bell dropped a liquid transmitter, spilling acid upon his trousers, causing him to shout: "Mr. Watson, come here, I want you!" Watson heard him in another room *over the wire*.[7]

1877   **The Bell Telephone Company was formed August 1 1877.** At the time, there were only 778 telephones in operation.[7]

The 'liquid transmitter' used in the mouthpiece of the Bell telephone was not as efficient as the 'microphone' invented by Emile Berliner. So when the members of the newly formed Bell Telephone Company heard about it, they offered to buy the rights and give Berliner a job as research assistant. He worked for them for the next seven years.[14]

It was soon demonstrated that the combination of Berliner's microphone transmitter and Bell's magneto receiver made the perfect telephone circuit. Berliner was the first to introduce a battery current transmitter which increased the volume of the transmitted voice. He went on to add an induction coil, or transformer, into a telephone circuit.[7]

The microphone Berliner patented – as a caveat to Bell's telephone patent. April 14 1877. *Library of Congress. Washington, D. C. 20540*

The first practical sound recording machine, the 'phonograph' *demonstrated by Thomas Alva Edison (1847-1931).* The recording medium was a piece of tinfoil attached around a revolving brass cylinder. When Edison spoke into the mouthpiece, the diaphragm at the end of the mouthpiece began to vibrate from the effect of his voice. A stylus attached to the diaphragm produced a pattern of indentations in the tinfoil on the cylinder. When Edison put the stylus back to its starting point and turned the cylinder, his voice saying "Mary had a little lamb" could be heard – indistinctly, but comprehensively. The new invention was patented immediately.[1]

Original Edison
Tin Foil Phonograph.
U.S. Department of
the Interior, Edison
National Historic Site

1878   *The Edison Speaking Phonograph Company is formed.* The company was set up to demonstrate the wonders of recorded sound to the public for a fee. Edison sold the patent for his invention to the new enterprise for $10,000 plus 20% of the profits. Agents were employed in America, Europe and Scandinavian countries to demonstrate the wonderful speaking machine. By 1879, demonstrations were being given in Australia. But the novelty soon wore off and the public tired of the hand-cranked tinfoil phonograph. The machine had no practical application because when the tinfoil was removed from the cylinder, it could never be played again.[1]

Edison needed to improve the instrument, but during the next ten years he concentrated on other projects. For example, he designed the electric light bulb and contributed to the development of railways, moving pictures and the cement industry. In fact, he became a major industrialist.[1] Eventually, he was to hold a record 1,093 patents for his various inventions.

The carbon microphone invented by David Edward Hughes. Born in London, Hughes was brought up in the United States. His discovery of the carbon microphone was essential to the development of telephony.[16] The principle of the device is that carbon granules beneath a diaphragm are compressed to a greater or lesser extent as sound pressure waves hit the diaphragm. The carbon granules produce an alternating electrical resistance which modulates the current supplied by a battery.

Siemens introduces the loudspeaker horn that would be used on most phonograph players. German and British patents were granted for a nonmagnetic parchment diaphragm as the sound radiator of a moving-coil transducer. The diaphragm could take the form of a cone, with an exponentially flaring "morning glory" trumpet form.[10]

1881   ***Alexander Graham Bell purchases a controlling interest in the mighty Western Electric.***[6]

A demonstration of 'stereo' in Paris. French inventor, Clément Ader, set up a stereo experiment at the Paris Opera. He placed two telephone microphones on the stage and transmitted their signals separately via telephone lines to a number of people listening on earpieces outside the auditorium. The experiment had no practical use at the time, but it was probably the first stereo "broadcast" of a live theatre performance. Clément Ader is better known for inventing a steam-powered flying machine with bat-like wings. Although a steam engine was not suitable for sustained flight, he managed to remain airborne for a distance of 50m (160 feet); thus proving, before the Wright brothers, that heavier-than-air machines could fly.[22]

1882   ***Thomas Watson (Bell's associate) patents a "balanced armature" transducer for use in telephones.***

1885   ***The first permanent recording machine, the 'graphaphone'.*** Charles Sumner Tainter and Chichester Bell (cousin of Alexander Graham Bell) patented the 'graphophone'. It was, in fact, Edison's phonograph with the tinfoil replaced by cardboard cylinders covered with wax so that sound could be permanently recorded.[1]

1887   ***Emile Berliner patents his idea for the 'gramophone'.*** This used the same principle for producing sound as the phonograph and graphophone, i.e the vibrations of a steel needle fixed to a diaphragm in a sound box attached to a horn to amplify the sound. But there were two main differences: firstly, the cylinder was replaced by a flat disc, and, secondly, the groove was cut so that the needle vibrated laterally and not vertically. Berliner thought that a flat disc could open the way to mass production, rather than making recordings one by one.[1] Unable to find a suitable material for his discs, he did not produce a working machine until 1889.

Radio waves detected by Heinrich Hertz, a German physics teacher.[10] By making an electric charge jump from one metal rod to another, he proved that electromagnetic (radio) waves did exist and also that they moved at the speed of light. Hertz could find no practical use for this discovery, but his name lives on as the unit for measuring radio frequencies: cycles per second = 'Hertz'.

1888   ***Edison launched the 'Improved Phonograph'.*** Somewhat peeved at Tainter and Bell making money from his idea, Edison bought the assets of the near bankrupt Edison Speaking Phonograph Company, and produced his 'improved phonograph'. This was somewhat similar to Tainter and Bell's graphophone, but the likelihood of litigation about rights and patents was avoided when a rich businessman from Pittsburgh, Jesse Lippincott, bought both patents. He set up the North American Phonograph Company and invested more than a million dollars to exploit the invention commercially. Lippincourt marketed the device to offices and businesses as a dictating machine, but the technology was not yet up to the task. Secretaries, fearing for their jobs, emphasised its unreliability. Lippincott lost a fortune.[1]

1889   ***Emile Berliner produces the first discs for his gramophone.*** Initially, the gramophones were crude affairs as the turntables had to be turned by hand. It took some years before a successful motor-driven gramophone was available.[1] Having experimented with etching sound on to zinc discs and trying to press records on to various materials, Berliner's first discs were made of a hard vulcanized rubber. He then moved to wax compounds, but finally settled on shellac, a tough natural resin used in making telephones.[5]

Berliner's
Gramophone, 1895.
Library of Congress.
Washington,
D. C. 20540

1890   ***Emile Berliner produces the first lateral-cut disc records.*** The first 5-inch (13cm) shellac discs were manufactured under licence by a German toy making company. Berliner then founded the Berliner Grammophon Gesellschaft which later became the world-famous Deutsche Grammophon Gesellschaft.

1891   ***Birth of the recording industry with the regular production of recorded music cylinders.*** When Jesse Lippincott died, Edison acquired the rights to his phonograph from the bankrupt estate. He originally sold the rights for $435,000, but he reacquired them for only $135,000.

New markets were tried for the phonograph. One of the ideas was to record music on a wax cylinder and place it into a coin-operated machine. The first 'jukeboxes', installed in amusement parlours, proved more profitable than the dictating equipment hired to offices. This gave the idea of producing music recordings for sale to the general public. Edison and Lippincott's agents in Washington, the Columbia Phonograph Company, began the regular production of recorded music cylinders – and the recording music industry was born.[1]

It was not possible to mass produce cylinders in those early days, so ten phonographs would be placed in front of the performers to create ten recordings. The process was then repeated as many times as necessary. Later, ways were found to copy cylinders in small batches, but it was not until the turn of the century that they could be copied industrially.[1]

1894 ***British scientist, Oliver Lodge (1851-1940), became the first person to transmit a radio signal.*** The demonstration took place at a meeting of the British Association at Oxford. To receive the radio waves, Lodge had perfected and named the "coherer" (forerunner of the vacuum tube or radio valve), based on a radio-wave detector invented by the French physicist Edouard Branly in 1890. The coherer was a glass tube filled with metal filings. In their loose condition, the filings are non-conductive to electricity but *cohere* and conduct when subjected to electromagnetic waves.[12] Oliver Lodge was knighted and made a Fellow of the Royal Society in 1902.

Although Marconi is widely known as the "grandfather of radio", Lodge was certainly ahead of him. Indeed, he later brought a successful law suit against the Italian for making use of his patents. As a result of the case, he was appointed scientific adviser to the Marconi company.[10] Lodge also made a major contribution to the motoring industry by developing electric spark ignition for the internal combustion engine and inventing the 'spark plug'.

Despite the vital work of Lodge and Marconi, a Croatian physicist, Nicola Tesla, is now credited with the invention of modern radio. In 1943, the year Tesla died, the Supreme Court overturned Marconi's patent in favour of Tesla. After emigrating to the US in 1884, Tesla invented fluorescent lighting, and developed the alternating current (AC) electrical supply system. The Tesla coil, invented in 1891, is still used in radio and television sets and other electronic equipment.[26]

1895 ***Radio signal transmitted 600 yards by Russian scientist, Alexander Popov (1859-1906).*** Within two years his wireless system was powerful enough to be installed in Russian naval vessels. In 1900 radio was used for the first time to launch a rescue mission for a ship in distress.[12]

Radio signal transmitted 1.5 miles by Guglielmo Marconi (1874-1937). Son of a wealthy Italian father and Irish mother, Marconi invented his spark transmitter with antenna at his home in Bologna, Italy.[10]

Electrophone Broadcasting. A forerunner of radio broadcasting, this was an audio distribution system using special headsets connected to conventional phone lines. It operated in the United Kingdom between 1895 and 1926, relaying live theatre and music hall shows and, on Sundays, live sermons from churches. The Electrophone Company, based at Pelican House, Gerrard Street, London, had an arrangement with the National Telephone Company. The subscribers had to ask the operator to connect them to a particular church service or performance in a theatre or opera house. The electrophone receiver was generally fitted as an extension to the telephone apparatus, being put in circuit by means of a switch. Queen Victoria was apparently a fan, and she had the Electrophone installed in Buckingham Castle and Windsor Castle.

In the Electrical Engineer (September 10, 1897) it states that the substantial transmitters (microphones) used in theatres were normally arranged *"in what is known theatrically as the "float" (i.e., the part of the stage just in front of or behind the footlights) and are, on an average, from 12 to 24 in number. The mounting consists of a rubber ring suspension on stationary wire hooks, this form of fixing having been found advantageous as offering immunity from actual stage vibrations."* The transmitter in a church might take the form of a dummy bible in the pulpit, augmented by one or two placed elsewhere within the building. Similar systems were set up in France (the Theatrophone) and Hungary (Tekefon Hirmondó). It was relatively expensive to hire and faded into obscurity as soon as wireless broadcasting became popular.

1896   *Edison launches a wind-up phonograph using a spring motor with a 'governor.'* The governor controlled the speed of rotation so that uniformity of speed was maintained as the spring ran down and power decreased. The 'Home phonograph' (using wax coated cylinders) cost $40, which was quite a large sum in those days. But the idea took off and in 1899 more than 150,000 were manufactured and phonograph shops were being set up all over the world. Edison developed a method by which an unlimited number of cylinders could be moulded [1]

Berliner launches a reliable wind-up gramophone for disc recordings. Berliner's 7-inch (18cm) discs were now gaining in popularity and, although the quality of reproduction was no better than the cylinders, it was possible to make copies much more easily and cheaply.[1]

In those early years, brass band recordings were popular. The public also enjoyed humorous and sentimental songs with piano or small group accompaniment, banjo and cornet solos, and comic monologues. By the turn of the century, the voices of famous opera singers like Enrico Caruso and Dame Nellie Melba were being captured, and most producers of recordings had given up cylinders in favour of the flat disc.[1]

1897 ***The British Post Office agrees to assist Marconi with his research.*** Marconi, who had moved to England when the Italian government showed no interest in his invention, demonstrated his radio system to the Engineer-in-Chief at the Post Office in London. He successfully transmitted a signal between two locations three hundred yards apart, and the Post Office gave Marconi backing to experiment with wireless apparatus on Salisbury Plain and in coastal locations. In the same year, aged only 23, he founded 'The Marconi Wireless Telegraph Co. Ltd' in Hall Street, London – the world's first radio factory.

1898 ***Major improvement in loudspeaker design by Sir Oliver Lodge.*** The improved loudspeaker had nonmagnetic spacers to keep the air gap between the inner and outer poles of a moving coil transducer.

The first practical magnetic sound recorder, the 'Telegraphone' patented by Valdemar Poulsen (1869-1942). Poulsen, a Danish electrical engineer, found that the variable currents generated by a telephone transmitter or microphone could be used to produce local magnetization of a steel wire, causing, in effect, a magnetic pattern whose magnetic variations exactly matched the variations of the current. The recording medium he used was magnetized steel piano wire wrapped around a drum. This grandfather of the tape recorder was given an award at the Paris World Exhibition of 1900. At that time, however, amplifiers were not available to exploit the possibilities of the invention.[5]

Poulsen
Telegraphone, 1898.

Amplification by compressed air. Edison considered the use of compressed air amplifiers to overcome the phonograph's lack of replay volume, but it was British inventor, Horace L Short, who was granted a patent in 1898. He demonstrated his 'Auxetophone' high up on a ridge of The Devil's Dyke in the English county of Devon. Apparently, it could be heard at a distance of ten miles. To amplify the sound, the Auxetophone used compressed air provided by an electric motor. The needle mechanism on the tone arm had a mechanism which opened and closed a valve to pulse air into the horn. In 1903, Short sold the patent rights to another Englishman, Sir Charles Parsons, who had been working independently on the same idea. The following year, Sir Charles demonstrated the Auxetophone to the Royal Society. The Victor Company manufactured a version called the 'new pneumatic Victor' in 1906 for use in large halls and open air events, but it did not catch on. Not only was it expensive, but extreme loudness could not make up for the poor sound quality. The Science Museum in London has an example of the Auxetophone.

1899   ***AT&T acquires Bell Telephones.*** The American Telephone and Telegraph Company (AT&T) was originally set up in 1885 as a subsidiary of the Bell Telephone Company to build and operate long distance telephone networks. In December 1899, AT&T acquired the assets of the Bell company.

1901   ***Marconi transmits a morse signal by wireless telegraph across the Atlantic.*** Three dots representing the letter 'S', just discernible within the background static, were sent from the southwest tip of Cornwall in England to a receiving station at St. John's, Newfoundland.[12] In the same year, the American Marconi Company was formed.[10]

1902   ***Marconi patents his 'magnetic detector' which becomes the standard wireless receiver for many years.***

Guglielmo Marconi, 1896.

1903   ***The first amplifier, called an 'Intensifier' patented in the UK by Sir Charles Parsons.***[12]

1904   ***The 'Thermionic Valve' invented by Sir Ambrose Fleming.***[12]

1906   ***The first vacuum tube or radio valve, called an 'Audion', announced by American scientist, Dr. Lee De Forest.*** The Audion was a three-element vacuum tube which could amplify radio waves. Although the vacuum was not very good at this point, it was a distinct improvement on both the "coherer" which Marconi had used in his initial experiments with wireless telegraphy and Sir Ambrose Fleming's "valve" which was, in effect, a diode.

A diode contains a filament which is charged with electricity and a 'plate' to which electrons flow from the filament. It was used to detect radio waves; not well, but sufficiently to prove their presence. De Forest added a third element which is now called a "grid". This was a sensitive device placed between the filament and the plate which could detect any changes in the flow of electrons between the filament and the plate. The audion, with its third element, was much better than anything that had gone before. Dr. Lee De Forest recognized the potential for installing audions or repeaters on telephone lines to amplify the sound waves at mid-points along the wires.

The 'Vitrola', a new type of gramophone is introduced. Looking more like a piece of furniture than the previous devices which resembled sewing machines with tin horns attached, the Vitrola was produced by the Victor company. The horn was concealed within the cabinet and the turntable was mounted beneath a lid. The sound came from a tapered hollow 'tone arm' connecting the sound box (needle/diaphragm assembly) to the horn. Around 1910, the cheapest Vitrola cost only $15 although it was possible to pay up to $900 for Louis XV, Louis XVI, Chippendale, Queen Anne and Gothic styles. For this kind of money, the machines were equipped with electric motors and the proud owners no longer had to wind up the spring between every record.

During the next few years, a number of companies made improvements to record players to enhance the quality of sound reproduction. In particular, the invention of the tone arm was a great step forward. No longer was the entire weight of the horn bearing down on the needle and affecting its performance. It also meant that steel needles could be replaced by fibre needles which were kinder to the records and produced a more mellow sound. Fibre needles required sharpening after practically every playing, but even steel needles had to be replaced on a regular basis when their points wore down.[1]

1907   *Western Electric form a new engineering division later to be known as Bell Laboratories.* The group was a consolidation of the engineering staff from Western Electric and the American Telephone and Telegraph company (AT&T), the latter being the direct successor of the original Alexander Graham Bell laboratory.[7]

1913   *Edison brings out a disc player.* The success of the Vitrola had a devastating effect of the sales of cylinder machines. Edison was forced to give in to the inevitable and, in 1913, brought out his disc player. But Edison's discs differed from Berliner's in several ways: rather than using shellac, they were made of much heavier Bakerlite. They revolved at 80 r.p.m. instead of

78 r.p.m. and were cut with the vertical ("hill and dale") groove used on the cylinders, rather than the side-to-side lateral cut. Consequently, in order to play them, you had to buy an Edison record player. Edison's cylinders remained in demand because of the thousands of phonographs in households all around the world and he did not cease production until 1928.[1]

Synchronised sound for movies attempted by Edison. Always keen to investigate new possibilities, Edison tried using his phonograph to add sound to moving pictures. The machine called the 'Kinetophone' used cylinders over 4-inch (10cm) in diameter and 7-inch (18cm) long and had a large horn to produce enough sound to fill an auditorium. Placed behind the screen, it was operated by the projectionist using a system of control wires and pulleys. Sadly, the experiment died a painful death at the hands of the theater audiences who made their feelings known when the sound failed to synchronize with the picture.[5]

1914 ***A practical amplifier developed by Harold D Arnold of Western Electric.*** This was based upon an improved version of the 'audion', the amplifying vacuum tube developed in 1906. Arnold found that removing the air from the tube with a vacuum pump greatly increased the flow of electrons across the grid electrodes. The device was used for amplifying sound in telephone cables, eventually allowing Western Electric to span the American continent with their telephone service[6]

Arnold's 1914 tube. Courtesy of AT&T Archives and History Center

1915 ***The first transatlantic telephone conversation by radio telephone – October 21, 1915.*** Bell engineers had been convinced that with the vacuum tube, radiotelephony was possible and that using wireless techniques for telephony would be much cheaper than stringing wires and cables. Although faint and garbled, a short transmission took place from Arlington in Virginia to the top of the Eiffel Tower in Paris.[7]

The first successful Public Address system devised by Danish inventor, Peter l Jensen. Arriving in America in 1909, Jensen had set up the Commercial Wireless and Development Company which later changed its name to Magnavox. After experimenting with the moving coil principle for sound reproduction, he built a dynamic loudspeaker using a one-inch voice coil, a three-inch corrugated diaphragm coupled to a horn about 34 inches (86cm) long, with an opening of some 22 inches (56cm). The first system employed a heavy duty carbon microphone, as used in early transmitters. The 'Magnavox' (latin for "giant voice") was officially presented as a working system on Christmas Eve 1915, to an estimated crowd of 100,000 people. *"They heard carols and speeches with absolute distinctness"* say the reports.[12]

1916   ***Western Electric unveil their "Electric Public Address System".*** With microphones, amplifiers and loudspeakers developed by the Bell Laboratories, demonstrations were given at Madison Square Gardens in New York and at the Velodrome in Newark.[12]

       When Western Electric entered the P.A. field, the Magnavox Company with its meager resources decided to concentrate on other applications of the loudspeaker. When radio broadcasting took off in a big way a few years later, Magnavox loudspeakers were installed in radio sets all over the world.

1917   ***The condenser microphone patented.*** Developed at Bell Laboratories by E C Wente, this device used a very thin steel diaphragm placed close to a back-plate, which was charged with a high voltage. Sound vibrations changed the distance between the plates, altering the capacitance of the circuit, producing fluctuations in voltage. These tiny electrical waves, mirroring the original sound waves, were then transmitted by a vacuum tube amplifier. It was improved over the years and in 1926 became the Western Electric 394-W microphone used to produce the first generation of motion picture sound.

1918   ***The first "balanced armature" loudspeaker for public address.*** Henry Egerton of Western Electric developed the loudspeaker based upon the 1882 balanced armature telephone transducer patented by Thomas Watson.

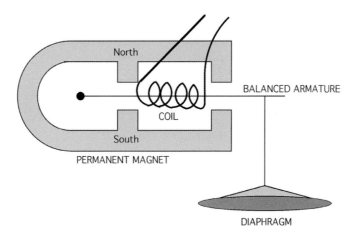

North

BALANCED ARMATURE

COIL

South

PERMANENT MAGNET

DIAPHRAGM

Magnetic forces from a permanent magnet and coil receiving varying electric currents work on a 'balanced' (or centred) armature or plate. Movements of the armature are reflected in the diaphragm to which it is connected.

1919   ***The first regularly scheduled radio broadcasting in Pittsburgh, USA.***
The commercially operated radio station KDKA, Pittsburgh, was run by
the Westinghouse Electric and Manufacturing Company.[19]

1920   ***A landmark British radio broadcast.*** On June 15 1920, the world
renowned diva, Dame Nellie Melba, gave a song recital from the Marconi
Company's experimental station MZX in Chelmsford in the English county
of Essex. Melba's microphone was a carbon granule type, similar to the
ones used in telephone handsets.[12]

1921   ***Electronic amplification comes to radios and record players.*** The first
radio sets were self-assembly, ran on batteries, and required an ear-tube to
hear the sound. Westinghouse and RCA were by now marketing single-
circuit receivers with loudspeakers.[5] The listener could enjoy an increase
in volume level and a much improved bass response. Once loudspeakers
had been installed in radio sets, this inevitably led to record players being
equipped with the same technology. The days of listening to sound
booming out from the depths of an acoustic horn were numbered.

1922   ***The British Broadcasting Company.*** The BBC (later the British
Broadcasting Corporation) was set up by a consortium of leading wireless
manufacturers including Guglielmo Marconi. The company acquired the
'2LO' call sign and transmitter from Marconi's Wireless Telegraph
Company and opened with a broadcast from Marconi House in the
Strand, London.

The first radio commercial. Aired by the New York Station WEAF on 28
August, it consisted of a ten-minute talk boosting the Hawthorne Court
housing development and was sponsored by the Queensborough
Corporation. October of that year heard the first radio broadcast of a
football game.[7]

Alexander Graham Bell died at the age of 75. As a tribute, all the
telephone bells in America were silent for a full minute.

1924   ***The modern moving-coil direct radiator loudspeaker patented.*** This was developed by Chester Rice and Edward Washburn Kellog of General Electric.[12] The audio quality was far superior to the balanced armature loudspeakers currently in use. Based upon the principle first described by Ernst Siemens in 1874, the direct radiator has a wire coil wound around a rigid cone, placed within a permanent magnetic field. The cone is attached to a large paper diaphragm. The two ends of the coil are connected to an amplifier, from which they receive alternating voltages. These positive/negative currents cause the coil to move within the surrounding magnet. The oscillation of the coil causes the movement of the diaphragm which, in turn, produces sound waves in the air. These are identical to the sound waves that had moved the microphone diaphragm at the other end of the system.

The birth of modern motion picture sound. Bell Laboratories research programme was responsible for introducing recording techniques of a higher quality than anything being used by the recording industry. This was because they needed more efficient equipment to test their new telephone systems. It was not long before someone asked the question: *"Why don't we see if we can apply this to the movies?"* [7]

The notion of introducing sound into the film industry was resisted both by the movie stars who were afraid that their voices would not be acceptable – sometimes with good reason – and by the producers who had a great deal of money tied up in soundless production equipment. But perhaps the overriding concern was the millions of dollars it would cost to re-equip all the movie houses in America. Resistance like that was difficult to overcome, but the Warner Brothers film company and Western Electric formed a joint company, the Vitaphone Corporation to exploit a disc-to-film system developed by Western Electric.[5]

The Western Electric system used a sensitive condenser microphone (first patented in 1917) to pick up sound and change it into varying electric currents, an improvement on the way that the microphone in the telephone turned speech into electricity. A vacuum tube amplifier increased the strength of these currents and used them to drive an electro-mechanical recording cutter to make a groove in the blank disc. The cutter was balanced to move precisely within a magnetic field, and as the varying currents from the amplifier influenced its movement, it transcribed wave forms on to the disc. On playback, the movement of the needle in the groove acted within the magnetic field of the electric pick-up to reproduce the varying currents that carried the sound signal. These currents were, in turn, amplified by vacuum tubes to drive a loudspeaker.[5]

Four months after forming the Vitaphone company, the Western Electric system had its first airing at the Warner's Theatre in New York City. Preceding the main film was a series of short sound films, replacing the usual live vaudeville acts. Then came the main feature, Don Juan, starring

John Barrymore and this had a complete recorded musical score by the New York Philharmonic Orchestra. The system was a hit, even if the film was not. Quinn Martin wrote in the New York World, *"You may have the* Don Juan. *Leave me the Vitaphone."* [6]

Vitaphone sound system for motion pictures used a new moving-coil loudspeaker developed at Bell Laboratories. The Western Electric 555-W speaker driver was coupled with a large horn having a 1-inch (25mm) throat and a 40 square foot (12m²) mouth. It was capable of 100-5000 hertz frequency range. It had an efficiency of 25% (compared to 1% today) which was needed because of the low amplifier power of 10 watts. [10]

Vitaphone 555-W.

1925 ***Western Electric forms a subsidiary to supply movie sound systems.*** Named Electrical Research Products, Inc. (ERPI) the company was to develop and distribute studio recording equipment and sound systems to the major Hollywood studios. ERPI equipped 879 movie theaters in 1928, and 2,391 in 1929. By 1932, only 2% of theaters in America were not wired for sound. The company continued to produce sound equipment for movie studios until 1956. [6]

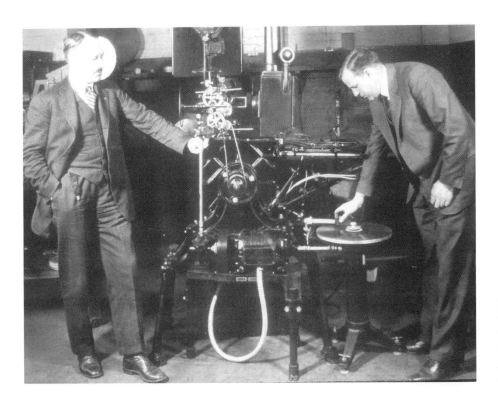

Disc synchronized with projector (ERPI Warner Vitavox). *Courtesy of AT&T Archives and History Center*

The first commercial 'electric' disc recordings. As soon as Western Electric demonstrated their new electric recording technique, the largest record company in America, Victor, bought the rights and Columbia negotiated a deal with Victor to use the new system. The first commercial recordings using this technique were made in 1925. [1]

Victor orchestra
recording in Camden,
NJ before 1925.
*Courtesy of
AT&T Archives and
History Center*

The wire recorder developed by German inventor, Curt Stille. This dictating machine was known as the 'Dailygraph' magnetic wire recorder.

A steel tape recorder developed by German inventor, Joseph Begun. Forerunner of recorders using paper and then plastic tape, the machine was called the 'Stahtonbandmaschine'.

Edison attempts the manufacture of 'long-playing' records. Using ultra-fine grooves, Edison managed to achieve twenty minutes of music on a record running at 80 r.p.m. Unfortunately, it was not a practical proposition because the records were immensely heavy, being about a centimeter thick, and the stylus tended to jump the grooves. [1]

1926 ***The first television pictures are demonstrated in London by Scottish inventor, John Logie Baird.*** This led to experimental transmissions of Baird's system by the BBC (British Broadcasting Company).

1927 ***The first fully electric record player is launched by the Brunswick company.*** Called the 'Brunswick Panatrope', it had a vacuum tube amplifier with a moving-coil loudspeaker, as used in the best radio receivers, and it incorporated an electrically powered turntable with a magnetic pick-up replacing the old soundbox. [1]

NOTE:

This is the earliest mention I have found of the word 'panatrope', a term used in the British theatre during the 1940s and 1950s for double turntable units with groove-locating devices for cueing music and effects from 78 r.p.m. records. There is a reference to the panatrope being used backstage for playing sound effects discs in New York in 1934 (See later chapter). The Oxford English Dictionary defines the panatrope as "an electrical apparatus for the reproduction of gramophone records through a loudspeaker" and states that the word came into common usage in 1926 – which seems to tally. The words 'pan' and 'trope' come from the Greek and mean 'all turning'.

Other companies followed suit and soon there were models with automatic record changing and with integrated radio receivers called radio-gramophones. The ability to turn up the volume control and, later, to adjust the 'tone modifiers' – treble and bass – was the start of tailoring sound reproduction to one's personal taste. *Everyone could now be a sound designer.*

Electric recording gave the engineers control of the recording characteristics to improve the sound quality. They were able to attenuate any strong bass frequencies which could not be handled in the disc cutting process, and they also came up with a method of reducing surface noise. To achieve this, the higher frequencies, where most of the hiss and crackle exists, were attenuated. Then, to reverse the process, the treble was boosted via the amplifier on the playback machine. The actual frequencies at which the various record companies attenuated and boosted the frequencies at both ends of the spectrum was not standardized until the 1950s when the RIAA (Recording Industries Association of America) curve was accepted.[1]

The first 'juke box'. A coin-slot machine with electronic amplification and a multi-record changer was produced in America by the Automatic Instrument Company.[5]

BBC receives Royal Charter. The British Broadcasting Company became the British Broadcasting Corporation when it was granted a Royal Charter.

The first radio 'disc jockey'. Christopher Stone was the first person to present Gramophone Record Recitals on BBC radio, or the "wireless" as it was known in those days. Thus, he became the world's first radio disc jockey. His weekly programmes began in July 1927. His avuncular relaxed manner made him so popular that he later topped the bill at London's Palladium theatre – playing records! He was also the first broadcaster to be given a three hour programme of his own, on a Christmas day. Christopher Stone was also editor of *The Gramophone*, the world's first record magazine, still being published in 2007.[4]

According to several sources, the first radio disc jockey was Martin Block who presented a programme called 'Make Believe Ballroom' from station WNEW in New York. However, his first broadcast was on February 3 1935, more than seven years after Christopher Stone established the idea.

Birth of the 'Talkies'. The first film to successfully demonstrate talking pictures was the Vitaphone film, THE JAZZ SINGER which synchronized discs with the projector. Although largely silent with sub-titles, during the presentation the public was astonished to hear Al Jolson sing a few songs, including "Sonny Boy", and actually speak a short section of dialogue.[5]

Optical sound tracks introduced. The 16-inch discs used in the early 'talkies' were very limiting because of their short running time and the difficulty of synchronization with the picture. To improve on this situation, a producer of newsreels, Fox Films, introduced the 'Movietone' system of sound-on-film. Based upon an idea patented by Theodore W. Case in 1919[19], this worked by converting sound waves into electrical impulses that modulated the light given off by a special lamp. The varying levels of light were then photographed on to the film to create the sound track. On playback, a lamp positioned one side of the film on the projector, sent a varying pattern of light to a photoelectric cell on the other side of the film. The varying light intensities were converted back into electrical impulses.[5] Synchronization was assured and the sound track could now run the whole length of the film.

Sound Equipment Manufacturing takes off in a big way. As the 'talkies' swept the United States and spread around the world, massive amounts of money were invested in Hollywood sound stages. Movie theaters were forced to re-equip with new projectors and install amplifiers and loudspeakers.[5]

Western Electric converted to sound-on-film and remained the major player in the industry as can be seen from the credit on the majority of films made in the 1930s and 1940s: "Western Electric Recording".[5] But they did not have it all their own way. There was strong competition, for instance, from RCA, and other specialist companies soon began to spring up.

The Lansing Manufacturing Company is registered as a Californian corporation. James Bullough Lansing (1902-1949) worked as an automotive mechanic before becoming an engineer at a radio station in Salt Lake City in 1925. He then worked for a loudspeaker manufacturing company where he met his future business partner, Ken Decker. He probably understood magnetic theory as well as any loudspeaker designer of his day and, just as important, had an understanding of basic manufacturing and tooling processes. He died at the early age of 47, but his position as one of the pioneers in professional sound is unquestioned.[9]

The Neumann microphone manufacturing company founded in Berlin. The microphones designed by Georg Neumann became famous world-wide for their quality. The CMV3 condenser (known as the "bottle" microphone) was the first model sold by his company. It was used by the German radio and recording industry in the 1930s and at the Berlin Olympic games in 1936.[10]

Neumann CMV3
"bottle" condenser
microphone, 1928.
*Photo: Georg
Neumann GmbH*

1928   ***Introduction of recording tape.*** Dr Fritz Pfleumer was granted a patent in
Germany for the application of magnetic powders to a strip of paper or
film as a recording medium to replace wire and steel tape.

1929   ***RCA introduces a mixing console.*** The use of two or more microphones
was now commonplace on a movie sound stage, and RCA developed a
sound mixing console for adjusting the level of several microphones.

Western Electric introduces 'equalization'. The film recording process
generated a high level of unwanted background sound, and this noise was
mostly concentrated in the frequencies in the form of hiss. The engineers
found a way of controlling the strength of signals at chosen frequencies,
allowing the unwanted frequency bands to be attenuated and the speech
frequency bands to be boosted. The result was a dramatic improvement in
sound quality and clarity.[5]

The development of 'compression'. Film soundmen were faced with the
problem of recording a volume range of 60dB – 80dB produced by the
actors on to a medium that could only handle a range of around 40dB –
50dB. Moreover, the dynamic range of the reproduction equipment in the
theatre was even more restricted. Compression techniques were devised
which automatically attenuated, or limited, the louder sounds to keep the
signal level within the capability of the system.[5]

Hollywood was responsible for many technical innovations, such as
equalization and compression, which were to become vital tools in all
types of recording and, later, in public address and theatre applications.

First demonstration of colour television. This was at the Bell Laboratories
on January 27.[5]

1930   ***The 'bass reflex' loudspeaker cabinet invented.*** Whilst working at Bell
Laboratories, Albert L Thuras filed a patent which was granted in July
1932. Early cabinets used a passive baffle to direct sound to the front,
allowing the back of the cabinet to be open for the low sounds. The bass-
reflex enclosure kept the low-frequency sounds from being lost from the
rear of the diaphragm.[10]

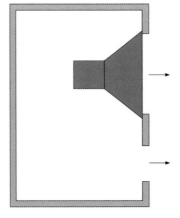

Bass Reflex Cabinet.

1931   ***The first three-way wide-range loudspeakers.*** Western Electric built these superior quality loudspeaker systems in which the sound was divided into bands of high, medium and low frequencies with each band being sent to a different set of loudspeakers. Four 15-inch (38cm) cone loudspeakers on a 4-foot (122cm) x 8-foot (244cm) baffle handled the bass, two 15-inch (38cm) long wooden exponential horns with 555W drivers handled the mid frequencies, and 3000A tweeters sorted out the high frequencies.[8]

A dual-range loudspeaker designed by RCA. The system used three 6-inch cone diaphragms with aluminum voice coils in divergent directions, with a response of 125-8000 Hz, and 10 foot long horns capable of 40-125 Hz.[10] This replaced their single 8-inch (20cm) cone transducer mounted on a straight horn.[9]

The Vitavox company founded in London by Len Young. One of the first companies outside America to manufacture high quality sound reproduction equipment, their loudspeakers were widely used in movie theatres all over Europe.[10]

The moving-coil, or "dynamic" microphone patented in America. It was developed at Bell Laboratories by W C Wente and A C Thuras. Unlike the earlier condenser design with a fixed plate behind the vibrating diaphragm, this microphone used a wire coil behind the diaphragm moving in a magnetic field to induce a voltage corresponding to the original sound. The sensitivity of the voltage output depended on the resistance, or "impedance" of the moving coil system. A low impedance of 30 ohms allowed transmission over long cables without loss of quality. It was, therefore, ideal for use as a boom microphone in film studios as, unlike the condenser microphone, it did not have to incorporate a bulky amplifier. The model 618A was unidirectional and the later model 630A was omnidirectional with a frequency response of 30-15,000 Hz.[10]

Western Electric 618A.
Photo: University of San Diego

The ribbon, or "velocity", microphone introduced by RCA. The model 44A became one of the most widely used microphones in vocal recording. It used a small ribbon 2 inches (50 mm) long and ⅛" (2.4 mm) wide that moved inside a magnetic field according to the difference in sound pressure on each side of the ribbon. The velocity of the moving ribbon was independent of the sound frequency, producing a high-impedance signal. The microphone was bidirectional with a pickup pattern like a 'figure 8', toward the front and back, eliminating unwanted noise from the sides. The large size of the microphone and weight of more than 8 lbs (3.6 kg) meant that it was only suitable for fixed locations.[16]

Bing Crosby using an RCA ribbon microphone in 1939.

The EMI 'Abbey Road' studio opens in London. It was the largest recording studio in the world.

The first Stereo microphone devised by Alan Blumlein. Alan Dower Blumlein, a young British inventor, produced the first stereo microphone. It comprised two ribbon microphone elements with a common magnet system. Each ribbon was most sensitive to sounds arriving at 45° to either side of the central axis.[17]

Blumlein had worked for one of Britain's leading manufacturing companies, Standard Telephone and Cables (STC) before moving to Columbia Graphaphone which in 1931 merged with the Gramophone Company to become Electrical and Musical Industries (EMI).

As an engineer at EMI, Blumlein assisted in the development of the "moving coil" microphone at the same time as Bell Laboratories was working on a similar project.[18] Their version was manufactured by Standard Telephone and Cables and was known as the STC 4017. It was a compact moving coil microphone with excellent performance which remained in widespread use for some twenty years.

Blumlein also patented a new stereo recording system which he called "binaural sound". It was installed in the new Abbey Road studio and a few stereo recordings (78 r.p.m. discs) and films were made there during the 1930s. These included two test recordings in 1934 of Sir Thomas Beecham rehearsing Mozart's 'Jupiter' symphony with the Royal Philharmonic Orchestra. Having no commercial potential, EMI shelved the technology and it was not until the 1950s that interest in stereo sound revived and Blumlein's work was remembered.[18]

Alan Blumlein registered one hundred and twent-eight patents in electronic and audio engineering. He died in 1942 when his plane crashed whilst testing an airborne radar system that could detect aircraft at night. He was thirty-nine.

Long-playing 'transcription discs'. RCA Victor presented the first practical long-playing records which revolved at 33⅓ r.p.m. The 16-inch (41 cm) discs had a groove width similar to the current 78 r.p.m. records because of the weight of the pick-ups used at the time.[1] The system was not commercially available, but radio stations started to use what became known as 'transcription discs' for recording their programmes.

1933   ***Multicellular horn loudspeakers introduced by Western Electric.***[8]

Live Stereophonic sound demonstrated in Washington. Before the National Academy of Sciences and many invited guests at Constitution Hall, Bell Laboratories set up a live demonstration of what they called 'stereophonic sound'. Transmission was over wire lines from the Academy of Music in Philadelphia and three channels were used with microphones respectively at left, centre and right of the orchestra stage and loud speakers in similar positions in Constitution Hall.[10] It was, in fact, a replica of Clément Ader's 1881 demonstration in Paris – but with amplifiers.

Introduction of the unidirectional or 'cardioid' micro-phone. RCA brought out their 77A ribbon microphone which had a front-only pickup pattern rather than the 'figure-8' pattern of the earlier model 44. Because this front-only pattern resembled an inverted heart, it became known as the "cardioid" pattern. This microphone had a velocity ribbon clamped in the center with the top half enclosed as a pressure-type ribbon.[10]

*RCA 77A Cardioid
microphone.
Photo: Darrin Warner*

1934   ***Birth of an iconic BBC microphone.*** The BBC designed their own version of the very successful RCA ribbon microphone. Called the Type A, it was built by Marconi and became the image that some people still associate with BBC radio studios. There were various modifications over the years until the final version, the type AXBT, appeared around 1944.

*BBC Type A
microphone.
Photo: Chris Owen*

The introduction of 'acetate' records. British inventor, Cecil Watts, made master recordings on a new type of disc which had much less surface noise than wax and could be replayed immediately without any sound degradation. Called 'acetates', they had a layer of cellulose nitrate on a glass or aluminium disc. Acetate discs were individually cut with selections of sound effects for theatre production in London until the mid 1960s (see later chapter).

1935   ***The first public demonstration of a tape recorder.*** The German company AEG exhibited a device at the Berlin Radio Fair called a 'Magnetophon', in which the steel wire was replaced by a paper tape coated with a metallic oxide developed by BASF. The speed of the tape was 76 cms per second (approximately 30 inches/second). The reproduction quality of the first magnetophons was clearly inferior to that of records.[1]

AEG
Magnetophon, 1935

1936   ***The first public recording using a tape recorder.*** A concert at BASF's own concert hall in Ludwigshaven with the London Philharmonic Orchestra conducted by Sir Thomas Beecham was recorded in November 1936 on an AEG Magnetophon tape recorder. For the recording, an improved tape was used based on a formulation of ferric oxide rather than the original carbonal iron. The ferric oxide tape had an improved dynamic range of 37dB, as opposed to less than 30dB with the old tape, and it was also chemically more stable.[10]

Lansing builds iconic 'bass bin and horn' systems for MGM. The sound department at Metro-Goldwyn-Mayer Studios was not happy with the augmented Western Electric systems. Douglas Shearer, head of the MGM sound department, got the idea of building his own system. James B Lansing was contracted to manufacture the components.[9] The Shearer system used high-frequency multicellular horns with the low-frequency section consisting of a large W-horn cabinet with 15-inch woofers.[9]

W-horn
bass cabinet.

The loudspeakers were installed in 12 theaters for the opening of Romeo And Juliet starring Norma Shearer, Douglas Shearer's sister.[10] There is no question that the Shearer MGM system set new standards for sound in the motion picture theater. The basic design was later adopted by many manufacturers around the world; both RCA and Western Electric adopted this approach for their later systems. [9]

James B Lansing went on to design a small two-way system using a 15-inch low-frequency loudspeaker and a small high-frequency driver, the 801 (later known as the Altec 802), driving a small multicellular horn. The iconic system gained wide popularity throughout the motion picture industry as a monitor loudspeaker. Many modern two-way monitors are only minor improvements on this early system. [9]

The birth of the Altec company. The United States government was not happy with the virtual monopoly Western Electric had in both motion picture sound recording and equipment manufacture, and the company was forced to sell off its equipment supply subsidiary, Electrical Research Products (ERPI). It was bought by a group of engineers who were working for them at the time. The new company, called the Altec Services Corporation (Altec being short for "All Technical") took on the maintenance contracts with theater chains all around the country.[9]

BBC launches the world's first regular television service from Alexandra Palace, London. After only two months, John Logie Baird's mechanical system was replaced by the electronic system developed by EMI-Marconi.

1938   ***The first column loudspeakers developed by RCA.***[21] Placing like loudspeakers on top of one another has the effect of decreasing the vertical distribution of the higher frequencies, concentrating more power in the horizontal plane. This fan-shaped distribution is very useful for focusing sound within an auditorium.

1939   ***The first successful single-element unidirectional microphone.*** The
American company, Shure, brought out the famous Unidyne microphone.
The single membrane design made it smaller and cheaper to manufacture.[12]
Previous directional microphones had to "mix" the signal from two
membranes to achieve the cardioid effect. The size, the styling, the
performance quality and the price made it one of the most popular
microphones of the era.

Far left
Shure 55A Unidydne.
Photo: Stan Coutant

Left
The Western Electric
639A unidirectional
ribbon velocity
microphone was sold
by Altec from 1939.
Photo: Stan Coutant

1940   ***Multi-channel film sound tracks.*** A three-channel sound system for
motion pictures was demonstrated at Carnegie Hall in New York by Bell
Laboratories. It apparently produced such a sound level that the New York
Times reported that the audience was at once spellbound and *"a little
terrified".* In the same year, the Walt Disney film FANTASIA was recorded
on eight separate tracks and mixed down for replay in the theatrers to
three tracks. Because of the costly replay system required, the three-track
version of FANTASIA only played in a few theaters.

1941   ***Dramatic improvement in the quality of tape recording.*** Weber and
Von Braunmuhl at AEG made the important discovery that applying a
high frequency current to the tape recording head along with the audio
signal significantly reduced tape hiss and
other forms of distortion. Magnetophon
tape recorders were installed in radio
stations across Germany to broadcast pre-
recorded propaganda messages for Hitler's
Nazi party throughout the Second World
War (1939-1945).[10]

The clarity of sound reproduction of the
German Magnetophon was now better than
sound on film and almost as good as discs –
and far outclassed the wire recorders being
used by the British and American forces.
Wire recorders were also being used by the
BBC for re-broadcasting news bulletins on its
colonial service.

An American
Webster wire
recorder. Spare
spools of wire can
be seen in the lid.
*Klaus Blasquiz
Collection, Paris*

The Altec Lansing Corporation created. Altec Service Company bought the Lansing Manufacturing Company and formed the Altec Lansing Corporation to manufacture former Lansing products. Altec Lansing launched their first power amplifier, Model 142B. [8]

1943 ***The first duplex® 12-inch (30cm) loudspeaker, Model 601 introduced by Altec.*** The 15-inch (38cm) version, the 604, appeared the following year.[8]

1944 ***The Altec A4 'Voice of the Theatre' loudspeaker.*** The A4 was a large two-way system standing about 8 feet high which produced a level of low-frequency performance not experienced in the theatre before. It virtually revolutionized motion picture sound [9]

1945 ***The Americans discover and 'acquire' the German tape recorder.*** At the end of the Second World War, when American troops were examining the radio stations of occupied Germany, to their surprise they found tape recorders that could reproduce sound considerably better than anything they had known. As a result of the war, AEG's patents fell into the hands of the Allied forces.[1]

Captain John T (Jack) Mullin of the Signal Corps took two Magnetophon tape recorders from Radio Frankfurt in Germany and shipped them back to America with fifty 1,000 meter reels of BASF ferric-coated tape. Later, he worked on them to improve the electronics with the AMPEX Manufacturing Company.[10]

Jack Mullin
demonstrates
the German
Magnetophon
in San Francisco.
*Department of
Special Collections,
Stanford University
Libraries*

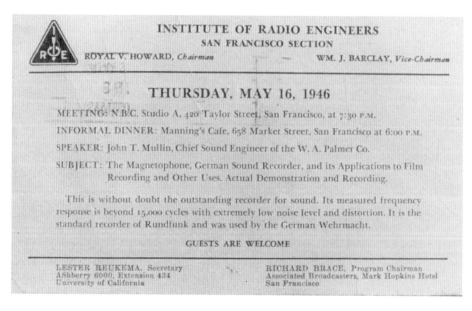

INSTITUTE OF RADIO ENGINEERS
SAN FRANCISCO SECTION
ROYAL V. HOWARD, *Chairman*   WM. J. BARCLAY, *Vice-Chairman*

THURSDAY, MAY 16, 1946

MEETING: N.B.C. Studio A, 420 Taylor Street, San Francisco, at 7:30 P.M.
INFORMAL DINNER: Manning's Cafe, 658 Market Street, San Francisco at 6:00 P.M.
SPEAKER: John T. Mullin, Chief Sound Engineer of the W. A. Palmer Co.
SUBJECT: The Magnetophone, German Sound Recorder, and its Applications to Film Recording and Other Uses. Actual Demonstration and Recording.

This is without doubt the outstanding recorder for sound. Its measured frequency response is beyond 15,000 cycles with extremely low noise level and distortion. It is the standard recorder of Rundfunk and was used by the German Wehrmacht.

GUESTS ARE WELCOME

LESTER REUKEMA, Secretary   RICHARD BRACE, Program Chairman
AShberry 6000, Extension 434   Associated Broadcasters, Mark Hopkins Hotel
University of California   San Francisco

1946 ***James B Lansing Sound Incorporated formed.*** James Lansing left Altec to form the company which became known as JBL, to pursue new directions in transducer and sound system design.[9]

1947 ***A revolution in recording.*** One individual who had a profound and lasting influence on mass media in the 20th century was not an inventor or a scientist or a film producer, he was a band singer. Bing Crosby embraced and changed for ever the use of the microphone in theatres and dance halls, for electric recording and for radio broadcasting. He inaugurated a recording revolution and was responsible for popularizing the tape recorder in America with repercussions across the world.

In June 1947, Jack Mullin demonstrated the Magnetophon to Bing Crosby who immediately understood how the tape recorder could increase the running time and possibly the sound quality of the 16-inch transcription discs used to record his radio programmes. He also realized the potential offered by the tape recorder of being able to assemble programmes out of separately recorded sections and editing out unwanted material as necessary. Bing signed Mullin up immediately and in the autumn of 1947 they began to tape record his radio shows.[3]

John T Mullin in 1988 with an Ampex Model 200, the machine he inspired that revolutionized the entertainment and information industries.
Photo courtesy of Eve Mullin Collier

From 1934-1954 Crosby completely dominated American entertainment. Nobody has ever had as many hit records. During his career, he recorded more than 1,700 titles, placing more records (368) and number one hit singles (42) on the general pop charts in the United States than any other artist. He sold more than 500 million records and had 22 gold discs. 'White Christmas' from the 1940 film HOLIDAY INN alone sold more than 40 million records world wide, a figure that no other singer has approached. He was the most successful radio and recording artist in history, going on to repeat this success in films (61 movies) and later, television.[3]

Born in 1903 of Irish parents, he started singing in pre-microphone days. Although a baritone, he sang in the tenor register to be heard over the band. But when microphones came in, he was able to bring the register down and develop an intimate style of singing that became known as 'crooning'. He was the first person to realise that the microphone was an instrument – and he used it. Placed in the mid-frequency range, with none of the extreme highs of the tenor voice or lows of the bass, Crosby's mellow baritone was ideally suited to the limited capability of microphones and loudspeakers of the period.

Whilst singing with the Paul Whiteman band, his new sound caught the public's imagination and he soon began to make records in his own right. Music publishers plagued him to sing their songs and in 1931 he got his own coast to coast radio show and his new sound soon swept the country. In 1932, he starred in his first full length movie, THE BIG BROADCAST, which was so successful that during the rest of the 1930s he averaged 3 films a year. Whilst making all these films, he recorded 21 of his 40 top hits. By the late 30s there were more than 300,000 juke boxes in the States and Bing's records were the main attraction.[3]

In 1935, he took over Paul Whiteman's prime weekly spot on NBC radio in New York to present his own show. He had such a busy schedule that he wanted to record the programmes, but NBC was bound by an agreement to keep music 'live'. Consequently, Crosby took his show to a relatively minor broadcasting company, ABC, in Hollywood. Up until then, NBC and CBC were the two big stations and no major stars would think of appearing on ABC. Such was his popularity and influence that, almost overnight, Bing made ABC into a major player with stars queuing up for the convenience of recording their shows. This was virtually the death knell of live broadcasting.[3]

1948   **Ampex produces the first American tape recorder with backing from Bing Crosby.** To improve the quality of the recorders and to make them available to the broadcasting and recording industry, Crosby Enterprises invested $50,000 in the Ampex Corporation to facilitate the production of the Ampex 200.[3] One of the changes he requested of Ampex was that the tape deck should be horizontal rather than vertical as he thought this was more convenient for editing, changing spools, etc.[22]

Bing Crosby with
an early Ampex
home model, 1948.
*Department of Special
Collections, Stanford
University Libraries*

The machine was bought by all the major broadcasting and recording companies. Suddenly, engineers could stop the recording, do re-takes, and make seamless edits. One of the first machines was given by Bing to his friend and famous guitarist, Les Paul. He had a machine adapted with an extra head so that he could use sound on sound to overdub many times his guitar and the voice of his wife, Mary Ford.[3] One of his biggest hits was "How High The Moon" in 1953. Adding a second recording head meant that it was simple to achieve stereo and the industry began to take the possibilities seriously; but it was another ten years before stereo recordings became available to the public.

In 1977, at the age of 74, Bing Crosby died of a heart attack on a golf course in Spain. A golfing addict, this is probably the way he would have wanted to go. He was still making records and giving concerts and he remained in remarkably fine voice up to the end, as I can attest. The previous year, I had been fortunate enough to design a sound system for his appearance at the London Palladium.

The transistor invented at the Bell Laboratories. John Bardeen and his associates William Shockley and Walter Brattain demonstrated that a piece of semi-conducting material – a slice of germanium crystal – could amplify or control electric currents. At the time, this pea-sized replacement for valves was only thought to be commercially useful for the manufacture of hearing aids. Transistor is short for "transfer resistance"

The forerunner of the commercial long-playing record. In June 1948, Columbia Records presented their new long playing record to a press gathering at the Waldorf Astoria hotel in New York. Instead of using shellac, the new LPs were pressed on a vinyl plastic called 'Vinylite'. This material was lighter, more durable and did not have the hiss associated with shellac recordings.[1] It also allowed for a much finer groove to provide a playing time of up to 20 minutes per side.[19] A few specially recorded discs were brought out, but the timing was wrong and these LP discs were withdrawn from the market. The idea of the long playing record was in the air, however.[1]

A pile of 78 r.p.m. records stands 2m (6' 6") high. Columbia's head of research, Peter Goldmark, holds a 40cm (16") high pile of LP records containing the same amount of music.

1949   **Altec acquires Western Electric Sound Products Division.** In the same year, Altec brought out their first microphone, the model 21 condenser.[8]

The 7-inch 45 r.p.m. disc introduced by RCA. This small disc revolving at 45 r.p.m. with a playing time of around 3 minutes per side was designed to take over from the old 78 r.p.m. record. A later 'extended play' version could accommodate two popular songs on each side.[1]

The first use of wireless microphones in a public performance. Two systems were used in a production of ALADDIN ON ICE at the Brighton Ice Rink in England. They were designed and built by Reginald Moores, who had been a Royal Air Force wireless operator flying in bombers during the Second World War (1939-1945). One of these systems is now in the Science Museum in London. There is more about Reginald Moores in chapter 15.

1950   *The LP becomes commercially available.* The 12-inch (30cm) long-playing record (33⅓ r.p.m.) and the 7-inch (18cm) 45 r.p.m. discs became standard over the next three or four years and the old 78s were gradually phased out. 10-inch (25cm) LPs were also issued, but did not really catch on.

1952   *The Shure Microphone Company brings out a commercial wireless microphone system.* The 'Vagabond' was powered by two hearing aid batteries and could transmit within a "performance circle" of approximately 700 square feet.[23]

The Rock 'n' Roll Era gets under way. Bill Haley's "Shake, Rattle and Roll" sold over a million copies. Elvis Presley cut his first record at Sun Records.

1953   *AKG brings out the classic D12 dynamic microphone.* The world's first high quality dynamic microphone provided the first true cardioid polar pattern. In addition to this improved directivity, it also had a remarkably low susceptibility to wind noise. The Austrian company, founded in 1945, had originally been set up to supply film equipment to movie theatres.

1954   *The 'silicon' transistor introduced by Texas Instruments.*[24]

The printed circuit board starts to become commonplace in consumer electronics around this time. A development of miniaturization was the printed circuit board where transistors, capacitors and other devices were all attached to a copper coated plastic board upon which all the wiring connections were etched. The PCB was probably invented in England by Austrian engineer, Paul Eisler, in 1936 as part of his design for a radio set. Around 1943, the USA began to use the technology on a large scale to make rugged radios for use during the Second World War. In 1948, three years after the war ended, the USA released the invention for commercial use, but printed circuits did not become commonplace in consumer electronics until the mid-1950s.[27]

The world's first transistor radio. An American company called Regency brought out a receiver that used four transistors. [13]

1955   ***Sony introduces the first Japanese transistor radio.*** Although they were just pipped at the post by the American Regency company, the mass produced Sony radios sold around the world and are often considered the first true transistor radios. [13]

1958   ***Setting a standard for stereo long playing records.*** An international agreement established technical standards for stereo recording which included the storing of the two signals on each side of the groove of a disc, at an angle of 45°. In the summer of that year, the first standard stereo LP was introduced by Columbia. [1]

     The beginning of professional multi-track recording. Initially, LPs were available in mono or stereo, and some studios began using three-track machines to record the stereo version on two tracks and the mono mix on the third.

1959   ***The first modern 'hand' microphone is introduced by Shure.*** [23] The Unidyne-lll was designed to accept sound from the top rather than from the sides and it immediately became popular with stage performers.

Shure Unidyne III.

The Integrated Circuit. Jack St Clair Kilby of Texas Instruments came up with a device for integrating several components into a single block of silicon – the integrated circuit (IC) solved the problem of interconnecting discrete electrical components to form a single complex circuit. [24]

1960   ***Birth of the minicomputer.*** The Digital Equipment Corporation (DEC) introduced the first commercial computer equipped with a keyboard and monitor. The PDP-1 (Program Data Processor) selling for US$120,000 was an important size and power step from mainframe toward personal computers. [25]

1962   ***The first international communications satellite.*** 'Telstar' was rocketed into orbit on July 10, 1962 by NASA. Bell Laboratories collaborated on the telecommunication systems.

1963   ***The tape cassette machine introduced by Philips.*** [1] Established in the Netherlands in 1891 by Gerard Philips to manufacture carbon-filament lamps, the company had become one of the world's leading manufacturers of sound and communication equipment and a major record producer. Their cassette machine was aimed at the domestic market and was designed for the completely non-technical user. The 'Compact Cassettes' used tape half as wide as the standard quarter inch tape and ran between two reels within a plastic case. The tape speed was 1⅞ inches per second compared with the 3¾ or 7½ inches per second of domestic and semi-professional recorders.[5] The cassette machine made it easy for the user to record from the radio and other sources and this inevitably led to the wholesale piracy of commercial recordings.

By the end of the 1960s, the compact cassette had become the standard for tape recording in the domestic market and the sale of pre-recorded music cassettes boomed. This despite the fact that, compared to disc recordings, cassettes had a poor frequency response and an unacceptable amount of hiss for the serious listener. The development of 'low noise' tapes helped, but a major improvement to the sound quality did not come about until the inclusion of Dolby noise reduction systems around 1971.[5]

Other cassette formats were tried out and around 1966 some cars in the US were being equipped with 8-track stereo cartridge players. These were not successful in the long term, but the technology was adapted for the endless loop cartridges which became extremely popular for playing jingles and commercials in radio stations – and then for sound effects in the theatre. The quarter inch tape ran around a central spool within an enclosed plastic shell – taking it from the inside and returning it to the outside of the spool. The cartridge could be slotted into the letter box opening of a cartridge record/replay machine.

A pre-digital version of the sampler, the Mellotron, is launched. Built by the British company Streetly Electronics, the Mellotron was an electro-mechanical device with a keyboard where each key activated a short length of tape playing back whatever was recorded on that tape. Conceived as a musical instrument, they had a bank of backing tracks and percussion tracks playing as loops, as well as individual notes played by single or groups of instruments. Over a thousand tracks (sounds) could be pre-selected from a bank of tapes. Each tape played for up to seven seconds. It was, of course, not possible to replay a tape until it had rewound (less than a second), so the sounds were often duplicated on two adjacent keys.

Alarmed at the prospect of one man replacing an orchestra, the Mellotron was not regarded favourably by the British Musicians' Union. They made their feelings felt, and the future of the Mellotron was severely threatened. Then in 1965, the BBC ordered several Mellotrons for playing back sound effects. These machines had the potential for storing 1,260 noises and they were used in many radio and television productions, including the famous 'Doctor Who' series. Later, I was contacted by the manufacturers to see if the Sound Effects Mellotron could be used in the theatre. The machine, looking exactly like a wooden organ console, was very impressive. I remember playing a sequence of keys with footsteps (two separate keys), footsteps stop and shuffle (another key), and then a series of keys for car door opening, car door closing, motor starting, engine revs, car departing, gear changes, speeding up, slowing down, etc. However, the price of the machine at £1,500 (equal to the cost of four or five tape machines) plus a copyright fee for the use of BBC sound effects was way beyond anything the theatre could afford in those days. Around 2,500 Mellotrons were built between 1963 and 1986 and they have now become collectors' items.

Mellotron Mark II
– upon which the
BBC effects machine
was based.
*Photo: Streetly
Electronics*

1964   ***The 'electret' microphone patented.*** Dr James West at Bell Laboratories, along with Gerhard Sessler, patented an electro-acoustic transducer. The electret microphone offered greater reliability, higher precision, lower cost and smaller size.[16] Among many other uses, this miniature device soon became standard for broadcaster's lapel microphones and wireless systems for theatre and film.

1965   ***4-track tape recorders being used by the Beatles.*** For the previous two years the Beatles had been recording at the Abbey Road studios in London in mono on 2-track machines, 'ping-ponging' backwards and forwards, adding instruments, backing vocals, etc. They had no noise reduction, but they did have compression.

1966   ***The concept of the 'slave' amplifier introduced by WEM.*** Charlie Watkins, founder of the British sound manufacturing company, WEM, came up with the idea of cascading amplifiers and produced a concert sound system of more than 1,000 watts, first heard at a jazz festival in Windsor. More about Charlie Watkins in chapter 9.

     The 'Moog Synthesiser.' During the 1960s, many people were making sounds electronically with white noise generators and variable frequency oscillators to produce pure tones and hisses for "space effects". As far back as 1956, BBC engineer Dave Stripp built a unit to synthesize machine-gun fire and by 1958 he had a machine capable of producing machine-gun fire, single shots (with or without ricochets) and heavy artillery. He went on to modify the circuitry to produce other realistic effects such as sea wash, thunder, steam trains, various rhythmic engine noises and, of course, science fiction noises.

In 1966, Robert Moog produced his Moog Synthesiser which could control the volume and pitch of a number of oscillators and could also add 'overtones', or 'harmonics', to change the sound. Later models were able to produce a greater variety of sounds which could be memorized and played back on a keyboard. The synthesiser, with its ability to make up sounds and store them for future use, soon became an indispensable tool for creative recording engineers and musicians.

The Dolby Noise Reduction System. British designer, Raymond Dolby, came up with a system to reduce the increasing problem of tape hiss as more recording tracks became available. His invention was based upon the pre-emphasis of certain high frequencies (areas of tape hiss) during recording and the de-emphasis of the same frequencies during playback. The Dolby system became a vital piece of equipment in recording studios across the world and remained so until the advent of digital sound. The next few years saw an explosion of processing devices for limiting, expanding, equalizing and generally controlling and changing the audio signal.

1967 ***Professional 8-track recorders come into use in the larger studios.***
When the flexibility of multi-track recording was fully realised, the studios demanded more and more tracks and they soon had 16 and 24 track machines. During the 1970s, even 32 track systems became available.

The first reliable solid state high power amplifier. As solid state technology developed, ways were found to crowd more and more transistors, capacitors and resistors on to one piece of semiconductor and it became possible to replace the bulky valve, or vacuum tube amplifier.[5] The American company, Crown, introduced their DC-300 stereo amplifier rated at 150 watts per channel.

1968 ***Altec develops a graphic equalizer and introduces Acousta-Voicing®.***[8]
Acousta-Voicing used a frequency analyzer to determine the accentuated frequencies of a sound system within a particular acoustic. The third-octave graphic equalizer was then used to reduce these problem areas. This was the forerunner of what later became generally known as 'room equalization'.

Into the Digital Age

1970 ***The first digital delay line from the US company Lexicon.*** The 'Delta-T 101' provided a variable time delay for loudspeakers placed at a distance from the source of sound in a reinforcement system. This was to compensate for the fact that sound transmitted electrically along a cable travels much faster than natural air-borne sound thus causing a pre-echo.

1971 ***The microprocessor developed by Intel***. Refinements in integrated circuit technology led to the development of the microprocessor – which combined the equivalent of thousands of transistors on a single, tiny silicon chip. This paved the way for the development of personal computers.

1977   ***The first successful home computer.*** The Apple II had a monitor and keyboard, along with 16 K RAM and 16 K ROM. Two previous home computers sold in kit form did not take off with the public. These were the MITS Altair computer in 1975 and the Apple I in 1976.

1979   ***Philips demonstrates the CD (compact disc) developed with Sony.*** The audio signal on a CD, converted into binary digits, is stored using a laser beam to engrave microscopically small pits in the disc's surface. Instead of the stylus on a traditional gramophone record, the information stored on the disc is read by a laser beam.[1] Here at last was a system of recording in which there was no surface noise, no tape hiss and no background hum. Music was now being 'sampled' rather than recorded. The compact disc had a frequency range that matched that of the human ear and it could store up to 75 minutes of playing time.

1980   ***Pressure Zone Microphone (PZM) introduced by Crown.*** Also known as a 'Boundary' microphone, the PZM has a miniature condenser microphone capsule mounted on a metal plate in the "Pressure Zone". This is the region where direct sound reaching the capsule will be added to sound reflected into the capsule from the metal plate at almost the same instant. This means that the direct and reflected sound waves are virtually 'in phase' and there is a potential for doubling the effective sound amplitude. Consequently, when placed properly, they are remarkably sensitive and can increase the level before feedback in sound reinforcement systems.

1981   ***IBM 1550 Personal Computer.*** Although the Apple II was on the market, the IBM 1550 is recognized by many as the first popular personal computer with global sales.

1982   ***Commercial CDs and players unveiled in the USA by Sony.*** Launched in Tokyo, they became available in Europe and the States the following year. By 1986, CDs were outselling LPs in Japan and by 1988 there was a similar situation in America.

         MIDI (Musical Instrument Digital Interface) introduced. MIDI is a standard system for linking computers with electronic musical instruments. Musicians were now using digital keyboard instruments to 'sample' the sounds of real instruments and memorize them on a computer. This technology soon began to be employed by theatre technicians. All the sounds required for shows, from natural sound effects to pieces of pre-recorded music, could be sampled and played back via the keyboard.

1988   ***DAT (digital audio tape) recorders become available in Japan.*** These small tape cassettes were based on the digital technology used for U-matic video recorders developed for television. Because of the high price of the equipment and lack of interest from the record industry, DAT recorders were mainly used by professionals.[1]

1991   ***Introduction of an affordable digital studio recorder from Alesis.*** Using a standard S-VHS cassette, the Alesis ADAT 8-track recorder allowed 60 minutes of recording with better quality than a CD. As they were far cheaper than the big open reel multi-track analogue recorders, they took the recording industry by storm. However, they only had a short life span because within a few years most studios were recording digitally on to computers.

1992   ***MiniDisc (MD) launched by Sony.***[13] Only 2½ inches in diameter and as thin as a floppy disc, the MiniDisc had the sound quality of a CD. Designed as a successor to the compact cassette, it had a major advantage over both the analogue and the DAT cassette in that track access was almost instantaneous. Despite these advantages, the record companies and the public remained loyal to the poorer quality compact cassette until the start of the 21st century.

1994   ***The first "affordable" digital multi-track mixing desk, the ProMix 01, unveiled by Yamaha.***[21] When sound mixing desks became digital, the problem of 'noise' inherent in the analogue recording process had virtually disappeared.

Digital technology continues

DURING THE 1990s, most recording studios abandoned digital tape recorders (which were only around for a few years), and were recording digitally direct to computers. Audio editing and processing on a computer screen where one can actually view the wave form is much simpler than with the old tape systems. Sections of sound can be selected and deleted, moved, copied, overlayed, or shifted to another track with ease and accuracy. Audio processing (equalization, compression, reverberation and a host of other effects) can be introduced, including altering the running time of a recorded item without changing the pitch. It was then but a short step to the emergence of 'memory' mixing desks which could remember and recreate complex arrangements of faders and other controls. This technology made possible the control of sixty or more microphones necessary for musical theatre when orchestras are amplified and every cast member wears a radio-microphone.

Not long after the professional recording engineers moved to tapeless recording, affordable computer programmes designed for sound recording and processing became available for personal computers. With the rapid advances and falling cost of digital technology, personal computers soon had the facility to record sound on CDs. Further developments brought in the CD-I (Interactive) for entertainment systems and the CD-ROM (Read Only Memory) with an enhanced storage capacity for sound and images. The CD-ROM is particularly useful for samplers because it can store thousands of pieces of sound.

PART THREE

Sound Recording and Amplification

7 AMPLIFIED SOUND IN THE THEATRE

When Did It Start?

WORKABLE LOUDSPEAKERS HAD been around from the end of the 1800s, but a practical power amplifier was needed before an effective public address system could be developed. When, in 1914, Western Electric unveiled their vacuum tube device for amplifying sound in telephone cables, the way was paved for Peter Jensen to design his 'Magnavox' system. This was first demonstrated in 1915 at a gathering of some 100,000 people in America. Realising the massive potential for live sound amplification, within twelve months the big boys, Western Electric, entered the market. Improved microphones and loudspeakers were soon to follow; but the real impetus for research and design in the audio industry was generated by Hollywood's massive financial investment in the 'talkies'.

Moving-coil horn loudspeakers were developed for motion pictures by 1924 and when, in 1927, the 16-inch discs used for early sound-on-film were replaced by optical sound-tracks, 'talkies' swept the United States and spread around the world. By 1930, The Lansing Manufacturing Company had been formed in California to produce loudspeakers, the Neumann company had been founded in Berlin to manufacture condenser microphones, RCA had introduced a mixing console for use on the Hollywood sound stages, and Western Electric had developed 'equalization' to combat the background sound inherent in the early film recording process. Two-way and three-way loudspeakers and multi-cellular horns followed during the next three years, along with the moving-coil dynamic microphone and the unidirectional (cardioid) ribbon microphone.

A spin-off from the burgeoning sound technology of the movies was the development of a brand new audio industry devoted to 'live' sound. This was highlighted in the Bill Board magazine of April 15 1933:

"From out of the depths of the depression, there has been created a new industry, that of the manufacture, sale and installation of public address amplifiers. Sound engineers have perfected a new series of low-priced amplifiers ideally suited to all branches of the show industry. In a very short period of time this industry has sold an enormous amount of equipment to showmen. Junior p.a. systems provide amplified sound for small gatherings, either indoors or outdoors; on the other hand, there are immensely powerful systems capable of deafening the ears of 20,000 to 100,000 people. Many fairs and expositions are now using fixed and mobile public address systems. Trucks equipped with p.a. systems tour the area to promote the events. Many fairs now have loudspeakers placed throughout the grounds for keeping the crowd advised of the events about to take place. Some enterprising theatre promoters have placed loudspeakers outside their theatres so that passers-by can hear the actors or the music coming directly from the stage. Then,

when a crowd has gathered, the sound is faded out to be replaced by a recorded promotional talk."

Band singers were using PA systems in dance halls during the early 1930s, but microphones used by crooners singing with the big bands were bulky devices only suitable for close-up work. It is unlikely that sound reinforcement was successfully employed in stage musicals before the 1940s when more suitable microphones were being developed. THE EARL CARROLL VANITIES (1940) is sometimes credited as being the first Broadway show to use the microphone, but reinforcement did not become common in New York and London until the 1960s.

In contrast, many civic theatres and arts centres installed audio systems of some sort from the early days of public address, if only to make announcements and play interval music.

According to "Theatres and Auditoriums" by Harold Burris-Meyer and Edward C Cole (first published in 1949), the first permanent installation in a theatre with completely flexible apparatus for the control of sound was installed in New York's Metropolitan Opera House in 1940. Designed by Vincent Mallory, the Stevens Sound Control System had six low level inputs routing to three master controls which, in turn, were switchable to eight output channels with gain controls. Four loudspeaker circuits could be selected to output channels 1-4 and four to output channels 5-8. There was also some basic equalization available for insertion. For the time, this was an amazingly flexible and sophisticated system.

Certainly by the 1950s, some American universities were carrying out fairly advanced experimentation with sound, often designing and building their own control systems. By 1965, according to an article in Theatre Design and Technology, Indiana University had a custom mixing desk in their 400-seat theatre installed in a sound booth with a large window which opened! The console had 10 inputs, 4 group masters and a section of loudspeaker switches and level controls along with a 3-position pan potentiometer. State theatres and opera houses built in Germany from the 1950s incorporated control rooms at the rear of their auditoriums with studio quality mixing consoles and ancillary equipment. Sound control rooms were not incorporated into professional theatres in Britain until the end of the 1960s.

As we have seen, mechanical sound effects were used well into the 20th century. Recorded sound only crept in gradually as equipment improved and became less expensive. Progress was relatively slow because there was no tradition of electric sound in the theatre and no department to foster its cause. The situation was very different in the movie business when the talking pictures came along. In this new industry, whose very existence relied upon technology, the audio technician was king. When the first Western Electric recorders were brought into film studios, the operators of this fantastic equipment (soon called "soundmen") were held in such awe that they actually took charge of filming. The soundman was the one who gave the signal to start the take, and he was the one to approve the take – not the director or the actors. He also had the power to stop the filming if he was not satisfied with the sound quality. Douglas Fairbanks Junior said that the soundman was: *"...a magician. He was like Merlin or the Wizard of Oz, and a bit of a faker in some ways, as he was experimenting himself at that time."* Nothing much has changed, has it?

It would be very many years before the theatre had the equivalent of the movie soundman. In America, microphones and disc turntables became the responsibility of the chief electrician. The stagehands who worked the mechanical effects were precluded by union rules from touching anything electrical. Compared with the lighting equipment, the sound system comprised a very small part of the equipment rental bill and many chief electricians looked upon it as an irritation. When a show moved into a theatre, the lighting rig was normally completed before anyone thought of unpacking the audio equipment – leaving little or no time for rehearsal. Making matters worse, because the chief electrician's main concern was for the lighting, the responsibility for operating the sound equipment usually fell to the most junior, or the most ineffectual, member of the electrical team. Quite often, one or other of the lighting board operators would perform sound cues between lighting operations. The operation of sound was not generally recognized as a specialist skill until large and complicated mixing desks became common on the big musicals in the 1980s.

The handling of sound equipment in the UK theatre developed in a slightly different way. As the big heavy mechanical noise-making machines went out of favour, fewer stage hands were required and it became the responsibility of the propman to blow bird whistles, slam doors, rattle thunder sheets or turn the handles of wind machines. As time went on, because the creation of such effects was regarded as artistic rather than technical, the task was taken over by stage management. So, when productions began using effects discs and even microphones, it remained the province of the stage manager. But, just as the junior electricians in American tended to be placed in control of the sound, in Britain it often fell to the lot of the least experienced assistant stage manager. This person was unlikely to have much interest or expertise in anything technical because, well into the 1970s, members of the stage management team would be expected to understudy the cast. Consequently, most assistant stage managers were budding actors desperately waiting for the opportunity to get on stage.

Although the art of creating sound for the theatre was taken very seriously by a few British directors as far back as the mid 1950s, it took another fifteen years or so before producers reluctantly agreed to pay for an individual whose sole job was to operate the sound equipment.

The first recorded sound effects

THERE IS MENTION IN Michael Booth's book, 'Theatre in the Victorian Age' of a phonograph being used for a baby's cry in a London theatre in 1890. Sixteen years later, Herbert Beerbohm Tree definitely used recordings in his London production of Stephen Phillips' tragedy NERO. The event is marked in the Theatre Magazine (1906) with two photographs; one showing a musician blowing a bugle into a large horn attached to a disc recorder, the other with an actor recording the agonizing shrieks and groans of the tortured martyrs. *"In the theatre,"* the article states, *"these sounds are all realistically reproduced by the gramaphone".*

Using direct-recorded discs played back through a large horn could not have produced a very faithful or, indeed, loud sound. Electric recordings and record players with amplifiers and moving-coil loudspeakers were not generally available until after 1927. Wire recorders emerged in 1925 and no doubt some enthusiasts experimented with these. It took a few more years before ready-made effects could be obtained from commercial sound libraries.

The American theatre did not have access to pre-recorded effects until the radio companies began broadcasting drama, and suddenly there was a requirement for instant noises-off. To fulfill this need, the Starr Piano Company of Richmond, Indiana, set up a subsidiary in association with NBC. Trading under the name of Gennett, the company was formed around 1932 to specialize in the production of sound effects transcription records. This was new technology, because RCA had only just started producing their heavy 16-inch long-playing (33⅓ r.p.m.) transcription discs for radio stations.

As broadcasting flourished, other companies such as Standard, Silver Masque and Major Records came into the field. Gennett was based in Richmond, but later had offices in Los Angeles and New York. The trade mark name for their record library was 'Speedy-Q'. Discs were sold outright to customers free of any further payment for royalties or public performance. By 1944, a double-sided 10-inch record from the comprehensive Speedy-Q library cost $2.00.

One of the first documented examples of records used in the theatre was for a production of Hamlet in New York in 1932. The pioneering director, Norman Bel Geddes, had a sound system engineered by a firm called Research Products, Inc. which included twin turntables for long-playing transcription discs. An article in the Scientific American (vol 146) says: *"The prelude, overture, and entire musical accompaniment to the show were reproduced over the system – there being no orchestras or other conventional music used in connection with the play."* Three years later, Bel Geddes was still pushing the boundaries of technology. For his production of Dead End at the Belasco Theatre, this innovative director hired a motion picture sound truck and spent four days recording river front noises, traffic sounds and crowd effects with his cast of actors.

The use of discs in the theatre obviously caught on rapidly. In 1934, according to the Herald Tribune, the union of stage hands in New York, Theatrical Protective Union No. 1, was decrying the fact that only 60% of their members were in employment, as opposed to 90% in 1927. The reason for this decline was largely because the old-time spectacles had disappeared and the new productions with, perhaps, three or four effects were using disc recordings. Previously, the manipulation of thunder and wind machines and all the other devices to create a storm or a spectacular battle gave employment to fifteen or twenty property men, but the introduction of the 'panatrope' had reduced this number to just one electrician.

The 'Panatrope' was the brand name of the first fully-electric record player launched by the Brunswick company in 1927. The term 'panatrope' was adopted by the British theatre and used well into the 1950s to describe double turntable units with groove-locating devices for cueing music and effects from 78 r.p.m. records. Strangely enough, although the panatrope was an American device, I have never come across a soundman in the States who is aware of it. In the UK, well into the 1970s when we were using tape, the older stage managers still referred to 'pan cues' rather than tape or sound cues.

The early use of recordings was not without its problems. When several critics writing about the play HELL FREEZES OVER made fun of the strange noises emanating from a dodgy wind machine, a reporter from the New York Sun (January 18, 1936) decided to investigate. To his amazement he discovered that it was not a wind machine at all. *"The odd noises which emerge from behind the scenery are, instead, the howls of the winds themselves, indented on phonograph disks by Rear Admiral Byrd."* The involvement of Rear Admiral Byrd was not explained in the article. Born in 1888, Byrd was one of America's greatest explorers and aviators. He made the first flight over the South Pole in 1929 and received a medal of honour for his exploits in the polar regions. Perhaps he took a wire recorder with him.

Soon disc players were being produced specifically for theatres and other live events. They were a little more robust and powerful than domestic versions, but there was no cueing device. To locate the start of the required track, the customary procedure was to place the pick-up on a white chinagraph pencil mark previously made on the disc. The 'Catalog of the Theatre' published by Cleon Throckmorton, Inc. in New York, listed all kinds of theatrical goods and services from box office equipment to scenery, properties, wigs, costumes and technical equipment. Recommended in the March 1937 edition was the Ansley 'Dynaphone' phonograph: *"it has a very light pick-up, which doubles the faithful life of the records and almost eliminates surface noise, and it is supreme in tone and reproducing quality."* The model 12, priced at $110.00, had a crystal pick-up with tone and volume controls, and was suitable for 10, 12 and 16-inch transcription discs. The 8-inch Magnavox speaker was separate.

The Ansley Dynaphone phonograph from Throckmorton's Catalog of Theatre, 1937. *New York Public Library*

The company points out that modern recordings are realistic and more reliably controlled. And in an editorial comment on the same page, a most perceptive truism is stated – that the *suspension of disbelief* which we claim from a theatre audience does not extend to sound: *"This board, you may say, is a tree, this muslin a wall and that spotlight the tropical sunlight – and the public will imagine it. But a dog's bark must sound like a bark, and a train like a train!"*

In Britain and other parts of Europe, there were no commercial radio stations. Consequently, there were no commercial sound libraries to service them. The BBC compiled an extremely comprehensive library, but this was solely for their own use because, under the terms of their Royal Charter, they were not allowed to indulge in commercial activities. A few soundmen in the film industry catalogued their recordings and eventually offered them for sale, but the amount of money per second they were able to charge film production companies was way beyond theatre budgets. As we shall see later, a specialist theatre sound company was set up in London in 1939 to provide sound effects and equipment.

8   PIONEERS OF BROADWAY

Masque Sound

MASQUE SOUND WAS FOUNDED in 1935 by three of the stage crew employed at the Playhouse Theatre in New York. They were Sam Saltzman, the electrician, Mac Landesman, the property man, and John Shearing, the stage carpenter.

When I talked to John Shearing's son, Jack, in July 2003, he told me that Masque Sound was probably the first company providing a sound rental service to the professional theatre. As I know that the first such company in Great Britain was not founded until 1938/39, three or four years later, this is almost certainly true.

The founders of
Masque Sound:
John Shearing, Mac
Landesman and
Sam Saltzman

The new enterprise (yet to be named) needed a base in New York and Sam Saltzman knew that Pat Green, who ran the Silver Masque Record Company, had some spare space in her premises just off Broadway. Silver Masque was one of the first companies providing sound effects to the radio and movie industry. They had a press for making 78 r.p.m shellac copies from their standard catalogue, and could also cut the less durable acetate discs with effects required for a specific production.

Having equipment rental and sound effects under the same roof (in fact, in the same room), had obvious advantages for both parties and, although the two operations were initially entirely separate, it was decided to call the new company Masque Sound.

Pat Green of Silver Masque Records in the rental shop circa 1940. The equipment in the rack is RCA. The metered unit on top is a Port-O-Vox receiver, one of the first wireless microphone systems.

In the early days, John Shearing built the cabinets for the equipment and installed all the electronics – which were very simple at that time. Mac Landesman turned out to be a good businessman and Sam Saltzman was a superb salesman. It was a good team and the business became very profitable, not least because the equipment lasted for years. From around 1935 to 1955, virtually the same equipment was being rented out. This was largely because the number of audio manufacturing companies was very limited and, unlike today, they did not keep launching new models. Masque Sound used mainly RCA equipment from the movie industry to begin with, later augmenting this with products from Altec Lansing (created in 1941). The famous Altec A4 'Voice of the Theatre' loudspeaker, introduced in 1944 ostensibly for use in movie theaters, also became a standard in the live theatre.

By the time America joined the Allies in the Second World War, at the end of 1941, the nation's industries were focused on servicing the armed forces. As a consequence, the purchase of new theatre equipment became almost impossible. However, when Irvine Berlin wrote THIS IS THE ARMY, a famously successful musical designed to entertain the troops, Masque Sound was fortunate enough to secure the audio contract. As the show was sponsored by the government, obtaining equipment was no longer a problem. THIS IS THE ARMY toured extensively both at home and overseas.

During the early years of Masque Sound, there was a general resistance to the use of microphones for speech reinforcement. Although the design of microphones was improving and better quality loudspeakers were being developed, the technology of the time was not able to produce a naturalistic sound. Moreover, the very suggestion of microphones was an affront to most stage performers. Not only had they been trained to be heard, but they also understood quite a bit about acoustics. Arriving at a new theatre, the 'stars' would go on stage to discover where their voices had the strongest resonance. This was known as the "sweet spot". Then in a performance, they knew exactly where to place themselves.

From the outset, Masque Sound had to cater for a growing demand for recorded sound effects and one of the first things John Shearing invented was what he called a "spotter and dropper". This was a 78 r.p.m. record player incorporating a device for ensuring that the pick-up would drop into the right groove. This had five adjustable rods which could individually flip up and down. In the down position, the pick-up arm could be backed against the screw which had been adjusted, via a screw thread, for the correct groove location. For the next cue, you flipped that one up and put another one down. The pick-up arm itself had a hydraulic mechanism so that pushing a button caused the pick-up to drop gently down into the groove. It was not until the early 1950s that tape recorders began to appear in the rental shop. The first of these was manufactured by Magnavox.

Masque Sound's
"Spotter & Dropper"
and two Presto
tape machines
on the table.

Saki Oura

SADLY, PAT GREEN OF Silver Masque Records died during the mid 1940s and Masque Sound took over the company. The recording studio became the responsibility of a Japanese-American gentleman called Saki Oura, whose name kept cropping up when I was investigating the history of Broadway sound.

Saki Oura, a graduate of the Massachusetts Institute of Technology (MIT), became interested in the theatre during the mid 1930s. Before long, his reputation for innovative work with audio systems led to an appointment as consultant to the Schubert Theatres. Then, like John Shearing before him, he teamed up with two theatre technicians and formed a company called Sound Associates. Unfortunately, the arrangement did not work out as Saki ended up doing most of the work. In 1946, he sold the company to a theatre electrician in New York named Tommy Fitzgerald. Sound Associates became the second sound rental company in New York. It is now run very successfully by Tommy's sons, Richard and Peter.

Shortly after selling the business, Saki Oura was offered a job with Masque Sound. Jack Shearing admitted that Saki was the first person they employed who had any real technical knowledge of audio, but he went on to stress that it is not technical knowledge alone that counts; success comes to the person who is best equipped to handle what is available technically during any particular era. And Saki Oura was one of these. Richard Fitzgerald made a remarkably similar comment to me the very next day. He said that Saki Oura was one of the real pioneers who was able to handle the equipment and get more out of it than most people.

When sound effects became commercially available on LP records during the early 1960s and tape machines took over for playback in the theatre, Masque Sound stopped producing new discs. With their studio facilities and extensive library, Saki Oura concentrated his talents on the creation of sound tracks specifically designed for each customer and each show, a process continued by John Kilgore when he joined the company in 1986. The only other significant studio facility in New York for theatre recording now, in 2007, is owned by the rival company, Sound Associates.

Jack Shearing – 2003.

The Shearings have been involved in the theatre for four generations. Founder of Masque Sound, John Shearing, was formerly head carpenter at the Metroplitan Opera House where his father had been property master. John's son, Jack, joined the company to become involved in sound design and contracting in 1955 and went on to run the company until the grandsons of the founder, Geoff and Jim Shearing, assumed responsibility. Masque Sound remains the biggest rental operation on Broadway with their main competition coming from Sound Associates and the more recent Promix, a wholly owned subsidiary of the lighting and sound operation PRG (the Production Resource Group).

Disc gives way to tape

WHEN JACK SHEARING came into the company in the mid 1950s, Masque Sound was still hiring out the 'spotter and dropper' record players, but tape was taking over. Records were mainly used in shows with only two or three effects, as this was easier and cheaper than having the effects recorded on to tape and renting the more expensive tape machines. Driven by the competition to invest in tape, they standardized on a machine from a local manufacturer named Presto. Jack modified these machines with an auto-stop mechanism triggered by a piece of metal foil stuck to the tape at the end of each cue. Although not good enough for quality recording, the machines were perfectly adequate for playing sound effects. Sound Associates went for the more expensive Ampex machines which became the most widely used tape recorders in the American theatre from the mid 1950s right through into the 1970s.

Growing acceptance of sound reinforcement

MANY PRODUCERS HAD acknowledged the need for sound reinforcement by the 1960s and although it was not a natural sound, people were able to hear the performers more easily, so they accepted it. According to Stephen Sondheim, reported in the New York Post (1978), foot-microphones were used on the original production of WEST SIDE STORY in 1957, but when A FUNNY THING HAPPENED ON THE WAY TO THE FORUM was produced in 1962, director George Abbot was against any form of amplification. They tried it without sound in New Haven – but nobody could hear a thing. By the time they got to New York the show was miked. (The London version opened later that year and I remember arranging a basic sound system with five microphones spaced equally along the front edge of the stage).

The early microphones used on Broadway were mainly RCA and then Shure. The Shure 545 'Unidyne', a directional microphone designed for vocals, was very successful as a foot-mike. Normally, five were placed along the front edge of the stage, mounted on little wooden stands sitting on foam rubber mats to minimize vibrations from the stage floor. The favoured mixer was the Altec five-channel unit with rotary controls. Should more channels be required, a second mixer was simply fed into one of the channels on the first mixer.

Early Altec
1599-A mixer.
*Klaus Blasquiz
Collection, Paris*

Getting enough gain out of the system was always a problem, particularly with a number of open microphones lowering the feedback threshold. So, to make life easier for the electrician operating the system, Jack Shearing devised a switch panel. Microphones could then be switched on and off rather than having to keep resetting the levels on the knobs.

Electronic equipment was not as reliable as it is today, and Masque Sound had a policy of supplying a back-up for everything. If an amplifier or a preamplifier stopped working, there was another one available at the flick of a switch, and two tape machines would be running at the same time – just in case.

The favoured loudspeakers were from Altec. A temporary rig would often have four or six of the big A5 or, later, A7 "Voice of the Theatre" systems mounted either side of the proscenium. The A5, launched in 1945, had a 15" (38cm) driver in a bass horn/reflex enclosure with an 8-cell horn mounted on top. The A7, which came out in 1966, was a bass horn/reflex cabinet crossing over at 500 or 800 Hz to a 4-cell sectoral horn. The frequency range was given as 35 Hz – 22 kHz.

Altec "Voice of the Theatre" loudspeaker.

During the 1970s, some soundmen opted for a cluster of loudspeakers mounted centrally above the proscenium. A good central array produces a cleaner sound than a number of widely spaced speakers and, if correctly set up, the sound appears to come from the stage. A typical cluster used ALTEC multicellular and radial horns with folded horn bass bin cabinets and a 500 Hz or 800 Hz crossover. Of course, the central system did not work in theatres with overhanging balconies because every seat in the house has to see the loudspeakers in order to hear them properly.

Jack Shearing recalled that back in the 1950s there were people who were adept at operating the equipment, but there were very few who understood sound technically. There were no consultants advising on new theatres being built and terrible mistakes were made. Everyone was experimenting and learning by their mistakes… or most of them were!

Jack Mann

ONE OF THE PEOPLE who did have some knowledge of electronics and was one of the great pioneering sound designers was Jack Mann. I had the good fortune to meet him in 1970 and benefit from his experience when he was working on the Stephen Sondheim show COMPANY, before I handled the London production. In November 2002, I had the great pleasure of renewing our acquaintance at his home near Philadelphia. At the end of my visit, he told me that he never discussed sound and the techniques he had used during his career with anyone. "The only person who has got me to talk about it is you", he said. I felt most privileged. His story encompasses the development of Broadway sound from a black art into a recognized skill and respected profession.

Having married his high school sweetheart, Jean, in 1942, Jack was drafted into the army where he soon found himself playing clarinet in a band to entertain the troops. At the end of the war, he got a job in the theatre in Michigan where his father was a stage electrician. He joined IATSE (International Alliance of Theatrical Stage Employees) and learned all about lighting. He also took a correspondence course in electronics.

Jack and Jean Mann
– November 2002.

At the beginning of the 1950s, after five years as assistant electrician, he became chief electrician at this 4,000 seat theatre in Michigan. In this capacity, he was responsible for designing a new sound installation which turned out to be the first Altec-Lansing PA system using 500 Hz crossovers. Until then, their crossovers were always up in the 2500 Hz area.

To replace the existing centre cluster, he installed Altec bass cabinets and wide dispersion exponential horns with the highest frequency drivers in the catalogue. From a theatrical point of view, Jack was never happy with the performers' voices emanating from way up in the ceiling, so a pair of small horns and bass cabinets were installed at the side of the proscenium for the main floor with another pair for the balcony.

Amazingly, the whole system was run from one ALTEC 70w amplifier running into a 70 volt system, balanced by tapping the 70 volt transformers at each loudspeaker. The level obtained from this one amplifier was more than adequate because the loudspeakers were extremely efficient and, unlike transistor amplifiers, the old tube amplifiers did not clip when being driven hard.

This was Jack's first experience at designing a sound system and was the start of a learning curve that led to a career on Broadway spanning twenty eight years. As he said: *"I learned my craft mainly by doing. People think they can find out how the equipment works and then they can create wonderful sound. It takes years to become a good soundman. It is like the boy who goes to the music shop and buys the best trumpet they have. He gets back home, opens the case, and expects to be able to make wonderful sounds. He has no idea that it takes seven years of hard work to become a mediocre trumpet player. And that assumes he has some talent in the first place."* Jack was fortunate in that he did have talent. He knew how the equipment worked, had a knowledge and love of the theatre and, being a musician, possessed a very good ear.

Jack Mann moved to New York late in 1959 with the idea of becoming a lighting director. The night he arrived, he visited an old friend, Robert Maybaum, who was to become one of the first Broadway soundmen and like Jack, was a trained musician – a trumpet player. Robert Maybaum had only been in New York for three months and was operating the sound on the musical DO RE ME. By chance, that show happened to be the last show to be lit by an electrician. The scenic artist's union had brought in a rule that any scenic designer had to light his own show or hire one of his scenic artist brothers to light the show for him. With the end of an era came the end to Jack Mann's ambitions in theatre lighting.

There is reference to Robert Maybaum in the Newark Sunday News (October 16, 1960) operating the equipment for a new installation in the St James Theatre on 44th Street. The play was BECKET by Jean Anouilh starring Laurence Olivier and Anthony Quinn. The reporter says: *"Theatre-goers have been treated to a new sensation in the theatre: hearing every sigh and whisper. The system includes seven microphones on stage, a battery of amplifiers in the basement and sixty six loudspeakers distributed around the theatre and up under the proscenium arch. The sound system is operated during the performance by Robert Maybaum, a radio engineer and graduate musician from Flint, Michigan, who never sees the play. He listens to the actors, turns the pages of the score and twirls amplifier dials."*

System designer
Richard Ranger (left)
and Robert
Maybaum in the
St. James Theatre.
Newark News.
Courtesy Newark
Public Library

Meanwhile, Jack Mann needed a job. Fortunately, Jack's father had worked for many years with one of the original partners in Masque Sound, Sam Saltzman, and he offered Jack employment in their workshops. One day in January 1961, Sam told him to get down to the Eugene O'Neil Theatre where they had trouble with the sound system on a Carol Channing revue called SHOWGIRL. The first preview had been disastrous as nobody had been able to hear a word. Jack was surprised to discover that the sound control (an Altec five-channel mixer) was placed between two lighting switchboards all facing the back wall of the stage. It was obvious that he needed to see and hear the show properly in order to do a good job, so he got the manager to agree that all the equipment could be moved into a box in the auditorium. Having only just arrived in New York, he had no idea that this was unusual. It just seemed to make sense. The proof was that the audience was able to hear the show that night. The producers were relieved and Jack's reputation as a Broadway soundman was launched.

Soon after that, he had a call from the chief electrician on a play directed by George Abbot called A CALL ON KUPRIN (1961). They need a soundman to cue in the sound effects, which were still on disc (the first time Jack used a tape machine was on a musical called ANJA in 1963). That phone call turned out to be the start of a long association with producer Hal Prince and his assistant Ruth Mitchell. In 1963, Hal Prince asked him to sort out the sound on a musical called SHE LOVES ME and in 1964 he worked on Hal Prince's next production, FIDDLER ON THE ROOF. There was no operator on that show; George Abbot, one of the greatest Broadway directors of all time, told him to turn the sound up until he could just tell it was on – and then back it off a little. The orchestrations were suitable for singers (no brass or loud instruments when anyone was singing) and the musical director controlled the sound balance between the performers and the orchestra. It was vital that the audience were not aware that the actors were miked. That is why Jack did not have a credit as sound designer for many years. The whole thing was meant to be a secret. As a union man, the only mention in small print in the programme was "Electrician (sound)".

After FIDDLER had been running a few months, Jack saw an advertisement for a new mixer from a company called Interface in Houston Texas. It was solid-wired and had very basic equalization. *"I contacted the boss, Louis Stevenson, and he sent me the first Stevenson 100A mixer ever to be used on Broadway. I took it into the theatre one night and plugged everything in and – Holy Moses! – that sound system just came to life. You think that a mixer is a mixer is a mixer.... Oh, no! Suddenly, there was clarity. The mixer did not get in the way of the sound. That mixer was the link between the old mixers and the big mixing desks of today. Years later, A CHORUS LINE had several road companies using the same little Stevenson mixer."*

By the second year of the run of FIDDLER, there were a lot of different people playing the lead – understudies and replacements – and some were not as vocally strong as others. The producers did not want to employ a sound operator, so Jack installed an Altec compressor unit, designed for motion picture recording, which automatically lifted the level of the microphones when an actor was not projecting properly. The show ran for another six years with this system.

After FIDDLER ON THE ROOF, the Hal Prince office asked him to design the sound for their next musical, CABARET (1966). Once again, the sound control was backstage with pre-set levels on the mixer.

It was around this time, the mid-sixties, that Jack Mann and his old friend Robert Maybaum (working on HELLO DOLLY which had opened in 1964) started specifying the type of equipment they wanted on shows, rather than accept the standard packages sent out by the rental companies. In many ways, the equipment suppliers were happy with this situation because the responsibility was no longer theirs. The producers were now paying a consultant or a sound designer – although no one called them that – to produce results.

From 1965-1972, Jack ran his own company, Theatre Sound, Inc. It was financed by Pete Feller Studios, a major New York scenery company. Pete Feller, who had started his career as an apprentice carpenter in a scenic workshop run by John Shearing (the theatre business is a small world), had the ambition to expand his scenery business into a complete theatrical service. He already owned the Four Star lighting company and Theatre Sound was another add-on.

One of the partners in Theatre Sound, Inc. was Jack Mitnick, a self-taught soundman, who began his theatrical career selling candies in the Schubert Theatre. He had been responsible for the sound on GYPSY (1959) and CAMELOT (1960). Later, he worked for Masque Sound.

Soon, Theatre Sound, Inc. owned enough equipment to service several large shows, and it was the type of equipment Jack needed to develop his own individual sound. Based upon AKG microphones and, most importantly, Bozak loudspeakers, this was very natural and subtle *speech reinforcement* rather than an obviously miked *public address* system.

Jack first came across Bozak loudspeakers at a concert in New York's Central Park. There was a huge stage with six large three-way column loudspeakers mounted above the proscenium, two or three on either side and more arrays on trucks in the auditorium. This was similar to the installation used for the big concerts in the Hollywood Bowl at that time. Jack recalled his experience that night: *"During the concert in Central Park, I walked away from the stage until the musicians looked like ants – and you could shut your eyes and swear that the orchestra was just in front of you. No horns, no bass bins, just beautiful quality."* Jack introduced himself to the designer, Rudie Bozak, and they struck up a relationship which lasted until Rudie died.

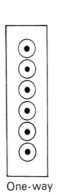

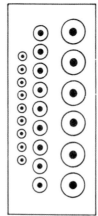

Bozak line-array loudspeakers.

One-way   Two-way   Three-way

In the theatre, Jack mainly used the two-way columns with their very defined wide horizontal and narrow vertical dispersion produced by the lines of six 5-inch (13cm) and twelve 2-inch (5cm) cone tweeters. Jack never did like sound systems relying on a central cluster and his columns were placed on the sides of the proscenium. When correctly positioned, the maximum power output could be directed at the rear of the auditorium, while the front rows only received the benefit of the lower drivers in the speaker. As he said: *"You have to spray the audience with sound – but the trick is to get the audience wet without wetting the walls of the auditorium. You have to stop the sound at the side aisle. You have to spray the people with an equal amount of sound. It is no good if two thirds of the audience get more sound than the other third. You might think it easy, but it takes a lot of experience to make it work."*

Various people have laid claim to discovering the 'boundary' or 'pressure zone' microphone, but Jack was certainly one of the first people to use the technique in the theatre. Apparently, he was sitting one day on the verandah of his country home looking across a big lake, when he began to wonder why a passing train, some two miles or more away, sounded so close. The answer had to be the flat lake. So he took some RCA-77 microphones to the theatre he was working in at the time, laid them on foam rubber platforms just clear of the stage floor, and tried them out on a show. *"It sounded beautiful. I had a cleaner sound and more gain."*

Jack cannot remember exactly what show that was, but my colleague, Richard Pilbrow, thinks it was in 1968. Richard was lighting designer for ZORBA in New York and remembers the soundman coming on stage one day during the previews and taking all the microphones off their stands and placing them on little pads on the floor. Richard thought that he would return later and, perhaps, place them on different stands, but he left them there for the show – and it sounded great. When Richard returned to England and told me about this, I said that he must be mistaken. It could not possibly work. He should stick to lighting. Nevertheless, I later did some experimenting and introduced the technique to the British theatre in 1969.

By the time Jack was working on Stephen Sondheim's COMPANY in 1970, he was using the AKG C451, a neat slim condenser microphone, suspended in small shock-absorbing stands. On a visit to the AKG factory in Austria, he explained what he was doing and they manufactured a special hinged knuckle joint (which became known as the A51) to fit between the body of the microphone and the capsule. That way, the microphone could be positioned low down parallel to the stage with the head tilting down at 45° almost touching the floor.

One of Jack's idiosyncrasies was that he always carried phase-reverse connectors with him. This was because the whole sound system might be in phase with itself – all the loudspeakers pushing and pulling in the same direction at the same time to create harmonious sound waves – but sections of it might not be in phase with the acoustics of different areas of the auditorium. Many engineers were very unhappy when Jack inserted a phase reverser because the system was no longer technically 'in phase' and there was a loss of gain. But, as he said: *"Loudness has nothing to do with it. You can always turn up the volume. It is the quality of sound that counts".* For example, he changed the phase for the balcony speakers in the St James Theatre for ON THE TWENTIETH CENTURY and in the Uris Theatre for SWEENEY TODD and it worked.

Theatre Sound, Inc. ceased trading in 1972 and Jack returned to freelancing. Sound systems were becoming too expensive for a small company and it was difficult to compete with Masque Sound and Sound Associates who could afford the equipment and had a reputation for doing a good job. Also, John Shearing had a way of ensuring that producers remained loyal to Masque Sound by quoting cut-price deals. He could afford to do this because he knew that when the show was about to open out of town, there would inevitably be panic phone calls for extras and items they had overlooked – and these were charged at list price.

Jack and I discussed the fact that soundmen tended to quietly get on with their jobs and often had minimal contact with the cast and crew. However, he told me a story to prove that the work of the soundman does not always go unnoticed or unappreciated. One night in 1983, at the end of a performance of PRIVATE LIVES, Jack was called on stage by the company manager to be confronted by the entire crew and cast of actors. Someone had discovered that it was his birthday. Completely overwhelmed, he was presented with a birthday cake while the entire ensemble, including the stars, Elizabeth Taylor and Richard Burton, sang "Happy Birthday".

Sound Associates

SOUND ASSOCIATES GREW FROM the small operation Saki Oura sold to Thomas Fitzgerald in 1946 into a major player. Initially, Thomas had to continue working as an electrician in order to supplement his income. He was nominated for Tony Awards for his work on two plays as "stage technician (sound)" in 1956 for LONG DAY'S JOURNEY INTO NIGHT and in 1958 for WHO WAS THAT LADY I SAW YOU WITH? Despite this recognition, the company was still struggling during the early 1960s when his son Richard came into the business. Not until 1975 could Richard give up his job as electrician at the Vivien Beaumont Theatre. Richard's younger brother, Peter, started to work for the company in 1969, and with both of them having full-time jobs in the theatre, they had to work nights and all through weekends to maintain the business.

Around 1967, Thomas Fitzgerald set up a company in California to manufacture silicon control dimmers and before long Sound Associates was largely being run by his two sons. Although he eventually moved out west permanently, he remained involved in the New York sound business and in 1974 received a Tony Award nomination for the musical GIGI at the Uris theatre, this time billed as "master soundman". Sadly, he did not receive an actual Tony Award in his lifetime. It was in 1974 that an award had a citation as follows: *Thomas H Fitzgerald, to the gifted lighting technician of countless Broadway shows and many Tony telecasts. (Posthumous)*

Thomas H Fitzgerald

Richard told me how difficult it was being a soundman in the sixties: *"There were only a few of us doing this at the time and we were all scratching around, experimenting with equipment and making up the rules as we went along. Nothing was designed specifically for live theatre. We had to adapt what was available".*

Richard Fitzgerald
– 2003.

In the 1950s and 1960s, Sound Associates was mainly using Altec "Voice of the Theatre" loudspeakers fixed to pipes on the sides of the proscenium. But around 1962, they installed possibly the first central cluster in a New York theatre for a show called SOPHIE at the Winter Garden. Although the loudspeaker array was very successful, it took a lot of installation time to hang a group of heavy loudspeakers in an inaccessible position. Consequently, central arrays were not seen very often in New York for some time.

When they saw how successfully Jack Mann was using the Bozak columns, they decided to invest in them and eventually owned around a hundred. As Richard said: *"The steerabilty was remarkable and they had a frequency range which was certainly equal to the amplifiers and mixers available at that time. The beauty of a good line array is that you do not know it is on until you turn it off. That technology is, of course, the forerunner of the line arrays that many people are using now".*

With the advent of the rock musical, followed by a wave of 'High Tec' British musicals like EVITA and STARLIGHT EXPRESS transferring to Broadway, everything became bigger, brighter and louder. Producers were no longer impressed by a subtle enhancement of the actors' voices to achieve audibility. They began to demand a larger than life unnatural sound. Budgets for the sound systems increased to unprecedented levels and the theatre audio business moved into a new era.

Sound Associates has continued providing audio systems for some of the largest Broadway shows, but they are also specialists in infra-red listening systems providing amplification for the hearing impaired. They installed the first such system on Broadway at the Lunt-Fontanne theatre in 1979.

9   THE BRITISH PIONEERS

When the 'crooner' became a popular feature on the bill during the 1930s and 1940s and stand-up comedians saw the advantage of delivering their patter into a microphone, basic public address systems were installed in the major touring theatres around Great Britain. The stand microphones and, later, the central 'riser' microphone appearing through a small trap at the front of the stage, were normally controlled from a small mixer in the prompt corner by an electrician. Similar systems were installed in a few London theatres devoted to staging popular entertainment and in the large cinemas where the feature films were interspersed with lavish stage shows.

Just before the Second World War (1939-45), a firm called Simon Sound seems to have been the first company in Britain to produce a unit for playing sound effects discs in the theatre. This was a big metal coffin with two large 78 r.p.m. turntables, a groove locating device made by Simtrol, and one enormous valve amplifier built by Pamphonic Limited. *(For the technically minded, they were single ended amplifiers with three stages of amplification, direct coupled so that the anode of one valve was connected to the grid of the next. One of the valves stood about 12" high.)* These machines were called 'panatropes' a name which was to become synonymous with all theatre disc replay units in the UK.

BBC 'TD/7' grams unit, circa 1937, with parallel-tracking arm and groove locator as employed on the Simon Sound panatrope.

The groove-locating device and the pickups (EMI Type 12) seem to be identical to the ones used in the BBC radio studios. It is possible that the BBC purchased these from Simtrol for their TD/7 machines.

The development of speech reinforcement and recorded sound effects in the commercial West End theatre in London was largely due to two individuals, neither of whom had any theatrical background. Although very different characters, they shared an enthusiasm for finding out how things worked and seeing if they could improve them. It was this typically British amateur approach that led to the formation of two companies that were to dominate the theatre sound business in Great Britain for many years.

Bishop Sound And Electrical Company

BISHOP SOUND AND ELECTRICAL COMPANY was founded in 1939, the year Britain declared war on Germany. The founder, Jack Bishop, whose real name was Joseph Lipowski, was educated at the Cooper's Company School in London and at Brussels University. He enlisted in the Royal Army Service Corps in the First World War (1914-1918) and was wounded in the Battle of the Somme. Jack had a fascination with radio and wireless telegraphy and soon after the war he began his career in electronics by repairing radios, or 'wirelesses' as they were called in those days. In December 1922, he was granted one of the first licences permitting him, on CAL2VM, to send and receive radio signals. His experiments with television led him to become one of the first members of the Royal Television Society. He was also keenly interested in sound recording which, in those days, was on film.

In 1927 he took over a radio shop in Roman Road, near Bethnal Green in east London. The shop was called Bishops and rather than change the name of the business, he changed his own name and was thereafter known as Jack Bishop. This could have been prompted by the fact that there was a good deal of anti-Semitism around at that time.

The shop in Roman Road, London, circa 1927.

The mechanical sound effects commonly used in the theatre were complicated and cumbersome and, through contacts he had made in the theatre, he was asked to provide recorded effects for shows. His earliest recordings, supplied on specially cut 78 r.p.m. discs, were for a play called FROG which apparently had a spectacular fire effect, and for two farces at the Gaiety Theatre, GOING GREEK and RUNNING RIOT, the final production at that theatre before it closed in 1939.

In the same year, just before the start of the Second World War, Bishop met a man called Killick who was chairman of the West End Managers Association and lessee of the Comedy Theatre. He also had a company which supplied theatre bar staff, ushers, and gallery stools. Until some time in the 1960s, the cheap seats in the gallery (upper balcony) of West End theatres were not numbered and could not be booked in advance. Consequently, people turned up early and queued in order to obtain the best seats. Most theatres provided rows of collapsible stools on the pavement outside the gallery entrance (usually at the side of the theatre) to alleviate the long wait.

Killick was a useful contact who could see the future for recorded sound, and he became a director with Jack Bishop of a new venture called the Bishop Sound and Electrical Company. Two rooms in the Comedy Theatre were made available as offices and a new era in theatre sound began.

During the blitz, when London was being bombed every night by the German Luftwaffe, Jack Bishop installed a disc recorder in the basement of the Comedy Theatre wired to a microphone on the roof, and he often stayed up all night recording the air raids. These incredible recordings were added to the library of sound effects which he had begun compiling.

Jack Bishop recording
a train, circa 1949.

When the war ended, Jack Bishop was approached by a leading production company, First Shepherd, who owned some Simon Sound panatropes and needed them serviced. Always on the lookout for a good deal, Jack refused to service the machines but said that he was prepared to purchase them and rent them back to the company on a weekly basis with a maintenance guarantee. This arrangement formed the basis of the Bishop Sound rental operation which was eventually to have systems in nearly every West End theatre and most of the regional touring and repertory theatres in England, Wales and Scotland.

As the demand for panatropes grew, Jack Bishop produced his own version with an important innovation, the 'cuebar', an ingenious but very simple device for lining up the pick-up so that it dropped into the right groove on the record. A block to the right of the turntable had a lever which lifted and lowered a piece of perspex fitted to the pick-up arm. On top of the block there was a groove into which the "cuebar", a 6" long metal rod, could be slotted. The pick-up was held against a domed plate at the end of the cuebar by magnetism. The position of the pick-up depended upon the adjustment of a locking collars on the bar. This was similar in concept to the variable-stop used on industrial lathes. Later, when magnetic pick-ups were replaced by crystal pick-ups, a special housing was devised incorporating a magnet.

Each separate sound effect would have its own cuebar with a collar locked off in the right position. You simply put the record on the turntable, inserted the correct cuebar, and lifted the handle to drop the pick-up; always remembering to keep the fader closed until the pick-up had hit the disc! The controls were very simple – volume, treble and bass, plus a monitor loudspeaker and four loudspeaker switches labelled FOH, PS, OP, US (Front of House, Prompt Side, Opposite Prompt, Up Stage).

To withstand the rigours of touring, the panatrope was housed in a strong metal box. The amplifier was usually located behind a panel in the front of the unit, but a few came with two amplifers, each within a pedestal upon which the panatrope could sit. This was to provide an emergency back-up, particularly when on tour. Amplifiers tended to blow valves and fuses rather frequently. By the early 1950s there were Bishop Sound panatropes in theatres all over the country. The weekly hire price for the standard kit of a panatrope with two 12" cabinet loudspeakers and cables was £4. Additional cuebars could be hired for sixpence (2½p) each. A microphone and stand was £1.

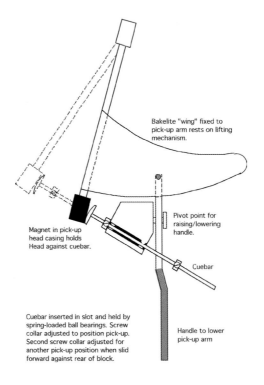

Bakelite "wing" fixed to pick-up arm rests on lifting mechanism.

Pivot point for raising/lowering handle.

Magnet in pick-up head casing holds Head against cuebar.

Cuebar

Cuebar inserted in slot and held by spring-loaded ball bearings. Screw collar adjusted to position pick-up. Second screw collar adjusted for another pick-up position when slid forward against rear of block.

Handle to lower pick-up arm

Bishop Sound 'cuebar' system

A 'cuebar' in the
block with two more
beside the turntable
with different
settings.

Far left
Two Bishop
panatropes with
amplifiers in the
pedestals.

Left
Amplifier in the front
of the panatrope.

Standard Bishop
Sound hire kit.

In 1946, just after the Second World War had ended, Bishop Sound and Electrical Company moved to premises in 48 Monmouth Street in London's Covent Garden area. This was a shop with the ground floor used for testing and repairing equipment, the first floor fitted out as a small recording studio and an office located on the second floor. Initially, the studio recorded straight to disc but by the time I was using their equipment, as an assistant stage manager in the mid 1950s, they were mastering on a mono quarter-inch Ferrograph tape machine. Jack Bishop's daughter, Mamie, was then in charge of most of the recording activities. Small, dark haired and with a ready smile for everyone, Mamie revelled in her work and was popular with her customers.

Jack and daughter, Mamie, with the PA recording van.

The business grew rapidly and around 1946 William (Bill) Spragg, an electronics engineer, joined the company and was later to marry Mamie. In January 2000, I traced Bill to a flat in north London where he was living alone, Mamie having died some years before. I had not seen him for some thirty years but, although now 82, he was still enthusiastic about electronics and still highly opinionated. His blunt way of informing you, albeit with a smile, that your ideas or way of doing things were wrong had ruffled the feathers of many a client. In fact, he declared this book to be a waste of time as nobody would want to read it, but he was perfectly prepared to talk to me if it made me happy. Despite this bluff façade, I knew that he was pleased to be approached and we had two lengthy and most interesting meetings.

Bill Spragg in 2000, aged 82.

Bill Spragg was working for Strand Electric Limited, the country's leading manufacturer and supplier of lighting equipment, when he met Jack Bishop. He was installing some lighting equipment at the Phoenix Theatre and Jack was setting up a sound system. They got talking and Jack offered him a pound to rig six loudspeakers on the proscenium and wire them back to the equipment. Jack was not known for his generosity, but a pound was not an unreasonable amount in those days as the weekly wage for an electrician was around £7. Unfortunately, the pound was not paid at the time, and although Bill visited the offices on several occasions to collect what was owing, there was always some excuse. Fortunately, Bill found this reluctance to pay the debt quite amusing and it did not sour their friendship. When Bill was asked to join the company, he accepted on the condition that he first received the outstanding pound.

Bill related an interesting story concerning the use of panatropes in a production of A STREETCAR NAMED DESIRE starring Vivien Leigh as Stella at the Aldwych Theatre in 1949. Towards the end of the play when Stanley, played by the American actor Bonar Colleano, screams "Stella!", the director, Laurence Olivier, wanted the word to be repeated like an echo. To obtain the effect, the actor's voice was recorded and three panatropes were installed understage. At the appropriate moment, four members of the stage management team joined forces to play the effect one after the other. The first panatrope had a loudspeaker placed near the stage and the other two had loudspeakers progressively further away. Thus, the effect was: "Stella!.... Stella!.... Stella!.... Stella!.... Stella!.... Stella!

Six turntables to achieve an echo effect for STREETCAR NAMED DESIRE at the Aldwych Theatre, 1949.

Seven years later, in 1956, for the first production of Samuel Becket's WAITING FOR GODOT at the Arts Theatre Club, London, the youthful director, Peter Hall, wanted to use music by Bartok recorded on one of the new long-playing records. For some reason, instead of copying the extracts on to 78 r.p.m. lacquer discs, Bill Spragg changed one of the turntables for one that played at 33⅓ r.p.m. The cuebar was pretty accurate locating a sound in the wide grooves of a fast spinning 78 r.p.m. record, but was not designed for the fine grooves of a painfully slow moving LP. As the sound operator for the show, I remember marking the label on the record so that the pick-up could be dropped when the mark came round to a certain position. In this way, I was either spot on, a second early or a second late. There were two sequences when a particular piece of music had to start every time one of the characters, Lucky, moved and cease whenever he came to a halt. Under the circumstances, my success rate was remarkably high. I believe that I was the first person, and probably the last, to attempt this folly.

Bishop Sound booklet of equipment hire prices and catalogue of sound effects.

To sell to the amateur theatres and smaller regional theatres, Jack Bishop produced a series of pressed discs with a selection of standard sound effects recorded over the years. For West End productions, they would cut acetate discs, selecting the required effects from the library and adding, when necessary, special sounds or voices recorded in the studio. Being made of aluminium with a soft lacquer coating, the discs were easily scratched and had a limited number of plays before the sound quality deteriorated. A West End show would normally have two copies of each disc and replacements were ordered every eight weeks or so. I always asked for the effects to be recorded so that the inner bands came first in the playback sequence. This allowed me to remove the cuebar whilst the inner band was playing and set up another cuebar for the next track towards the outside of the record.

Although he normally had a gentle and friendly manner, Jack's mecurial temperament and dogmatic views often brought him into sharp conflict with the people who worked for him, and sometimes even his customers. Bill Spragg was also not slow to put forward his opinions, and the working relationship between these two strong willed people was, to put it mildly, volatile. Bill had more knowledge of modern electronics than his boss, but Jack had the experience and a very annoying habit of being right. He would often end a technical argument by saying:

"All right, do it your way. When it doesn't work, do it my way". After one particularly serious row, Bill decided that he had had enough and walked out. This caused tensions in other directions as he was about to marry Jack's daughter. When, later, he was asked to rejoin the company as a director, Bill was very reluctant. An offer of twice the salary plus a director's fee of £400 finally persuaded him.

As an example of how Jack could behave in a completely irrational manner, there was an incident concerning a show at the Globe Theatre in 1946. Called Morning Star, it relied heavily on air raid effects. That morning, a director of the production company, H M Tennent, rang up to request a reduction in the hire bill on the grounds that the show had been running for some months. Jack was affronted. He considered that his prices were reasonable and he could see no argument for taking a cut when the show was making a lot of money. The director continued to insist and, incensed, Jack finally said: *"All right, if you want a reduction, I will give you one".* He slammed down the phone and told Bill to get out the van. They then proceeded to the theatre and removed all the equipment with total disregard for any consequences to the show that night or, indeed, thereafter. This was an incredible action to take with any customer, but even more so as H M Tennent was the UK's leading drama production company and Bishop Sound had equipment in several of their shows in the West End and on tour.

Gradually the equipment came back from all the shows as H M Tennent made alternative arrangements and there was no further business from that management for many years. Eventually, Bill brokered a peace with Tennent's lighting director, Joe Davis (the doyen of British theatre lighting design) and Bishop Sound did work for them again, but never exclusively as before.

One of the ways that Bishop Sound obtained such a strong foothold in the British theatre was with the introduction of his 'cuecall' system, installed in dozens of theatres in London and around the country. Up until the early 1950s, it was normal practice for actors to be called to the stage for their entrances by "call boys". Originally young boys, similar to pageboys in hotels, they stood beside the stage manager in the prompt corner with a list of calls. When the stage manager gave them the nod, they would trot off to the dressing rooms and politely inform the next actor or actors on the list that they were due on stage. This all changed when Mr Bishop's Cuecall was installed.

The system had a microphone positioned in the footlights to relay the performance to a loudspeaker in each dressing room with a second microphone in the prompt corner to allow the stage manager to call the actors. Along with the paging and show relay facilities, Cuecall also had an intercom allowing the stage manager to communicate with the lighting switchboard, the fly gallery and other technical areas. Up until then, the only way of making contact was by telephone. Later versions of Cuecall provided paging calls to the foyers and bars to replace or augment the old system of bells.

A number of companies around the country specializing in paging systems for hotels and railway stations and for outdoor events also provided systems for theatres, but theatre owners tended to opt for Cuecall because it was a standard proven system. Another advantage was that it was familiar to stage managers touring from theatre to theatre. Jack Bishop had a canny policy of never selling any equipment, so once a rental contract was agreed and Cuecall was wired into a building, the owners were virtually locked in. The weekly rental was only £2.00 per week but there was very little maintenance involved and, once installed, the systems remained in place for years and years. Soon they could be found in nearly every West End theatre and a large proportion of the regional touring theatres. Between stage management jobs in 1957, Jack very kindly employed me for a few weeks and I remember the piles of cheques arriving through the letter box at 48 Monmouth Street at the beginning of the month.

Cuecall was not always popular with the acting profession. As a stage manager, I remember how some of the older actors detested having the show piped to them in their dressing room; and they were positively affronted by being summoned to the stage by a disembodied voice. Some 'stars' insisted on having a personal call. In 1958, the Theatre Royal in Brighton still retained a call boy. I use the term loosely as he was a dapper and diminutive middle-aged gentleman who wore very tight trousers and sported a very obvious wig. The theatre had no audio system to the dressing rooms, neither did it have any form of communication to the technicians, other than cuelights. This caused a problem at the end of one particular show when the stage manager gave the cue to the fly gallery to lower the curtain – and nothing happened. He flashed and flashed the cuelight to no avail. Fortunately, the theatre's stage carpenter happened to be standing near the prompt corner and to our surprise, he turned swiftly to the wall and blew into a rusty old piece of conduit which no longer had any electrical socket box attached. After a short pause, the curtain came down. The carpenter explained that the flyman sometimes fell asleep while waiting for his cue, but fortunately the other end of the conduit came out just beside his ear where he was sitting. Who needs modern technology?

It is interesting to note that Max Culver in "A History of Theatre Sound Effects Devices" states that the Metropolitan Opera House in New York had a stage manager control desk as far back as 1897 equipped with electric bells to cue back-stage staff and warn the audience that the performance was about to begin. Silent cueing using electric lights was introduced in 1899.

During the course of a long career, Jack Bishop became acquainted with many famous artists, one of whom was the popular actor/author/composer Ivor Novello. Apparently, Bishop recorded several live performances of Novello's Drury Lane musicals, including PERCHANCE TO DREAM and KING'S RHAPSODY, using a single microphone placed in the footlights connected to two 78 r.p.m. disc recorders under stage. The 12" laquer discs only ran for about five minutes, so it was necessary to keep swapping machines, taking care to overlap. Although a successful and prolific composer, apparently Novello was unable to notate music, so Bishop set up two disc recorders in his house so that he could send recordings of the compositions to his arrangers. Another famous artist who became a friend was the comedian and star of the old time music halls, George Robey, renowned as the

"Prime Minister of Mirth". Towards the end of his career, Robey invited Jack Bishop to his house and, in a number of sessions, they recorded all of Robey's famous monologues. These priceless recordings, along with the sound effects library, were given by Bill Spragg to the British Sound Archive.

Basic amplification systems for the actors had become standard in many large touring theatres around the UK by the 1960s. Permanent installations were provided by large PA companies, such as Westrex and STC (Standard Telephone Company), usually based on five microphones along the front of the stage, a mixer in the prompt corner and four or six loudspeakers on each side of the proscenium. These could be single 12" speakers in cabinets or the more efficient Vitavox cinema loudspeaker (single driver in a cabinet with a multicell horn), although these were hardly in the same league for power or performance as the Altec loudspeakers widely favoured by American soundmen.

Just like Broadway, there were no permanent PA systems in the commercial West End theatres. The show promoters hired in what was required for any particular production, as is still the case. Bishop Sound's business was based upon panatropes and Cuecall systems, but they inevitably became involved in the occasional sound reinforcement system for musicals. Bill Spragg liked to think of this as "acoustic correction" rather than amplification. Usually he employed three large black microphones on short stands in the footlights with an amplifier feeding just two cabinet loudspeakers on the proscenium. The microphones were Standard Telephone 4033A which combined ribbon and moving coil elements to achieve a uni-directional characteristic. Designed for the 'talkies', it became a standard television boom microphone for many years.

People became so used to seeing these large black objects in the footlights that when, in 1962, I tried to use a much smaller moving-coil microphone (STC 4105) for a musical called BLITZ!, the producer, Donald Albery, was outraged. I explained that they were manufactured by the same company and that they had designed this more directional microphone specifically for sound reinforcement, but he would have none of this technical clap-trap. It was obvious that a big fat microphone would produce a far better sound than a little stick less than half the size. He would not even agree to hear them in a rehearsal. They were to be removed immediately. This was one of my earliest experiences of everybody being a sound expert.

 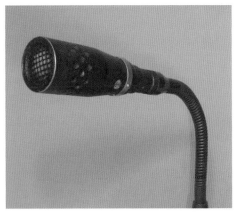

Far left
STC 4033.
Photo: Chris Owen

Left
STC 4105.
Photo: Chris Owen

R G Jones

FOR SOME TWENTY YEARS from its inception in 1946, Bishop Sound appeared to have a monopoly in British theatre. Jack Bishop was adept at promoting his company and the success of 'Cuecall' meant that he had constant dealings with theatres and managements throughout the UK. But Jack Bishop did not have it all his own way by any means. R G Jones became active in the theatre around 1945 and his company had equipment in theatres well into the 1970s. According to his son, Robin, his father claimed to have installed equipment in every West End theatre except the Criterion. I am sure this is true. Looking through the company diaries, although a couple of years were missing, I found mention of thirty four West End theatres.

Ronald Godfrey Jones was born in the town of Caerphilly in South Wales in 1912. From an early age, he loved designing and building things and, although entirely self-taught, he was equally skilled at carpentry and metalwork and became quite capable of constructing a power amplifier or other pieces of electronic equipment.

Known as Geoff or "RG", his first job on leaving school at the age of fourteen was for a company called Milton, a renowned manufacturer of a sterilising fluid for baby's feeding bottles. He became a salesman for the company and from a caravan, in which he also lived, he sold his wares in town markets all round Wales. Shouting above the general hubbub to attract his customers was hard work and he was attracted by the idea of using electrically amplified sound. Undaunted by a lack of any training in electronics, he procured all the necessary components and had soon assembled a system. Two large horn loudspeakers, the flares constructed by himself out of timber, were mounted on top of the car which towed his caravan. Inside, he installed a microphone connected to an amplifier powered by four twelve volt batteries and a rotary (48v to 230v) convertor. It worked. The young RG Jones was now able to advertise himself effortlessly to the crowds and at a volume level which gave him a distinct advantage over the other retailers. Such was the success of this enterprise that his employers asked him to build fifteen more systems to equip the rest of the Milton sales force. This gave him the opportunity to go into business on his own account. By the tender age of eighteen, this precocious young entrepreneur had not only set up his own company, but he had also met and married his wife, Nora.

RG Jones with his
first PA system,
circa 1928.

In 1933, R G Jones decided to advertise other people's products from his own van. The first client, on October 7 that year, was Candle King Limited of Cardiff – presumably a manufacturer of candles – who paid twelve guineas (twelve pounds and twelve shillings or £12.60) for an "Advertising Broadcast". Quite a sizeable fee.

Later, he and his wife moved to South West London in their caravan home, and rented space in an orchard within the grounds of Morden Manor. Here, they erected a shed for his office/workshop and with Nora looking after bookings and dealing with the accounts, they generated a business producing and hiring out public address systems. By 1942, they were able to move out of the caravan into a house in the grounds of Morden Manor, and there RG built his first proper recording studio.

RG in his original
studio.

The business prospered and he was soon hiring out equipment for all kinds of events. Dance bands provided the popular music of the day and RG put together what he called 'Crooner Sets' – an amplifier, two Vitavox K/12/20 loudspeakers and a microphone for the singer. For those who could not afford a group of professional musicians, he hit on the idea of providing dance music from amplified records. In an article for the Electrical Trading and Radio Marketing magazine of October 1943, he describes how to run 'PA Dances'. For a dance floor of up to 250 people, he recommends a good quality amplifier with an output of 10 watts and a 12-inch (30cm) loudspeaker on a baffle with a 36-inch (92cm) horn speaker to give brilliance. Two turntables are necessary as it is essential to avoid a pause in the music while the disc and the needle are being changed (the fibre needles would need to be sharpened after each play). To add realism, all the equipment should be hidden behind a muslin curtain on stage, except for the microphone needed for announcements. The microphone is connected to a separate amplifier feeding two 10-inch loudspeakers, one placed either side of the stage. This avoids feedback and, with the microphone remaining live, amplifies the music from the loudspeaker behind the muslin to good effect.

Not only did he invent this form of entertainment, but he also acted as impresario, hiring the hall and promoting the event. Sometimes, to create a better effect, he would hire three or four people to dress up in dinner jackets and sit on stage with instruments 'miming' being musicians. I wonder if any of the modern DJ's with their megawatt disco systems know what they owe to RG and his PA Dances. In a BBC radio interview in 2002, I heard the veteran disc jockey, Jimmy Saville, claim that he had: "invented disco in 1944 using two wind-up gramophones for a small local event". It seems that RG was well ahead of him, and with rather more technical sophistication.

During the Second World War, mobile PA equipment from RG Jones was used by the Home Guard, the Red Cross and even at Liverpool docks for controlling the landing of thousands of American troops. Always keen to try out new ideas, he pioneered the 'Public Address Pageant' in 1944. Hailed in the Electrical Trading and Radio Marketing magazine as *"a new art form created by that well known specialist, Mr R. G. Jones of Morden"*, this was a piece of drama performed by a large cast of 400 amateurs miming to a play devised, written, produced and recorded by R G Jones.

RG with the twin-turntables and Vitavox loudspeaker for the Public Address Pageant, 1944.

Ten years later, his obvious theatrical flair came to the fore again when he scripted and recorded all the voices and effects for two mammoth events at the Bell Vue arena in Manchester. Using large scale scenic effects, pyrotechnics, lighting, and a cast of hundreds, THE STORMING OF QUEBEC was modestly billed as *"The Most Gigantic Spectacle in the World"* and, in 1955, THE RELIEF OF LUCKNOW was called *"The World's Most Prodigious Scenic Spectacle"*.

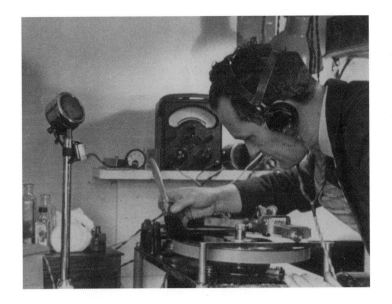

RG cutting an
acetate disc.

RG Jones first became involved in the theatre after seeing a show at the Kings Theatre in Hammersmith, London. His son, Robin, believes that this was soon after the war ended in 1945. Money being tight, RG purchased a seat in 'the Gods' (Upper Gallery) from where he had great difficulty hearing the actors. He mulled this over for a few days and then returned to the theatre to put a proposal to the management. He convinced them that with a microphone and a few loudspeakers, he could make the actors voices carry right to the back of the gallery. Thus came about one of the earliest *speech reinforcement* systems. Recommendations followed, and soon R G Jones found himself in the theatre business. The company diaries show that equipment was supplied to seven West End theatres during the following year, 1946.

To handle sound effects, RG designed and manufactured a panatrope. It was a beautifully engineered piece of equipment with specially designed cueing devices for the two 78 r.p.m. turntables. Each pick-up arm was held in place over the record by means of an electro-magnet. This was attached to a rod which, in turn, was fixed to the groove locating mechanism adjusted by means of cue bars (although slightly different to Bishop's patented 'Cuebar'). Each bar had a screw collar and was dropped into a slot in the mechanism. Moving the collar altered the position of the rod with the electro-magnet holding the pick-up. When the correct groove was located, the collar could be locked off with a screwdriver and was thus set for the start of the effect on that particular record. When the "go" button was pressed the power to the electro-magnet was switched off allowing the pick-up to drop on to the record. As this was an electrical device, the panatropes were equipped with remote "go" controls so that a stage manager could activate an effect from the prompt corner whilst, perhaps, giving a lighting cue.

The cabinets, which he also made himself, were of timber with beautifully rounded corners. The turntables were set in a choice piece of polished wood and the inside of the lid had a 'flock' spray, giving a soft velvet effect. RG took great pride in sending the panatropes to customers in pristine condition and was quite upset when they were returned from touring around the countryside covered in marks and scratches.

This was a more sophisticated and better engineered device than the Bishop panatrope but, as I never had the opportunity of using one, I cannot say if the changing and cueing of records was as speedy. Setting up the next effect with the 'Cuebar' was remarkably quick under skilled hands.

Although Leak amplifiers, Vortexion mixers and Vitavox K12/10 and K12/20 loudspeakers formed the basis of his theatre equipment, by 1955 RG had built up a stock of his own equipment with the help of Peter Woodroof who was "the staff". Peter had been in the RAF during the war and had some training in electronics.

Peter Woodroof,
"the staff", with an
R G Jones panatrope.

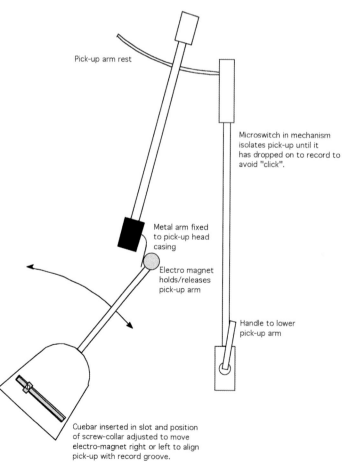

Pick-up arm rest

Microswitch in mechanism
isolates pick-up until it
has dropped on to record to
avoid "click".

Metal arm fixed
to pick-up head
casing

Electro magnet
holds/releases
pick-up arm

Handle to lower
pick-up arm

Cuebar inserted in slot and position
of screw-collar adjusted to move
electro-magnet right or left to align
pick-up with record groove.

R G Jones
panatrope groove-
locating device.

Service calls recorded in the diaries often refer to "noisy turntables" or "noisy volume controls" or "bad hum". I remember how the old 78 r.p.m. turntables needed a little oil to stop them rumbling, and a squirt of switch cleaner usually fixed the crackling volume control. The nightmare was when a turntable motor decided to make loud groaning noises during a show and you knew that anything played on it would 'wow' horribly. Many sound systems seemed to have built-in hum and one had to insist that the suppliers cured this before a public performance. I have been in the audience on more than one occasion where the sound effects were ruined because each one was preceded by a low frequency hum as the loudspeaker was switched on.

R G Jones column loudspeakers

APART FROM A VALVE amplifier, RG designed a high quality line array loudspeaker. The column speakers being produced in the UK at the time were mainly for budget PA systems and were consequently not high quality. So when the American producers of the original London production of PORGY AND BESS (Stoll Theatre, 1952) specified column loudspeakers, RG set about designing something better. He went on to develop several line arrays using 10-inch (25cm) Celestion drivers, but the most successful was a four-foot column with five Celestion 7-inch x 5-inch (18cm x 13cm) elliptical drivers, power tapered using Sowtar custom transformers. The array was 'tapered' to provide maximum sound output from the centre loudspeaker, with slightly less to the adjacent pair, and less again to the top and bottom pair. Thus, if positioned correctly, full power would be delivered to the rear of the auditorium where it was needed, with less being received by people sitting near the array. I experienced these on the original London production of A FUNNY THING HAPPENED ON THE WAY TO THE FORUM in 1963. The sound coverage of the auditorium was very good. This was the first of several Broadway shows co-produced in London by Hal Prince and Richard Pilbrow, lighting designer and founder of the Theatre Projects Group. Within Theatre Projects, I was at that time creating sound effects but was not yet involved in miking musicals. It was the custom in those days for producers to call in Bishops or RG Jones to put in a system and set the microphone levels.

The RG Jones arrays were so successful for speech reinforcement that a special version was commissioned by BBC television for their live audience shows. The columns were mounted at 45° above the auditorium with an STC 4033 microphone suspended immediately underneath, and because the loudspeakers were so directional, the microphones picked up a clean audience sound. During the 1980s, a development of these arrays was provided for the Centre Court at Wimbledon and St Paul's Cathedral. At the time of writing, they are still in place.

A little while before RG designed his first column loudspeakers, Bill Spragg of Bishop Sound had read an article about their efficiency for theatre use and decided to build some. Unfortunately, this caused another heated argument with Jack Bishop who did not understand the principle and was unwilling to spend any money on experimentation. He would only consider the investment if Bill could take him to a theatre where he could hear them working. No such theatre could be found, so the project was shelved. Not one of Jack's better decisions.

Electronic thunder

FOR THE PRODUCTION of NO TIME FOR SERGEANTS at Her Majesty's Theatre (1956), RG was asked to reproduce the sound of an atomic bomb. To achieve this, he constructed an 'electronic thunder sheet' based upon a square of wire mesh held taut in a wooden frame measuring about 4 foot square (120cm x 120cm). At the top of the frame, the wire mesh was connected to the moving coil part of a gramophone pick-up. Thus, the wire mesh became a gigantic microphone diaphragm – and we all know what happens if you touch or blow on a diaphragm...! The thunder sheet was connected to several meaty valve (tube) amplifiers driving six 30-inch (76cm) loudspeakers in bass reflex cabinets placed in the orchestra pit. The concept of the electronic thunder sheet might possibly have come from "Theatres and Auditoriums" (first published in 1949) where Harold Burris-Meyer and Edward C. Cole describe a similar 'thunder screen'.

Apparently, the initial test at Her Majesty's Theatre was so loud that glasses fell off shelves in the stalls bar. The poor lady working in the bar at the time was seriously distraught, complaining that it sounded exactly like the German V2 rocket that had demolished her neighbour's house during the war. Needless to say, they had to reduce the power a little!

In 1959, I hired this device to create the sound of an avalanche for Ibsen's BRAND at the Lyric Theatre Hammersmith. The sequence started with a gentle vibration of the mesh with one hand to achieve a sinister rumbling, gradually increased in volume and intensity by adding more speed and pressure until both hands were drumming on the screen to produce the final crescendo. To add texture, I mixed in recordings from two turntables of wind, landslides and rocks falling. The actor portraying Brand had to shout above the approaching avalanche and because the thunder sheet was 'played' like an instrument, one had complete flexibility to vary volume and intensity between the actor's lines so that he could be heard.

There is an anecdote concerning the atom bomb in NO TIME FOR SERGEANTS. The sound was synchronized with the triggering of several flash boxes lining the front of the stage. On the final performance, one of the stage electricians decided to have a bit of fun (!) and, instead of using the specified thimble-full of explosive powder, foolishly he filled the containers. When they went off, the wall of fire singed the bottom of the house curtain and the metal boxes completely disintegrated. Although pieces of shrapnel were found embedded in some of the front row seats, miraculously nobody was hurt. I believe that a few members of the audience did have their cleaning bills paid.

R G Jones moves away from the theatre

THE R G JONES COMPANY was becoming progressively involved in the supply of PA systems for large outdoor events and other non-theatrical work. A new store was built to house the ever expanding rental equipment together with a larger recording studio. When, in 1952, Bill Haley recorded 'Shake, Rattle and Roll' and Elvis Presley cut his first disc at Sun Records, the pop music scene exploded. Publishing companies funded unknown groups to make demo recordings and the new R G Jones studio was often working around the clock recording artists, some of whom became major stars. Working in the theatre with all its difficulties became less attractive. Manufacturing and installing the specialist equipment was extremely costly and time consuming and, with the company located some miles from the centre of London in Morden, it became increasingly difficult to compete with the West End based Bishop Sound and the emergence of a new company called Stagesound. According to the diaries, R G Jones still had equipment in nine West End theatres in 1969, but this side of the business tailed off noticeably during the next few years.

Having obtained qualifications in radio and television servicing and tele-communications, RG's son Robin had officially joined the company in 1963, although he had, in fact, been working alongside his father since his early teens. Fascinated by the music side of the business, a trip to a studio in Nashville was arranged so that he could discover how they obtained 'The Nashville Sound'. He was privileged to sit in on sessions with such artists as Brenda Lee, Floyd Kramer, Chet Atkins and Jerry Lee Lewis. The sound was amazing, but there was nothing special about the studios or the equipment. He decided that the magic ingredients were the combination of brilliant musicians and talented engineers.

The only items of equipment he did envy were the limiter/compressors and the equalizers, not available in England at the time. Shortly after his visit, Robin obtained a Marconi limiter/compressor for the R G Jones studio. These were operated with valves (tubes) in those days, of course. In 1969, a new studio was opened with 4-track capability, quickly upgraded to eight, sixteen, and then twenty-four tracks. Robin was recording with such illustrious names as the Bee Gees, the Rolling Stones, the Springfields, Tom Jones, Engelbert Humperdinck, Lulu, and David Bowie. During the 1990s, the pop music business changed and there was less money available for artists to hire independent studios for demos and experimentation. Recording work tailed off and the R G Jones studio was closed in November 2001.

When RG retired in 1971 and Robin took the reins, the equipment side of the business was extremely busy designing permanent systems for churches, school halls, corporate lecture centres, etc., and hiring out PA systems for outdoor events. When I interviewed Robin during 2002, the company had just provided enormous PA systems for the Queen's 50th Jubilee celebrations outside Buckingham Palace with audio relays to the adjacent Royal parks.

Robin Jones – 2004

Ronald Godfrey Jones died in 1987 at the age of 75. Robin Jones retired from the business in 2005.

Stagesound

THE COMPANY THAT CAME to the fore in the 1960s and eventually caused the demise of Bishop Sound, was called Stagesound. It was founded in 1948 by Bill Walton, who, unlike Jack Bishop and R G Jones, was a theatre practitioner. Born in 1922, Bill had an interest in technical things from an early age and took up electronics as a hobby. As a young man during the Second World War, he served in the Merchant Navy sailing convoys across the Atlantic before transferring to the Royal Navy where, between other duties, he lectured on radio communications. He was injured when a bomb hit the ship and nearly had to have his leg amputated. The metal plate inserted in his leg gave him trouble for the rest of his life.

Discharged from the Royal Navy because of his injury, he promptly joined the Army where he attained the rank of Sergeant Major. Some of his time was spent mending searchlights in Kent, but he also worked on a system for "bending" radio waves from German bomber target-locating systems so that the bombs would miss. It was during this period that he first became involved with the theatre, helping out with the lighting for the Army entertainment group called ENSA (Entertainments National Service Association – also affectionately known as Every Night Something Awful) putting on shows at the Players Theatre in London.

After the war, bitten by the bug, he got a job as chief electrician at the Lyric Theatre Hammersmith, an outer London theatre being run by the Company of Four, an offshoot of the major West End producers, H M Tennent, as a try-out venue for new plays and *avant garde* productions. Seven or eight new shows were mounted there each year, two or three of which would transfer to the West End.

In those days, the chief electrician would set up the lighting as requested by the show director. Should the show go on tour, it became the responsibility of the company manager (then known as stage director) to take the cue sheets and recreate the lighting with the local electrician. There was no 'design' as such, as the lighting rigs were very basic. However, an exception to this method of working was introduced by H M Tennent whose production standards, including stage lighting, were extremely high; and because they produced a constant stream of shows, they could afford to employ a permanent expert. This was Joe Davis who, with Richard Pilbrow and Michael Northern, was one of the three original giants of theatre lighting design in Britain.

Joe Davis, lighting
designer for
H M Tennent

Bill Walton and Joe became friends and, as Joe had more work than he could handle, Bill began lighting all the shows at the Lyric Theatre Hammersmith and was often asked to light shows in other theatres. Through this involvement with lighting design, Bill Walton became friendly with Jack Madre who ran the hire department of the UK's leading lighting equipment manufacturer, Strand Electric. Jack recommended him for lighting jobs and Bill would fill his 3-ton ex-army van with equipment and head off to theatres all over the country. It is not clear how he managed to cope with these projects alongside his responsibilities as chief electrician, but he did work very long hours at the Lyric, so perhaps he arranged time off in lieu for his other activities.

Bill's assistant at the Lyric, Dick Lock, told me a story demonstrating Bill's uncanny foresight into future technology. During a pause in a lighting session, he stated that one day it would be possible to sit in the stalls and set all the lights by means of a tiny portable control unit. Considering this was in 1949, many years before the first crude electronic switchboards, it is not surprising that his young apprentice treated the notion with a deal of scepticism. As far as Dick was concerned, the height of technology was the massive Strand Electric "Grand Master" switchboard with dimmers operated by banks of wheels and levers.

When Bill offered him a job at the Lyric, Dick was working at the Ambassadors Theatre in the West End as a 'call boy' on a salary of seven shillings and sixpence (37.5p) per show, with as much again in tips from the actors. The £6 or so per week for merely turning up for eight shows to call the actors to the stage, was a much better deal than working the punishing schedule offered by Bill Walton for two pounds ten shillings (£2.50); but to the sixteen year old, the job at the Lyric seemed much more interesting – and Bill had an extremely seductive personality. Family pressure for Dick to have a "proper career" caused him to hand in his notice after eighteen months, but he was to return to Stagesound some five years later and eventually became manager of the rental operation. When I caught up with him in 2003, he was still in the audio business, running a small rental operation from his home.

Bill Walton's interest in all things technical included sound, and he would record the effects for the Lyric productions. One of these, AN ENGLISH SUMMER, took place on an RAF fighter base during The Battle of Britain. (This was a period during the Second World War when England was under constant attack by German bombers and, at enormous cost to themselves, a small band of English fighter pilots eventually proved so effective that the Germans curtailed their raids.) The play not only required dramatic lighting for the bombing raids, but it called for realistic sound effects. This was, after all, only five or six years after the war had ended, and most people in the audience would have experienced the real thing. Bill wanted to startle the audience with airplanes, guns and bomb explosions coming from all directions, so he engineered a sequential loudspeaker switching device by adapting an ex-RAF bomb release mechanism. Instead of bombs being released in sequence at the touch of a switch, loudspeakers were connected in sequence at the touch of a switch. Perhaps this was the first automated sound system?

In 1948, Bill Walton decided to enter the audio business in opposition to R G Jones and Bishop Sound. Stagesound Limited was formed with a board of directors who were all friends, but were also extremely useful to the company.

There was Diana Plunkett, manager of the Lyric Theatre Hammersmith, Jack Madre of Strand Electric bringing all the contacts of the country's major lighting company, and Alison Colville who was a senior company manager for H M Tennent.

Operating from the basement of the Lyric, Bill put together a range of equipment. Power amplifiers and mixers were bought in from Vortexion and a firm called Whiteleys built some effects loudspeakers with 12" (30cm) drivers. He developed his own panatrope, initially using a groove-locator made to his design by Simon Sound who had introduced the first panatropes in the late 1930s. This had a rod marked in sections (A, B, C, etc.) supporting a cradle holding the pick-up arm over the disc. To set a cue, the cradle would be placed in one of the sections and turning a wheel, marked in numbers, at the end of the rod moved a fine tuning locator to push the cradle into position. Thus, a particular cue set up might be C37. The pick-up was lowered on to the disc by a small lever beside the wheel. This arrangement was later replaced by an improved version using a flat rod with grooves at each section to hold the pick-up and the wheel moving the whole rod backwards and forwards for fine tuning. The flat rod turned through 90° to lower the pick up.

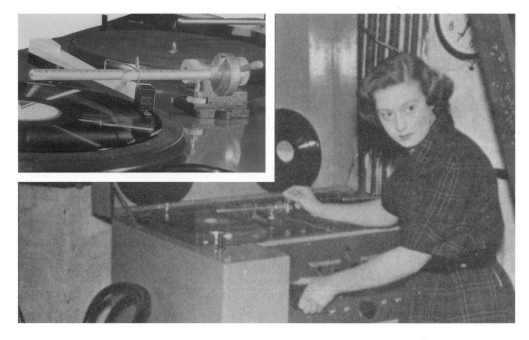

Early Stagesound panatrope. To cue a record, the pick-up arm support was placed within sections A-K along the bar by turning the wheel on the right to move the locator. Fine tuning was achieved by setting the numbers on the wheel.

Later groove locator where pick-up arm support was placed in a notch on the bar and the fine tuning wheel moved the bar to and fro. When the lever was pulled, the flat bar turned 45° to drop the stylus in the groove.

In my opinion as a 'pan operator', the Stagesound cueing system was not as good as Bishop's cuebar because the pick-up arm had to be positioned for each cue by twiddling a little knob, whereas the cuebars were all pre-set and just had to be slotted into the holder. Changing records was also easier with the Bishop system because the cuebar could be removed as soon as the sound effect was playing, leaving the turntable completely accessible. The Stagesound pick-up arm support bar could be raised, but it always remained over the turntable.

In my last few months at the Arts Theatre Club in 1957, the theatre manager decided to hire a Stagesound panatrope to replace the one we were using from Bishops. He had been persuaded that this smart new equipment would be more reliable and had undoubtedly negotiated a good deal. Unfortunately, my mentor, Bob Batey, was no longer in charge backstage and the director Peter Hall had also moved on to better things. So it was left to me to protest.

I requested an interview with the manager in which I explained the speed and accuracy of the cuebar, citing several sequences on previous shows where this flexibility had been essential. He remained totally unmoved by the opinions of a 19 year old youth, and it was pointed out that these machines were being used successfully on many major West End productions and that, with a little practice, I would find them equally good – if not better. During the next few years, I used both machines on many productions and I have to state that the man in the front office, who never appeared backstage, was wrong.

1948 was an eventful year for Bill Walton as he was also to meet his future wife, Judy, who was kind enough to talk to me in 2002 about the company and her husband's background. They met at the Old Vic Theatre School where Judy was a student and Bill gave lectures on lighting. This was a highly acclaimed course because working theatre technicians, like Bill, were brought in to give lectures and the school was actually run by practitioners: including Michel St. Denis, one of the greatest theatre directors from the 1940s to the early 1970s and George Devine, who was to become artistic director of the Royal Court Theatre and was responsible for such ground-breaking plays as Look Back In Anger and The Entertainer. Occasionally, a promising student was offered a job at the Lyric Theatre Hammersmith as assistant electrician. One of these was Judy, who found the physical work and the hours she was expected to work utterly exhausting, but, as she told me: *"It was the most enjoyable period of my life".* Apart from her daytime work replacing bulbs and rigging lighting equipment, Judy operated lighting and sound equipment for the shows. She recalled how Bill favoured non-technical people for these tasks as they tended to be sensitive to the production, being more interested in their contribution to the performance than in how the equipment worked. As a non-technical person myself, my career was based upon the same premise and, as a designer, I always favoured sound operators with a stage management background over the keen 'boffin' types.

By 1950, Stagesound had outgrown the little office at the Lyric and running the business had become a full-time job. The company moved to a small warehouse building in Dansey Place, a mews located a stone's throw from Shaftesbury Avenue in the heart of London's theatreland. Here they installed a store for the hire department, a workshop to develop and build new equipment, and an audio dubbing facility. Their sound effects library was compiled from records Bill had acquired whilst in the Forces and from recordings he had made himself. On the floor below, there was a small recording booth. This was not large enough for music recording and I discovered two references in the R G Jones diaries for Stagesound using their studio. There are also ten references for equipment supplied or installations carried out on behalf of Stagesound. One of these, on October 3 1950, was a delivery of equipment to 3 Dansey Place for the new Jack Buchanan musical GAY'S THE WORD. The last mention of Stagesound is in 1954: *"Deliver four tripods to Bill Walton – SS"*. After that, presumably, Stagesound had enough equipment and staff of their own.

The marriage of Bill and Judy Walton took place in December 1952 at a church in Covent Garden. Bill was working that day (of course!) and was delivered to the church door by a Strand Electric van. After the wedding Bill and Judy headed for Scotland, not for a romantic honeymoon but to install some lighting equipment for Strand Electric for a production of ROSE MARIE at the Murrayfield Ice Rink. The "honeymoon" proved fortuitous for the company because Bill struck up a friendship with the owner of the ice rink, a Scottish solicitor named Alastair Walker. A shrewd businessman with a finger in a number of pies, he was intrigued by the new sound company and later became chairman, playing an influential part in the growth of the company.

Bill Walton recording footsteps in Dansey Place, circa 1954. In the van, Eric Turner who ran the hire department.

Around 1956, the expanding rental department moved from Dansey Place to an unused scene dock in the Coliseum Theatre near Trafalgar Square, with its own entrance just beside the stage door. By then, the equipment hire operation was managed by Eric Turner, a businessman who had served with Bill Walton in the army. He was assisted by Dick Lock, the junior electrician from the Lyric Theatre Hammersmith, who was persuaded to rejoin the company. When Eric later took on a central managerial role and became a director of the company, Dick took over as hire manager. It is interesting to note that neither of these people had any training in electronics.

Equipment hire charges were the same as their rivals, Bishop Sound, who were now experiencing, for the first time, serious competition from a larger company with a new range of equipment. The weekly fee for a panatrope and two loudspeakers was £5.5.0 (£5.25) and a microphone was £1.1.0 (£1.05). One pound and one shilling was called a guinea in those days, so five pounds and five shillings was five guineas.

By the 1960s, Stagesound had their own loudspeakers and microphones for speech reinforcement. As I recall, the heavy 6-foot (180cm) column loudspeakers, incorporating a row of 10-inch (25cm) drivers, had poor bass response and were also distinctly lacking in the high frequency department.

The microphone was designed by the managing director of Reslo Sound, Roland Westgate, whose son, Roger, later became a Stagesound engineer. The microphone was very similar to the famous Reslo ribbon used by the Beatles in the early days, but as it was for use in the 'floats', it was much more sensitive at the front than the rear. In the UK, we have historically used the term float-mikes rather than foot-mikes. The word 'foot' derives from the foot-lights on the front edge of the stage which were once the main source of lighting the actors. The pre-electric foot-lights were lighted wicks floating in oil – hence the term 'floats'.

Stagesound ribbon
float-microphone.

Back in Dansey Place, the manufacturing workshop employed qualified electronics engineers who designed the Stagesound range of mixers and amplifiers. The PF60 and the PF100 amplifiers were manufactured by the company until the mid 1970s when they were replaced by transistor amplifiers purchased from the British company HH Electronics and the American company Crown. But many people were never entirely happy with the transistor versions, saying that the difference in quality could actually be heard.

The Cue Tape

LIFE WAS MADE EVEN more difficult for Bishop Sound when Stagesound brought out their Cue Tape machine based on the mechanically robust 'Wearite' tape transport, manufactured by Wright and Weare Limited and used in the semi-professional Vortexion and Ferrograph tape recorders. For theatre use, Stagesound added an auto-stop mechanism activated by pieces of metal foil stuck to the tape running across two contacts on an insulated pillar placed after the playback head. The foil shorted out the contacts causing the power to the capstan motor to be disconnected. Because the motor took a little time to get up to speed when the start button was pressed, it was necessary to have a second or two of blank tape before the recorded sound. It was a crude arrangement, but it worked.

The first major show in London to use the Cue Tape was the block-buster musical MY FAIR LADY, transferred from Broadway to the Theatre Royal, Drury Lane in 1957. A year or two before this, Jack Shearing at Masque Sound in New York had brought out his auto-stop tape machine using a similar mechanism. Masque had provided the sound for the original Broadway production of MY FAIR LADY. It could be that Bill Walton was prompted to copy Jack's idea in order to obtain the contract for this prestigious show.

Right
Stagesound
Cue Tape.

Far right
Cue Tape machines
for MY FAIR LADY
Theatre Royal, Drury
Lane, 1957.

We know that R G Jones had a tape machine by 1957 because of a diary entry for a service call to London's Savoy Theatre. Robin Jones told me a story about installing tape machines for Agatha Christie's THE MOUSETRAP at the Ambassadors Theatre in 1960. Apparently, at the age of nine in 1952, Robin had recorded "Three Blind Mice" on the piano for his father, little realising that this was to feature in the longest running play in theatrical history. Some eight years later, when replacing the original panatrope with a double tape machine, Robin suggested to producer Peter Saunders, that he was perhaps by now due a royalty payment.

Mr Saunders was amused but did not feel obliged to pursue the matter. (The Ambassadors is the only theatre in the West End in which I have never installed a sound system. This is partly due to the fact that the THE MOUSETRAP played there for twenty two years from 1952 to 1974. It then transferred to the larger St Martin's Theatre next door where it is still running in 2007.)

The tape machine had a great deal to do with the demise of Bishop Sound. It certainly speeded up the process. Suddenly, the big old panatropes with their piles of 10" and 12" records seemed very old fashioned. Many producers were impressed because the hire charge for a tape machine was the same as for the panatrope, but there was no requirement to replace the acetate discs every few weeks. Moreover, Stagesound's Cue Tape had a simple press-button operation which meant that there was no need to employ a skilled "pan operator". Anyone could do it.

The end of Bishop Sound

NOT WITHOUT CAUSE, Jack Bishop was furious when Bill Walton used the name Cue Tape. His whole business was based on Cue Call and the Cue Bar, but he had not had the foresight to register the name Cue Tape. During the next few years, tape became the norm and cuebars were eventually relegated to history. Bill Spragg at Bishop Sound brought out a few tape units, but Jack Bishop resented spending the money because he had a warehouse full of panatropes. Also, he was getting elderly and even more set in his ways. Soon Jack retired and Bill Spragg found himself in charge of a flagging business that had failed to keep up with advancing technology. Stagesound had already taken over the lucrative H M Tennent contracts, via director Alison Colville and lighting designer Joe Davis, and other producers followed suit.

Bishop Sound tape
deck with RCA
preamplifier.

By the late 1960s, Bishop Sound was also facing competition from my company within the Theatre Projects Group and, apart from supplying a few sound effects records and servicing equipment on long term hire contracts, their theatre work virtually dried up. The ground floor of the building in Monmouth Street was turned into a shop and Bill was reduced to selling electrical goods to the public. Very bitter at how life had turned out, Bill finally decided he had had enough when his wife Mamie became ill and died. One day, on a whim, he loaded his car with the archive recordings and the library of sound effects, locked up the building in Monmouth Street and never returned. Without even bothering to sell the lease, which had some years to run, he put the keys in the post to the landlord with a note stating that he no longer had any interest in the building or its contents. It must have been a little disconcerting for the landlord to find his premises full of recording equipment, old panatropes and a large stock of electrical goods. This was a very sad, but typically Jack Bishop sort of way to end the most important pioneering company in British theatre sound. Bill Spragg died in March 2002, aged 84.

Charlie Watkins and WEM

THERE IS ONE OTHER pioneer who, although not working in the legitimate theatre, did make important contributions to the development of public address for live music concerts. In October 2003, I interviewed Charlie Watkins, founder of WEM (Watkins Electronic Music), and the man they call "The father of British PA". During the 1950s, he was responsible for producing an early electric guitar called the Rapier with one of the first guitar amplifiers, and this was followed by his famous 'Copicat' echo machine that became a major contributor to the 'sound of the sixties'. But, most significantly, he was the first man to use 'slave' amplifiers to achieve a 1,000-watts PA system.

Like many early innovators in the audio business, Charlie had no technical training or background in electronics. He was an enthusiast who saw a problem and liked to solve it. After serving in the Royal Navy during the Second World War, he earned a modest living as an accordion player until, in 1949, he opened a record shop with his brother in London's Tooting Market. Two years later they moved to a small shop in Balham where they also sold accordions and guitars.

In 1957 the WEM factory was opened to produce their own electric guitar and amplifier. The launch of the Rapier coincided with the craze for 'skiffle' music and was an immediate success, selling thousands worldwide. Skiffle had begun by accident at a recording session with the Chris Barber Jazz Band for which Lonnie Donegan was playing guitar and banjo. Lonnie wanted to record an old Leadbelly song, "Rock Island Line", but the producer was not interested. The engineer agreed to stay on during a break and recorded the song with just Lonnie Donegan's vocal and guitar, plus double bass and washboard. The track was released in 1956 and became a number eight chart hit in the UK, creating a nationwide craze for skiffle. It also became a number eight hit in the USA. Suddenly, anybody could form a group and make music as long as they could master a few basic chords on a guitar. The rhythm backing was created by an improvised string bass, made by attaching a string to a broom handle stuck into a wooden box acting as a resonator, and thimbles strummed on a metal washboard.

Skiffle was a short-lived phenomenon that began to lose popularity when Bill Haley came to England in 1957 and Rock 'n' Roll swept the country. This new music provided the opportunity for talented musicians, attracted to the guitar during the skiffle era, to start forming rock 'n' roll groups. Charlie Watkins jumped on the bandwagon and brought out two guitar amplifiers, the 'Westminster' and the unusually wedge-shaped 'Dominator'. They were still only 10-watts and 15-watts output, but they both had the new "tremolo" effect. One of the competitors, VOX, had a 30-watt amplifier which, to Charlie's mind, was the best guitar amplifier ever made. The other competitor, Selmer, had a couple of amplifiers, but they were not in the same league. Originally priced at £38.10.00 (£38.50), the WEM Dominator was more affordable that the VOX A30 at £85 and more than 25,000 units were sold. VOX soon brought out 60-watt and 100-watt versions and Selmer produced a 100-watt amplifier, as did another company called Hiwatt. Guitar amplifiers became bigger and louder, but when you went to see a group in those days, all you could hear was guitars. The vocal microphones were plugged into the guitar amplifiers and whereas the guitar players could turn up the volume – which they did – the singers' microphones went into feedback when they tried to compete. There was a glaring opportunity for someone to produce an efficient sound system to help the singer. VOX introduced a column loudspeaker with four 10-inch (25cm) loudspeakers which was used by the Beatles in the early days. Charlie copied this idea using his own amplifier in a voice column, but these were only suitable for use in small indoor venues.

Meanwhile, a big hit record in 1958, "Como Prima", by an Italian group called the Marino Marini Quartet set Charlie thinking. Part of its appeal was a big echo sound created by recording on to a Revox tape recorder and playing back on to a second tape recorder placed alongside to achieve the time delay. Recording studios had echo chambers and steel echo plates, but these were enormous and cost a fortune. What was needed was a cheap device in a small box that could be carried around. Working with his electronics engineers, Charlie came up with a device based upon a recording head, four playback heads and a loop of tape. Called the 'Copicat', it produced a great guitar sound and WEM manufactured thousands of them. Other companies brought out their versions, but WEM had a good six month's start.

Musicians discovered that if you put a Copicat together with a VOX AC30 amplifier something special happened. There was a bit of chemistry. The system was used to great effect by "The Shadows", backing group for the English rock star Cliff Richard. The combination of The Shadows' musicianship and this special sound sold millions of records throughout the sixties. Charlie admitted that, for some reason, the results were less impressive with his own amplifiers and the Selmer was no good at all. Despite modern digital technology, sales of Copicats have continued into the 21st century because people just like the sound. An even more successful transistorized version was brought out in the 1970s, marketed in the USA under the Guild brand.

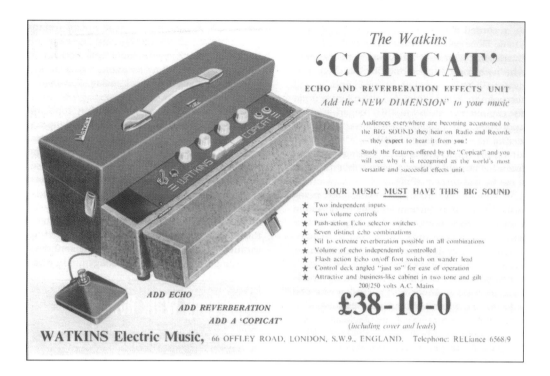

By the mid 1960s, many of the groups had become so popular that they wanted to play to larger audiences. The necessity for developing a really powerful PA system was highlighted when the Beatles played New York's Shea Stadium at the start of their American tour in August 1965. This was the first time in the history of music that a stadium was used for a rock concert. On stage, the Beatles had 100-watt guitar amplifiers especially developed for the tour by VOX. But these, combined with the PA system based on Shure column loudspeakers placed on the ground and tilted up at the audience all around the stadium, proved totally inadequate. As soon as the Beatles took the stage, the screaming from 55,600 fans was so loud that nothing from the stage could be heard. The Beatles could have been playing anything.

Around this time, Charlie had agreed a deal with the American group, The Byrds, to provide a free PA system for their UK tour in order to publicize his new transistor amplifier. The WEM column speakers he initially installed were a total disaster and they were quickly replaced by Tannoy columns, each with four 10-inch (25cm) speakers, and Vitavox multicell horns. Even so, the result did not compare with the system the group used in America with 100-watt Fender amplifiers and many more loudspeakers.

Having had this bad experience with The Byrds, Charlie Watkins was determined to crack the problem of underpowered PA. The first thing he came up with was a little 4-channel mixer called "Fred", forerunner of his 5-channel Audio Master. This was a novel idea, because there were no mixers on the market designed for groups. Then, while discussing with the French and Belgium importers of Copicat, both electronics experts, the need to generate more power from an amplifier, it was suggested that a new 100-watt transistorized amplifier from RCA might be the answer. Because it had no output transformer, it might be possible to feed one amplifier into another (which is not possible with an output transformer). Theoretically, there was no reason why one could not put ten of the things together to achieve a thousand watts – the magic figure! Back in London, Charlie's engineers were extremely sceptical about the idea, but within a week they had proved that the system worked. The first trial was carried out at the 1967 annual jazz festival at Windsor, just outside London. This took place in a field with an audience of only two or three hundred enthusiasts because a larger gathering would have found it difficult to hear the bands in the open air.

Fleetwood Mac at
Balloon Meadow,
Windsor in 1967.

Charlie installed ten of their largest loudspeakers plus twenty columns, each with four 12-inch (30cm) drivers, with high frequency horns mounted on top. To complete the system, he had six bass speakers with four drivers in each. It was all controlled from three WEM 5-channel Audio Master mixers linked together. When 'Fleetwood Mac' on their first appearance in the UK struck their first chords, the level of sound was awesome. Now there was a new problem; because only the vocals and acoustic instruments were being miked, it was the guitars that were in trouble. Their amplifiers could not compete. Charlie takes up the story:

"Our system was producing in excess of 1000 watts – power unheard of since Hitler's Nuremburg rally. The reaction was fantastic. People heard it from miles away and they came to see what was going on. The audience grew. People in the houses nearby were leaning out of their windows and cheering. I knew that this was the breakthrough we had been looking for. At last, you could hear the vocals. History was in the making. Then I was arrested.

Feeling a heavy hand on my shoulder, I looked round. It was the local Chief of Police accompanied by an entourage including the Lord Mayor, an official from the Noise Abatement Society and representatives from the local Residents Association. They wanted the system switched off immediately. However, when I pointed out that such an action could well result in the audience turning very ugly – by now there were thousands of them – they saw the sense in this and let us carry on.

By the end of the three-day festival, word had spread. I returned to the office and was besieged by everybody who was anybody in the music industry. Rod Stewart, The Small Faces, Manfred Mann, Pink Floyd, The Moody Blues, Freddie and the Dreamers, you name them. They all wanted a system. We were way ahead of America where they were mainly using combinations of folded-horn bass bins with

*mid frequency horns which were not good for voice and hopeless for guitar, and
their amplifiers were still limited to 100-watts, of course.*

*In 1969, Bob Dylan gave a concert in England to a crowd of more than 150,000
people at the Isle of Wight Festival, at the end of which he insisted on buying the
whole rig. Even JBL at the first Woodstock Festival in the same year could not equal
the power or the quality. American groups came over and bought systems. I had
people like Janice Joplin and Jimi Hendrix knocking on the door. Even The Byrds,
when they returned to England, bought a system. The fiasco of their first tour
forgiven if not forgotten."*

1969 was also the year that the Rolling Stones performed the first ever free concert
in London's Hyde Park to an audience of a quarter of a million people.

"Stones in the Park" was mixed by Charlie Watkins from a position at the side of
the stage. Soon after the event, Mick Jagger asked him to go on a tour of France
and Germany with them, insisting that the mixing position should be in the
auditorium. He even had a special scaffolding platform designed.

By then, WEM had just started using stage monitors and had added a foldback
output to their Audio Master mixer. This innovation came about when working
with a close harmony group called The Family. Charlie could see from his mixing
position at the side of the stage that they were in trouble. The band was so loud
that they could not hear themselves. So, he quickly connected a spare amplifier
into the headphone output of the vocal mixer, plugged in a loudspeaker and ran it
out on to the stage. Charlie said that the look on the lead singer's face was
wonderful. He even took his hand and kissed it. Bands like Harmony Grass doing
five-part harmony, King Crimson and Genesis all benefited from a good 'inward
mix' and could not perform properly without an efficient monitoring system.

For five years after inventing the slave amplifier, WEM more or less had a clear
run, before companies like CROWN and JBL came out with their big amplifiers
and more efficient bass bin and horn loudspeakers. By then, Charlie Watkins was
becoming disenchanted with the festival scene. Bands were making excessive
demands, asking him to produce bigger and louder systems, and audiences were
becoming unruly and sometimes violent. The fun had gone out of it. *"After I had
to produce 5,000-watts at one festival, I thought that's enough for me. Knowing that
I'd seen and been involved in the most exciting and loveliest time for music, 1966-
1972, I gracefully bowed out."*

10 FROM DISC TO TAPE
IN THE WEST END

As the quality of equipment improved during the 1950s and effects libraries became available, several young theatre directors became interested in the dramatic possibilities of sound. Following my experience at the Arts Theatre Club, I became one of three or four 'pan operators' (the others were all female) known for handling the really heavy sound shows in the West End.

I nearly lost the chance to work on one of these, CAT ON A HOT TIN ROOF directed by Peter Hall, because I refused to be an acting understudy. Stage management in those days were regarded as performers who happened to be doing a job backstage, and were consequently employed on a standard British Equity (actor's union) contract. This specified a requirement to play or understudy as directed. Even company managers and deputy stage managers often covered leading parts. I had never performed on any stage in my life and, in fact, suffered from a recurring nightmare where I found myself standing centre stage playing the lead and with absolutely no idea of what to do or say. So when I was summoned to the office of H M Tennent, the interview with the general manager did not go well. Indicating by his manner that he did not approve of directors meddling in the appointment of junior staff, I was informed that Peter Hall had mentioned my name as a possible assistant stage manager on this production. Then, assuming that I would gratefully accept the job, he placed before me a standard Equity contract. I desperately wanted the job, but when I explained that I was not an actor and could not possibly understudy, he was utterly astounded. His eyebrows shot up and he sat back in his chair. Then, fixing me with a beady eye, he informed me that they *never* employed stage management who did not understudy. After an awkward silence, I mumbled my apologies and made to leave. He let me reach the door before calling me back and, with extremely bad grace, struck out the understudy clause. In silence, I signed the contract and was then dismissed with the wave of a hand. I did not make a friend that day, but what it is to have influential people on your side. I never did join Equity and, at the time of writing, sound operators in the UK are a breed apart, not represented by any official organization.

That production of CAT ON A HOT TIN ROOF used four turntables for an almost movie-like soundtrack to generate a hot oppressive atmosphere with crickets, bullfrogs, bird calls, and plantation workers singing. There were also specific effects such as children shouting, an off-stage party and a firework display. As was usual, at the start of the rehearsal period I accompanied the director to Stagesound to select the sounds and record any special items with the cast. He then left me to work out how many discs I required and in what sequence the tracks should be recorded to allow for mixing and cross-fading. Thus, when we came to setting the sounds in the theatre, Peter Hall could ask to hear the croaking frogs, then add some chirruping crickets, adjust the balance of that, then try a bird cry, discount that and try an alternative bird call from a different loudspeaker location, and so on to build up the audio picture. We also used the extremely effective device that I call the heightened pause. This was achieved by introducing a background atmosphere and running it for a long time so that it was accepted by the audience as part of the scene. Then, just before some dramatic pause in the action, the sound is cut. The ensuing silence is electric. A variation on this was to build up two or three different sounds and then change the texture by cutting one or two of the elements. The audience is only subconsciously aware that something has happened, but the tension is heightened.

With a collection of discs, a number of turntables and a competent operator, all these subtleties and tricks could be tried out during rehearsals. But when tape came along, the director was expected to make a final choice of what sounds he wanted, how they were to be mixed, how long they should run and in what order they were required, all in the antiseptic atmosphere of a recording studio. And all this was to be agreed before the play was properly set in rehearsal. When the tapes were played in the vastly different acoustic of the theatre, the mix was inevitably wrong and the timings were out. To add to the frustration, when the director wished to hear an effect recorded in a different part of the tape, he had to wait while the technician spooled backwards and forwards trying to locate it. The impatient reaction of many directors under fraught rehearsal conditions, was simply to shout "Cut it".

For a few years, to get round this problem, discs continued to be used for the first few weeks of the run if there were complicated effects. Then, when the show had settled, we would time all the cues and transfer them to tape. Replacing the panatropes with tape machines made operation easier, provided better sound quality, and avoided the expense of having to replace the acetate discs every few weeks .

Nevertheless, the number of plays in the West End enlivened by the inventive use of music and background sounds dwindled during the mid 1950s to the late 1960s. Background music, sometimes specially composed, went totally out of fashion. It is true that part of the blame could be laid at the door of the Musicians' Union who tightened the rules for the use of recorded music but, to a great extent, I blame the inflexibility of the tape machine and the fact that if you remove the tools and the skills, the art dies. The ability to experiment creatively with sound in the auditorium did not really re-emerge until the digital sampler provided instant access and memory.

Paradoxically, when I became a sound designer, it was because of this loss of flexibility during rehearsals that my services were seized upon as someone who could relieve the director of these problems and create what he or she had in mind (hopefully something even better!).

Another example of how disc had the edge over tape was in BROUHAHA at the Aldwych Theatre in 1958. Yet another Peter Hall production. The play starred Peter Sellers as the Sultan of a small impoverished Arab state whose aim was to obtain foreign aid for his people. Unfortunately, his people were too lazy to become involved, so it was left to the Sultan to instigate various events, such as the simulation of a devastating hurricane (using wind and rain machines on stage as mentioned in chapter five) and to broadcast the resulting chaos to the world, or to invent a revolt by his starving people and then blow up the British Embassy to make the point. At the end of the play, he stands in the middle of the stage shouting directions into the auditorium at a flotilla of ships arriving with aid from England, Russia and America. Each instruction was followed by a sound effect of, say, a warning siren before two ships collide, men shouting, a ship going aground, another one sinking with bubbling noises, etc. During half a page of script, there were twenty or more sound cues using four turntables and a collection of records. To add to the fun, Peter Sellers tended to alter the script on a nightly basis at the sound operator's expense. He would suddenly call out to the Russian ship – which required a response from the Russian ship's siren – and if it did not come immediately, he would look off-stage and cry gleefully "Aha, that caught you out", amused by the spectacle in the wings of discs flying in all directions. We learned to cope with this situation by having the company manager make strange strangulated noises into a microphone whilst I hurriedly rearranged the turntables. Try doing that on tape!

I am reminded of an amusing incident in BROUHAHA, not exactly to do with sound, but hopefully worth relating. At the end of Act One when the British Embassy was blown up, there was a very loud explosion from a pyrotechnic in a bomb tank augmented by recorded explosions and falling masonry. Simultaneously, part of the set on stage collapsed, followed by an assortment of bricks, plaster, sheets of paper and a dead cat falling from above. After a long pause, once the audience laughter had died down, Peter Sellers, crouching at the front of the stage with fellow actor Jules Munchin, would ask anxiously "Do you think we have gone a trifle too far?" – Curtain. On one memorable night, the laughter died down during the pause and then started again. Somewhat surprised, Peter Sellers looked around and saw the cause of the amusement. On stage, there was an elderly propman studiously picking up the bricks, the plaster, the pieces of paper and the dead cat and placing them in a large basket. This process took quite a while and by the time he had finished the task and walked off-stage, seemingly oblivious of the mayhem he had caused, Peter Sellers was lying on his back, legs in the air, helpless with laughter. He made several unsuccessful attempts to say his final line, but eventually gave up, waving frantically at the stage manager to bring down the curtain. When the company manager asked the propman what on earth he thought he was doing, walking on to the stage while the curtain was up and the actors were still performing, he reacted with amazed innocence, totally denying all knowledge of the incident. "That wasn't me, sir. That wasn't me." This, despite the fact that he had been seen by the actors, the entire stage crew, and several hundred people in the auditorium.

On another night, I noticed someone standing at the rear of the stage right beside the bomb tank just before it was due to explode. This was odd because everyone knew to keep well clear. Unfortunately, there was a deputy fireman that night who had arrived on stage to lower the fire curtain in the interval, as is the law in all British theatres. Theatre fireman are often elderly people who have retired from the force and this one was no exception. Needing to rest his legs while waiting for the end of the act, he made himself comfortable – on the bomb tank. The thought flashed into my mind that I should try and make a dash for it to save him from a possible heart attack, when the green light came on. I reacted and performed the cue. The poor fireman had the shock of his life. Some time later that evening, I passed him shuffling along the dressing room corridor. He was shaking his head and muttering to himself "They nearly got me. They nearly got me."

Stagesound in the sixties

Around 1960, Stagesound began expanding its recording activities, including a lucrative deal with the BBC for recording schools radio programmes and selling tapes for replay in the classroom. The company took on premises at 7 King Street in Covent Garden to house their offices and recording facilities, including a dubbing suite for sound effects and a recording studio capable of accommodating a small group of musicians. The master recorder in the studio was an EMI TR90, a state-of-the-art stereo tape machine used by many major studios. In the dubbing suite there was another TR90 and several TR50 portable studio machines. It seemed that "professional sound" for the theatre had arrived at last! A year or so later, another building was taken over at 11 King Street for more recording facilities, and then a film dubbing suite was set up round the corner in Maiden Lane.

Bill Walton in the
new recording studio
in King Street, 1960.

Lorna Coates
creating effects in
the new King Street
dubbing room,
circa 1960.

The directors at the
opening of the
King Street studio,
from left to right:
Jack Madre (Strand
Electric), Alastair
Walker (chairman),
Diana Zwar (née
Plunkett), Eric Turner
and Bill Walton.

Some spectacular *Son et Lumiere* productions, including one for the Tower of
London and another for the Rock of Gibraltar, were recorded in King Street. This
was before the days of multi-track tape recorders so all the information had to
come from a standard quarter inch stereo machine. The audio programme was
on both tracks to allow for spatial effects, and the pulses to activate the lighting
were recorded over the audio at such a low frequency that their sound was not
reproduced by the loudspeakers. These pulses, sensed by a filter system, activated
a large telephone exchange stepping switch. Contacts on the switch were pre-
wired so that each time the switch stepped, a different combination of contacts
activated the fade up or fade down controls on selected lighting dimmers. The
same switch was used to connect different loudspeakers. I had occasion to use
one of these systems in 1964 for an exhibition in Stratford-upon-Avon celebrating
the 400th anniversary of the birth of Shakespeare. Theatre Projects was engaged
to create an automated light and sound production in a third scale model of

the Globe Theatre where the walls were made of gauze so that it could look solid when front-lit or skeletal when light flooded the wrap-around sky cloth behind. In a series of scenes, the voices of all the Knights and Dames of the British theatre were heard speaking their favourite purple passages, to which I added music and sound effects and Richard Pilbrow created visual magic with the lighting. This exhibition was memorable for two incidents, one comic and one tragic.

The comic story involved a push-button mounted in an old tobacco tin connected by a long piece of wire to the telephone exchange switch in the control room. To set and test the various lighting states, it was not possible to keep running the half hour tape from the beginning to arrive at the required scene, so Richard's assistant, Robert Ornbo, rigged the tobacco tin in order to quickly step through the switch sequence. This all worked fine and eventually the lighting states and loudspeaker switches were all programmed. On the morning of the Royal Gala Opening by His Royal Highness the Duke of Edinburgh, we decided to run the show one more time for luck. To our horror, the tape played but it refused to activate the cues. Dick Lock dived in with his screwdriver – but too late! We were told to stand by because the Duke's helicopter had just landed outside the building. Moments later, the Duke was escorted into the theatre by a group of officials and introduced to Richard. I started the tape and crossed my fingers. The Duke seemed to enjoy the show and, being interested in technology, asked how it worked. Richard explained about the tape, the pulses, the switch, and the pre-set dimmers. The Duke was impressed. "So the whole thing is automated?" he enquired. Richard nervously assured him that it was, praying that His Highness did not lean forward to peer over the 4-foot high barrier against which they were standing. If he had done so, he would have seen Robert Ornbo lying on his back amongst the cables and lighting equipment, clutching a tobacco tin and desperately trying to remember when to push the button for the next cue.

The other incident occurred when, during the set up of the exhibition, Dick Lock was called away to the telephone. He returned, extremely upset, to inform us that Bill Walton had been diagnosed with cancer. He died a few weeks later that year, 1964, at the all too early age of 42. His cherubic smiling face and confident, yet somewhat shy, demeanour endeared him to all. He was one of those rare people – especially in the theatre – about whom you never heard a bad word. His contribution to technical theatre in Britain was immense and one can only wonder what else he would have achieved if his life had not been so tragically cut short. Without his leadership and charisma, Stagesound went rapidly into decline.

11 BECOMING A SOUND DESIGNER

As already mentioned, my road to sound design was an accident, mainly due to the fact that directors became frustrated by the limited range of effects available from Bishop Sound and Stagesound. They also felt the need for someone on their team to be responsible for organizing the recordings and the playback equipment, rather than relying on an amorphous sound company.

It began in 1958 with the play Brouhaha requiring a range of weird effects and pieces of mock Indian music for scene links. The music was recorded one night in Peter Hall's flat where he played the piano and harpsichord, and a member of the cast, John Wood, played the penny whistle and recorder. My job was to operate the tape machine and provide the percussion section consisting of tambourine, small drum, and a variety of boxes and vases that sounded interesting when hit. Although only an assistant stage manager on the show, I was given the responsibility of ordering from Stagesound the panatropes with some better quality loudspeakers than their standard 12" (30cm) cabinets, and the bomb-tank from Strand Electric for the big explosion. Organising this equipment was normally the province of the company manager who, working on behalf of the producer, was expected to arrange the cheapest deal for the minimum amount of equipment to satisfy the director. My approach was slightly different.

During the run of the show, a few stage management friends who knew my interest in sound, asked me to assist on their productions by providing effects and specifying the best playback equipment. By default, I found myself becoming a sound expert.

One evening, I was discussing this turn of events with the star of Brouhaha, Peter Sellers. Always keen on gadgets, he asked me if I had one of the new Reflectograph variable-speed tape machines – very useful for creating effects. I told him that my budget only stretched to a second-hand Ferrograph recorder, a portable gramophone and a basic mixer; additional equipment being hired in when necessary. The next day, he called me into his dressing room and gleefully revealed a spanking new Reflectograph. He kept it there for a few days and we had fun experimenting with the speed control. One recording was of him singing as I slowed down the machine so that his voice rose to an incredibly high pitch on playback, at which point he called for his nurse to adjust his "Tenors' Friend Truss"! Then, after suitable adjustment noises, he completed the song as I quickly wound the machine back to normal speed. Having exhausted the possibilities of the machine and had a lot of laughs, he said that he would like to give it to me. Somewhat taken aback, I protested, but he said that it had given him sufficient enjoyment and he really had no further use for it. A few weeks later, he presented me with an expensive Garrard transcription turntable that he "had no further use for". I was not the only recipient of his generosity; during a break in rehearsals, he noticed one of the junior members of the cast strumming away on a guitar. They got talking about music and the next day he brought in his own very expensive guitar and they had several jam sessions. When the rehearsal period came to an end, the surprised young actor was presented with the splendid guitar on the grounds that it was only gathering dust at home and he would rather it was being used and giving pleasure.

On another occasion, at the end of a morning rehearsal during the pre-London tour, the stage management were having a drink in the pub when Peter Sellers walked by. The company manager asked if he would care to join us for a drink and he appeared genuinely pleased and surprised. Not only did we spend an amusing half hour in the bar, but he then treated us all to lunch in a local restaurant. To have a leading movie actor (he was currently making his second feature film) and a star of the country's most popular radio programme, "The Goon Show", treat everyone – cast and crew – as equals was not only remarkable but it was extremely good for company morale. Later, I worked on a couple of musicals with another member of the "The Goon Show" who had the same quality of being "one of the boys". That was Harry Secombe.

A turning point in my career came during the run of BROUHAHA when I was engaged to create the sound effects for a season of plays produced by the 59 Theatre Company at the Lyric Theatre Hammersmith. The success of this endeavour turned out to be significant in several ways. The young and talented directors, Michael Elliot and Caspar Wrede, made their names and ten years later were able to build the Royal Exchange Theatre in Manchester for their 69 Theatre Company. Reviews for the shows in the '59 season enthused about the sound (unusual to get a mention in those days) and the innovative lighting design by Richard Pilbrow, the creative genius with whom, it turned out, I was to work for the next thirty years.

In conversation with Richard Pilbrow during rehearsals, he explained his vision for Theatre Projects Limited. Although he was becoming renowned for his lighting (the first independent lighting designer to make a living at the craft), the word "lighting" did not appear in his company name, because his aim was to encompass all aspects of theatrical production. This seemed a grandiose plan for a young man with no financial backing but, by the end of the 70s, the Theatre Projects Group was to have the biggest lighting and sound rental operation in Europe, a recording studio, audio-visual and video suite, manufacturing facilities for specialist audio equipment and display lighting, plus a shop in Covent Garden with agencies for a host of leading lighting and sound companies. The group also encompassed the largest theatre design and consultancy company in the world (more than thirty employees) with offices in New York and Hong Kong; and although Richard spearheaded this theatre design operation, he somehow found time to win awards for lighting shows in London and on Broadway and to produce a major movie, SWALLOWS AND AMAZONS, a television series on popular music, and more than thirty West End shows – several co-produced with Hal Prince. In 1959, however, the two year old company consisted of just Richard, his assistant Bryan Kendall and Richard's first wife, Viki, running the office.

Working out of a one-room flat was proving inconvenient for me, so I asked him if he would like a sound department. He said that a space could probably be made in his office so, a little while later, I carried my equipment up the small rickety staircase past open doors where tailors toiled at sewing machines and steam irons, to the third floor of an old building in Whitcomb Street just off Trafalgar Square. I was given a corner in one of the two tiny rooms that comprised the 'Head Office'. Thus, Theatre Projects (Sound) was born.

To make ends meets for the next two years, it was necessary to have an evening job at London's Pigalle theatre restaurant, bringing in the princely sum of £7 per week for working from 7.00 p.m. until gone midnight. The sound system for this major night spot did not take much operating as it merely consisted of a 6-channel mixer/amplifier and two column loudspeakers. That was it. Stage monitors were not around in those days, so the musicians at the back of the stage could hardly hear the singer and he or she just sang along with the orchestra, assuming that the audience was enjoying a satisfactory experience. During my spell at the Pigalle, there was a season of international stars and I was fortunate enough to turn on the microphone for such illustrious performers as Tony Bennett, Peggy Lee, Patti Page, Shirley Bassey and Sammy Davis Junior.

In 1961, the Royal Shakespeare Company engaged me to work on five productions, one at Stratford-upon-Avon and four at their London base in the Aldwych Theatre. A letter from the general manager regarding THE CHERRY ORCHARD specifies that for the work involved in recording all the effects plus attending rehearsals over a period of five days, the fee would be £20. No wonder I had to keep doing the evening job. Another production, ONDINE, starring Leslie Caron, called for an effect to make the ondines (water sprites) sound other-worldly. There being no echo machines, I used tape-delay, whereby a signal is recorded and played back simultaneously, except that the time delay between the record head and the playback head produces an echo. Four microphones were placed strategically on the stage and to enhance the effects, the delayed voices were played through a horn loudspeaker located way up on the fly gallery. By accident, this echo device was switched on during the rehearsal for a Shakespeare play when a live fanfare was being played. The enlivening of the sound was so good that a duplicate system was set up in the theatre at Stratford-upon-Avon and 'switch on echo mikes' became a standard feature on the sound plot for all on-stage music.

For AS YOU LIKE IT at Stratford-upon-Avon, I installed loudspeakers around the auditorium to create a deep-in-the-woods atmosphere with bird sound. Although this seems a mundane thing to do now, at the time people were most surprised to be surrounded by tweeting birds. One critic urged people to see the show, saying that even if they did not agree that the production and particularly the performance of Vanessa Redgrave were unmissable – they could always sit back and enjoy the birdsong. The production was televised by the BBC in 1964 and I notice that I received a sound credit along with the composer and lighting designer.

The Royal Shakespeare Theatre at Stratford had two tape machines mounted in a home-made console with volume controls and speaker switching, but the control position was on a platform above the prompt corner. Being a permanent company receiving a government subsidy (similar to the Royal Opera House in London), the technician operating the equipment was part of the electrical staff. Consequently, despite the fact that there were a lot of cues to learn, and many of them were quite complicated, the electrician was not made available until the lighting had all been set and plotted. During the long sound rehearsals, the director would ask me to edit the tapes because of changes in timings or trying out new ideas, and this would inevitably mean working well into the early hours of the morning. Things were a little more advanced at the London operation of the Royal Shakespeare Company at the Aldwych theatre as this was a new venture. Here, they had a sound operator on the stage management team and a control room in the auditorium. Built into one of the side boxes at the front of the stalls, the room had a small window affording a partial view of the stage but, of course, it did not open!

1962 was an extremely busy year for me, marked by the achievement of having, for the first time in a West End theatre, the sound operator working in the auditorium with a purpose-built effects console. The show was BLITZ!, composed by Lionel Bart as a follow-up to his blockbuster OLIVER! Set in wartime London during the worst period of the bombing raids, the musical ran at the Adelphi for eighteen months. This gargantuan production also introduced ground-breaking technology in motorized scenery and the first radio cueing system for stage management.

I was engaged to produce all the sound effects and to specify the necessary equipment and to create very loud noises around the stage and auditorium. Because the sound was so complicated and vital to the show, I was given a separate contract as sound operator which meant that I could leave the job at the Pigalle and become a full-time sound designer. A telephone call from Bill Walton nearly changed all that. To my immense surprise, he offered me a job at Stagesound based in his plush new studio premises with access to his effects library and his state-of-the-art equipment, doing exactly what I was doing now – but for him. He pointed out that I would never be able to compete with his expensive facilities backed up by thousands of pounds worth of rental equipment, so I might as well join in. Still operating from part of a room in the Theatre Projects lighting design office with my three tape machines and gram deck, this was a tempting proposition; especially as he was offering £20 per week – 45% more than my temporary salary to operate BLITZ! Being stubborn, and preferring to remain my own boss, however poor, I politely turned him down. In my wildest dreams, I could not have imagined how, a few years later, Theatre Projects was to acquire Stagesound and I would be in control. For now, I turned my attention to BLITZ!

On a bare stage, the main elements of the innovative set by Sean Kenny (also designer of OLIVER!) were four three-storey 'buildings' made of steel measuring about 24 feet (7.5m) high x 5 foot (1.5m) x 10 foot (3m). Each of these structures was on castors and could move under battery power, controlled by an assistant stage manager sitting in a small camouflaged cabin. With the aid of a few push-buttons and a steering wheel, these juggernauts, weighing more than two tons, could move backwards and forward and turn, following white lines on the stage. At the same time, the drivers were able to revolve the entire structures about them. With four different fascias on each, one street scene could fluidly move into another. As if this were not complicated enough, a bridge spanned the entire width of the stage, supported by two steel towers containing staircases for the actors. Not only could the bridge go from floor level to 30 foot (9m) up, but when it was raised above the height of the moving buildings, the entire structure could track from the back of the stage to the front. Take a cast of forty actors working amongst all this free-ranging machinery, plus several large pieces of scenery flying in and out, and it is obvious that the strictest technical control was necessary.

The complexity of the production called for two technical stage managers working in unison. From the prompt corner, stage manager A gave all the lighting, follow-spot and special effects cues via cuelights and paging loudspeakers. Stage manager B was located high up on the non-working side fly gallery with a microphone and radio transmitter. Transistor radios, fairly new on the market, were purchased from the English company, Perdio, and adapted to receive a single frequency. These were distributed to the entire stage management team and the flymen. From his high vantage point, stage manager B gave cues to the four drivers of the mobile buildings and, when they were in place, cued the flymen and operated the massive bridge. In order to synchronize all the technical elements, stage manager A had a radio receiver and stage manager B could hear his cues via a paging loudspeaker.

BLITZ! Air Raid sequence. On the left, firemen are standing on the descending bridge. In the centre is one of the mobile structures. To the right at the back is the projection of St. Paul's Cathedral.

Sometimes things inevitably went wrong. For example, the heavy mobile buildings would get stuck if one of the castors came up against the tiniest object dropped on the stage. It was not unusual to see a man wearing what appeared to be a deaf-aid, walk along the street and give one of the houses a hefty push. Everyone – cast, crew and stage management – was in full view of the audience, but they were all wearing appropriate clothing so it did not matter. The only time the show actually ground to a halt was on the Royal Gala preview. The spectacular end to Act One was a full-scale air raid on London starting with distant air raid sirens followed by a nearby siren as the sound of far off anti-aircraft guns and the drone of German bombers grew louder, culminating in all hell being let loose: whistling bombs and explosions from all sides of the stage, sounds of falling masonry, burning buildings and fire engine bells, with airplanes passing low overhead through the auditorium.

At its peak, the four 100-watt valve (tube) amplifiers I was using managed to top a 30-piece orchestra playing flat out. Meanwhile on stage, bright flashes of light synchronized with the explosions as flames were projected on to the buildings. Firemen ran out their hoses and erected ladders to rescue people from high windows, ambulance workers carried people on stretchers, others ran through the streets in panic. Smoke gradually filled the stage, created by two stage managers walking around with smoke guns – unnoticed in the melee. The climax came when the buildings gradually parted (a magnificent sight in the smoke and flames) to reveal an enormous projection of the famous image of St. Paul's Cathedral wreathed in smoke as all London burned. Almost immediately, the projection screen was gently flown out – but the image of St. Paul's remained, ghost-like, projected on to the smoke, gradually dissipating.

The cartoon by JAK in the London Evening Standard makes fun of two events in 1962 – the Campaign for Nuclear Disarmament rally and the smoke incident in BLITZ!.

"CND HECKLERS, US? — WE'VE JUST SAT THROUGH THE LAST ACT OF BLITZ."

For the Royal Gala performance, it was decided to add more smoke because the projection had not worked properly the night before. Unfortunately, it all got out of hand and the smoke filled the stage until the actors were entirely lost from view, then it rolled forwards into the auditorium, filling the orchestra pit so that all one could see was the conductor standing waist high in smoke. The musicians could no longer see him, so the music petered out. The audience began to laugh. Although we could not see them, the cast on stage continued to shout and rescue people from buildings, and I continued to drop bombs and have ambulances arrive and planes roar overhead. But the dense fog surged onwards, filling the entire stalls and rising to the first balcony level where the Princess Royal and her party were sitting. Fortunately, someone backstage had the presence of mind to open the emergency skylight in the roof of the fly tower and the rising heat drew the smoke back on to the stage. As it cleared, the actors (by now becoming hoarse) came into view and were applauded wildly by the audience. Then, as the smoke cleared from the pit, the orchestra struck up and the show continued.

The sound control was positioned at the side of the upper circle with a good view of the stage, and from where I could actually hear what I was doing. At last! The producer was not happy with the situation, even though I had put to him what I thought was an unarguable case for the necessity of working out front. Initially, he would not countenance such a preposterous idea. He only agreed (with rather bad grace) that the equipment could occupy three not very expensive side seats in the auditorium when the company manager pointed out that there was absolutely no space available backstage.

The first show in New York that Jack Shearing could recall having an auditorium control position and a dedicated sound operator (although still an assistant electrician) was in 1968. Like BLITZ!, he needed to hear what was going on because it was a complicated tape show with sound all round the stage and auditorium.

The control of sound effects for BLITZ! called for something more than the standard equipment available for hire; i.e. two tape decks feeding either of two amplifiers with a loudspeaker switching panel. I therefore drew up a simple mixing console to be built by Stagesound. It was somewhat basic by today's standards, but seemed very daring at the time. Most importantly, it worked.

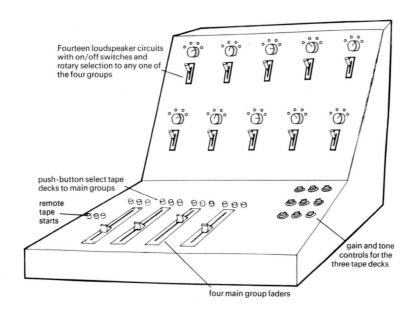

Fourteen loudspeaker circuits with on/off switches and rotary selection to any one of the four groups

push-button select tape decks to main groups

remote tape starts

gain and tone controls for the three tape decks

four main group faders

Sound effects console for BLITZ! – 1962.

The three tape machines, which had remote start, gain and tone controls on the desk, were selectable to any combination of four main 'group' faders each controlling the input of a 100 watt amplifier, and fourteen loudspeaker circuits were selectable to any one of the amplifiers or off. Thus, in the first scene where people were using an underground railway station as an air raid shelter, I was able to simulate a train passing through the station using four loudspeakers – two either side of the stage and two in the orchestra pit. With each loudspeaker connected to one of the amplifier faders, a mono recording of the train started stage right and as it entered the station, the other three faders were quickly opened. Then, as the train departed, the first three faders were closed in sequence leaving the sound to die away stage left. Synchronized with a flickering lighting effect, this was very convincing, although the noise created by 15-inch (38cm) Goodman speakers in the bass reflex cabinets I had specially built for the show might have been unpopular with some members of the orchestra.

The sound reinforcement for the show, specified by Stagesound, simply consisted of five microphones positioned along the front edge of the stage and four of their 6-foot (180cm) column loudspeakers – two for the stalls and the other two vaguely directed at the dress circle and upper circle. When it was found that people in the upper tier were having audibility problems, a 12-inch (30cm) loudspeaker was placed either side of the auditorium on a ledge above the side boxes. Of course, there was no time delay in those days, so these speakers might have added to the level but I doubt whether they did anything for the clarity. To control the microphones, I was given a 6-channel mixer with overall treble and bass controls and, as was standard procedure, turned up the master for the songs and down for the dialogue. If a song happened to be performed in a fixed area of the stage, one might turn off a few microphones in order to get a little more gain before feedback.

Sound reinforcement for BLITZ! – 1962. Two column loudspeakers on the proscenium and a 12-inch speaker on a ledge to boost the upper circle. On stage can be seen one of the three-story mobile structures driven by a stage manager.

I became friendly with one of the stage management team, Antony Horder, who occasionally took over as sound operator when I was engaged on other projects. Being handy with hammer and nails, he offered to help construct a recording studio in the basement of the Theatre Projects lighting store in Neals Yard, just off Monmouth Street, London. During the space of a few weeks, almost single-handed, he built a sound-proof studio and recording booth. He also began to assist with installing equipment, usually hired from Stagesound, into theatres where I was providing effects tapes or discs. As things became busier, he began helping with the recordings and within a year or so he had become the other half of the team. We worked together, with never a cross word, for more than fourteen years until he married a nice French lady and went to live in Paris. Many illustrious voices were recorded in the wooden studio until, in 1966, it was replaced by a smart recording complex with a 'proper' recording engineer.

Before leaving BLITZ!, I have to mention a memorable incident when Antony Horder most dramatically demonstrated his stage management skills. It came about in a scene where the juvenile lead emerged from a pub and went into a drunken song and dance routine. On this occasion, as he spun round, the bottle he was holding came into contact with part of the steel set and it shattered. With the stage covered in pieces of glass, it was inevitable that the small castors on one or more of the massive mobile 'buildings' would become jammed – and there was a big scene change coming up. With great presence of mind, Tony dashed to the prop room, grabbed a broom, then purloined an old trilby hat from one of the cast. The next thing I saw from my vantage point at the side of the upper circle, was an old street cleaner – a 'deaf' old street cleaner – calmly working around this singing and dancing drunk, occasionally giving him a disapproving look, as he brushed away the offending glass. That is what I call stage management. And, of course, the audience totally accepted that this was part of the action.

One last anecdote: near the end of the show, there was an enormous explosion when a landmine went off. For this we used a bomb tank placed at the back of the stage near the large door in the scene dock. On the other side of the door, in the street, there was a notice warning passers-by that there would be a loud explosion at approximately 10.00 p.m. each night and 5.00 p.m. Wednesdays and Saturdays. One summer evening, one of the stage management was out there having a cigarette break, using his receiver and earpiece to keep track of the show, when along comes a gentleman wearing a similar earpiece connected to one of those big old fashioned deaf aids clipped to the breast pocket of his jacket. Indicating his hearing aid, he said in a loud voice, *"Wonderful things, these, aren't they? I expect you have come along here like me, haven't you... to hear the bang?"*

Noel Coward is reported to have said of BLITZ! that it seemed: *"twice as long as the real thing, but only half as amusing."* The first night audience, however, was swept away by the spectacle and the applause was tumultuous. Because there had been teething problems with the lighting switchboard, Richard Pilbrow was sitting behind me at the sound control with an intercom – just in case any dimmers stuck and improvisation became necessary. When we reached the big air raid sequence with all the scenery moving through the smoke and the flames and the projection of St. Paul's, everything came together perfectly for the first time. Richard became so excited that he began thumping me on the back and shouting above the tremendous din: *"Isn't this exciting? Isn't this what it is all about?"* My reply was:

"Get off, I am trying to do a job here!" but I knew that this was possibly the most heart-stopping evening I would ever spend in the theatre.

First poster credit for sound

SEPTEMBER 1962 SAW the start of the final season of the renowned Old Vic Theatre Company before the Old Vic became the temporary home of the newly formed National Theatre Company, waiting for their complex to be built on the south bank of the Thames. I was engaged by the artistic director, Michael Elliot, to create the sound for MEASURE FOR MEASURE, PEER GYNT, THE ALCHEMIST and OTHELLO at a fee of £75 per show. For me, this season was particularly significant because Michael Elliot surprised me by stating that he regarded sound as important an element in a production as lighting or scene design and, for the first time, I received an equal credit in the programme and on the poster. As far as I can discover, this was the first time in the West End or on Broadway that sound was so acknowledged. A precedent was set and, from that time on, I was usually able to negotiate a poster credit either as "Sound by..." or, as in the case of PIPPIN (1973), "Sound Design by..."

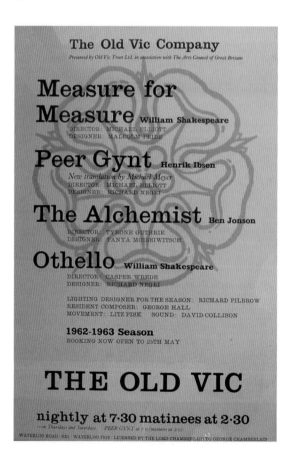

Equal billing for
sound, 1962.

The two Shakespeare plays were full of all the usual music and effects, and PEER GYNT seemed to have non-stop noises from beginning to end. For THE ALCHEMIST, however, nothing was requested. I told the director, Sir Tyrone Guthrie, that £75 had been allotted to his budget for my services and, after a little thought, he suggested that one scene could possibly be enhanced by the inclusion of an ancient clanking lavatory flushing effect. When we came to the run-throughs, I kept receiving notes to reduce the volume a little. Eventually, when I pointed out that it could hardly be heard at all, he said: *"Ah, but you and I know it is there".* That must have been the most expensive unheard flushing lavatory in the business.

Being on hand in case 'the effect' required any last minute adjustment, provided the ideal excuse to watch this legendary director at work. At the final run-through before public previews, the play was set and all discussions with the cast about their motivation and the meaning of the play had been resolved. As they ran the play, Guthrie would stop from time to time to ask individual actors to move a pace to the left or take half a pace up-stage or, upon an entrance, to pause between the chair and the table. With these minor adjustments, no actor was being masked or upstaged. Far more than that, the audience was now being presented with a series of the most wonderful stage pictures. I know that many modern actors would hate having their movements constricted in this way, but perhaps we all need reminding from time to time for whose benefit a show is being performed.

For the production of PEER GYNT, I was concerned about the complicated sound track for two reasons; firstly, the only space available for the two tape machines was in a little corner right at the back of the stage, and, secondly, the company manager had engaged the wife of the chief electrician to operate them. I was assured that, although she knew nothing about sound, she did have stage management experience and "was very bright". Fortunately, she turned out to be brilliant and had no problem in following the cue sheets I always prepared for a show. However, it demonstrates how, although directors were now accepting the importance of sound effects, there was no concept that the person making them happen every night was contributing anything more than pressing a few buttons.

Fortunately, attitudes were slowly beginning to change. The Association of British Theatre Technicians (ABTT) had been formed in 1961 to collect and disseminate information on technical theatre and to set general standards. In 1962, the ABTT issued a publication on Adaptable Theatres in which the audio section included recommendations for sound effects, speech reinforcement and communications systems. The following year, a lecture was given by the ABTT Sound Committee in which the importance of the sound operator was discussed, and chairman John Fernald, artistic director of the Royal Academy of Dramatic Art, stated that the sound operator should be considered as much of an artist as an actor – a somewhat scandalous idea to many of those assembled. Bill Walton of Stagesound and other committee members from Westrex, the Standard Telephone Company and Associated Television, talked about audio equipment and explained why different microphones and loudspeakers were required for specific jobs. They also stressed the necessity for standardizing cables and connectors – something the committee had already begun to address. Wireless microphones were mentioned and the fact that their use in the British theatre was limited because the GPO (General Post Office) refused to allocate frequency bands suitable for stable reception. As a new voice for the theatre, the committee promised to put pressure on the GPO. Then, by way of light relief, I gave a demonstration of cueing discs with four turntables and, because it seemed to be of general concern, used a tape machine to show how easy it was to cope if a tape broke in the middle of a performance.

In 1964, the Architects' Journal published a series of Information Sheets prepared by the ABTT providing guidelines for architects on auditoria, stages, ancillary spaces, fixtures and equipment. In a comprehensive paper on sound and communications, the desirability of having a control room in the auditorium and the need for the sound operator to *"hear the sound from the stage at the same quality and intensity as the audience"* was stressed. This was an important document because this information was now in print and being read by people responsible for building new theatres.

Sound design for musicals

BETWEEN WORKING ON THE last Old Vic season and the first National Theatre season, I received a phone call that was to have another profound effect on my career. The scene designer of BLITZ!, Sean Kenny, was working on a new musical called PICKWICK with Harry Secombe in the title role. It was a few days before the out of town premiere in Manchester. Once again, although on a more modest scale, he had designed a set with motorized structures moving around a bare stage. However, unlike BLITZ!, they were asking performers, and Harry Secombe in particular, to sing on platforms some 8-foot (2.4m) above stage level – with the platforms sometimes moving during a song. And nobody could hear a word. They had tried using the theatre's float-mikes (foot-mikes) with absolutely no success. Consequently, the chief sound engineer for the Stoll Moss group, owners of several London theatres and a chain of major touring theatres, had been urgently summoned to sort out the problem. His solution was to suspend six omni-directional microphones (STC 'Ball and Biscuit') above the set in the hope that they would pick up singers on the upper levels wherever they happened to be. With a hard echoey stage floor and no drapes or masking to soak up the sound, one can imagine the effect – that of a swimming pool in an echo chamber.

So, Sean Kenny suggested that I should get on a train to Manchester right away and sort out the problem. I tried to explain that I knew nothing about sound reinforcement; what I did was make recordings and create sound effects. But as far as he was concerned, it was all 'sound' and I could not possibly make matters worse. Anyway, he has already told producer Bernard Delfont that the leading sound expert in the country would be arriving the next morning.

In panic, I visited Stagesound and hired one of every type of microphone they had in stock, including a 36-inch (90cm) rifle and even a microphone set in a parabolic reflector (only useful, I later discovered, for recording high frequency bird sounds). My plan was to sneak into the theatre during the morning rehearsal, evaluate the problems and, during the lunch-break, spend some quiet time testing the various microphones.

When I sidled into the back of the stalls, an orchestral rehearsal was in progress with the entire cast on stage and a group of people clustered around the lighting designer's desk in the auditorium. Unfortunately, Sean Kenny looked round and saw me lurking in the darkness. *"Ah, David, you got here. Come and meet Mr. Delfont."* I shook hands with the famous producer who stopped the rehearsal and escorted me on stage to meet Mr. Secombe. *"Thank God you are here."* he said. *"Sean has told us that you are a genius, and that is exactly what we need. The rehearsal is yours. What would you like us to do?"*

The entire cast, orchestra and production team seemed to be holding their breath, waiting for the saviour to pronounce. To admit that I had not the foggiest idea would, I suspected, be less than a shrewd move. So, to gain time, I proposed that the rehearsal should continue so that I could study the extent of the problem. But when the orchestra struck up, my heart sank. I had never heard anything so awful. All you could hear of Harry Secombe's tenor voice was a thin strangulated sound something akin to a sub-standard PA system in a sports stadium heard from some miles away.

Logic told me that all those microphones hanging over the stage had to be turned off and some way had to be found of getting a microphone near the singer. That night, we rigged several directional dynamic microphones (Shure 545 Unidyne) from bars above the stage. Each cable ran through pulleys on the bar allowing the microphones to be raised and lowered from off-stage. Thus, when someone was about to sing from an upper level of a platform, the relevant microphone was lowered. If the platform moved during a song, the movement could only occur during an orchestral section so that when the scenery came to rest, another microphone could be lowered before singing resumed. The microphones were painted black, and as the space above the set was also black, they went almost unnoticed. Crude, but effective. Because of the excessive reverberation caused by the lack of masking in an empty fly tower (loft), I soon discovered that the fewer number of microphones switched on, the clearer the sound. So, contrary to tradition, the normal state for the foot-microphones was "off", and they were individually faded up and down as necessary. Stagesound sent up a twelve-channel mixer for the five dropping microphones and the five foot-mikes and it became obvious that a sound operator would be required. Not only that, but, because the operator has to see the stage in order to synchronise the fading of microphones with the movement of the cast, the mixer was installed in a box out front. Thus, when the show opened at the Saville Theatre, it became the first West End musical to have a multi-microphone rig, a control position in the auditorium, and a sound operator.

An amusing rider to this story was told to me by one of Stagesound's engineers, Roger Westgate. Apparently, after the show opened, Harry Secombe became worried that the sound system might fail during a show. There was no such thing as fold-back (stage monitors) in those days, so he would not be able to tell. So, to allay his fears, Roger purchased a sound-to-light controller (as used in the early discos for flashing lights to music) and rigged some lights backstage on either side of the proscenium. By this means, Harry could 'see' that the sound system was working – the brighter the lights, the louder was the sound.

Somehow, during that year of 1963, I also managed to cram in three productions for the Royal Shakespeare Company and a show in Las Vegas. THE WARS OF THE ROSES at Stratford-upon-Avon was adapted from Shakespeare's HENRY VI trilogy and Richard II into three plays. Although each play was full of recorded music and effects, my task was made easier by the fact that the company now had a member of the stage management team solely responsible for operating the equipment.

An experience in Las Vegas

At the end of an eventful year, I found myself on the way to Las Vegas with a selection of sound effects created for a spectacular revue with the original title of Les Follies to be presented at the Dunes Hotel. Once again, it was Sean Kenny designing extraordinary and complicated motorized scenery, this time operated by a computer (when it worked!), and it was he who had put my name forward for the job. The big theatre at the Dunes had a new sound system designed by a Los Angeles-based sound consultant, a species I had never before encountered. The budget he was given for the specially-built loudspeakers, the echo chamber, wireless microphones, and all the Altec mixers and amplifiers would have equipped a dozen theatres in the UK. In the luxurious new control room (but with no opening window!), there were even two Ampex tape machines, the like of which I had only seen in professional recording studios. And what, I wondered, was the purpose of all those microphones amongst the musicians? The orchestra was located at the side of the balcony, so I could not understand why any form of amplification should be necessary. When we came to the first full rehearsal, I was therefore not totally surprised when the orchestra was far too loud. A meeting was called to which I was invited. The sound consultant proposed glassing in that section of the balcony in order to contain the sound. The owner of the Dunes hotel asked my opinion and I was foolish (or honest) enough to query the logic of having live musicians shut off from the audience in order to produce a canned sound. My comments did not make me totally popular with the sound consultant who was forced to come up with plan B. This was to line the walls and ceiling around the orchestra with extremely thick sound-absorbent material which had the desired effect from his point of view. Unfortunately for the musicians, this extreme deadening of the acoustic had the effect of partial deafness and made it extremely difficult to play an instrument.

There was, of course, a permanent soundman in charge of all this equipment and I was intrigued to know exactly where he was going to place the wireless microphones and transmitters on the female singers, some of whom were only wearing sparkly G-strings and large feathered head-dresses. Visualizing large transmitter packs and chunky lavalier microphones, I somewhat facetiously suggested constructing special wigs. To my surprise, he said that I had got it in one. He then showed me the Edcor integrated microphone and transmitter – not much bigger than the familiar Shure 545 dynamic microphone. Although designed as a hand-mike and still quite large and heavy, the wigs were massive too. So, way back in the early sixties, here was a technique being used that did not become standard in the musical theatre for another twenty years or so when the miniature electret microphones were small enough to be taped to people's heads.

The LA sound consultant seemed to be held in awe by the chief soundman and his assistants and they would gather around him at coffee breaks to hear of the big projects he was designing and the new ideas coming out of his laboratory. *"Right now,"* he said, *"we are working on a tooth-microphone. Fits right there at the back of the tooth."* This announcement engendered raised eyebrows and expressions of admiration. *"Of course,"* he went on, *"we are having a little trouble with saliva right now."* Not quite comprehending, I asked him if it was really possible to fit a radio transmitter into the mouth. The answer was: *"No, at present there is a little wire coming out from the corner of the mouth, but we're working on it."* There followed a stunned silence as no one dared to pursue the subject further.

Having gained the friendship of the chief soundman, he took me into his confidence regarding the very expensive echo system that had been specially designed for the show. We had heard much about the sound-proof room built to a specific shape and size with reflective walls and a strangely shaped loudspeaker cabinet with loudspeakers at carefully calculated angles, and – above all – a revolving microphone! One day he asked me if I would like to take a peek at the chamber and see the famous revolving microphone for myself. As it was such a unique concept, he had the only key to the room and was not supposed to show anybody. As a fellow soundman, however, he was prepared to trust me because he thought I might learn something. And learn something I did. When the door was opened, all that was revealed was a small square room with a standard 12-inch (30cm) cabinet loudspeaker lying on its back at one end and, from a hook in the centre of the ceiling, a microphone hanging by a piece of string. That was it. It is true what they say – audio design really is a black art.

An experience in Philadelphia

WITHIN A FEW MONTHS, I was on my way to the USA again. A new musical, GOLDEN BOY, starring Sammy Davis Junior was on tour prior to opening on Broadway. The director was the Englishman, Peter Coe, who had been responsible for PICKWICK and my colleague, Richard Pilbrow, was devising the scene projection. One afternoon, the telephone rang in the studio and it was Richard calling from America. He told me that the sound on the show was a disaster and Peter Coe wanted me out there immediately. I was to pack my bags because the producer had booked a first class flight for me the following morning. Bearing in mind I had only been responsible for sound reinforcement on one musical and had only got away with that by the skin of my teeth, the prospect of telling a Broadway soundman how to do his job was more than a little daunting. However, the next morning I began to feel more relaxed after being plied with free champagne by the charming staff in the BOAC (British Overseas Airways Corporation) first class accommodation. More drinks appeared before, during and after the meal, so by the time we landed in New York, I almost had to be poured off the airplane. Once through customs, I was scooped up by a gentleman wearing a blue blazer and a peaked cap and whisked off to Philadelphia in a large black limousine. This was the life!

At the theatre, the show was about to begin. The producer, Hillard Elkins, told me that there was a new man mixing the sound that night because he had sacked the previous one on the grounds that he was deaf. Apparently, during rehearsals there

had been a terrible hum from the loudspeakers which the soundman, in his box at the side of the auditorium, claimed he could not hear. The rehearsal was held up while he tinkered with the wiring at the back of the mixers, occasionally shouting: *"Is that any better?"* – when it was patently obvious to everybody in the theatre that it was not. Just before Mr. Elkins was about to explode, the hum stopped. Merciful silence.
"Is that any better?"
"YES".

The rehearsal continued, but the performers on stage could not be heard. Hillard Elkins put his ear to one of the loudspeakers and discovered that the cure for the hum had been to switch off the entire system. That was it. The technician was banished from the building without consideration of who would mix the show that night. Nothing daunted, the producer decided to do it himself. It was at this point that director Peter Coe, in despair, requested my presence.

Mr. Elkins suggested that I should see the show and then attend a meeting in his hotel suite. There being no seats available, I had to stand at the back. It was hot, I had a cracking headache, and the change of pressure when the airplane landed had caused both my ears to block up. By the time the show ended, I was jet-lagged, badly hung over and deaf.

Production meetings in England are usually low key affairs, so I was not prepared for the extraordinary scene awaiting me in the sumptuous hotel suite. It was like walking into a Hollywood B movie. On one side of the enormous room, the composer was seated at a piano going through the score with the musical director; in a corner, the director was sitting with his secretary reviewing his notes on the performance; on the other side of the room, Sammy Davis, reclining on a leather sofa with a large bourbon and coke, was being interviewed by several members of the press as flash bulbs went off, and in the centre of the room, Hilard Elkins, clad in powder blue pyjamas, was stretched out face-down on a medical couch having his back professionally massaged while talking on the telephone, drinking whiskey and giving instructions to two secretaries seated at either side of his head. He broke off when he saw me and asked what I thought about the sound. I had to ask him to repeat the question. Not a good start. The amplification of the show had been abysmal but, not wishing to cast any slight on the technicians, I merely said that it was not the best I had ever heard. And when asked if I could fix it, my answer was that I was sure improvements could be made. There was a pause. This was not what they wanted to hear. They expected upbeat confident talk of dramatic changes. Then, Mr. Elkins laughed. *"Oh, I get it,"* he said, *"it's that famous British understatement".*

It was agreed that I should have the stage to myself the next morning with the new sound technician in order to go quietly through the system. What I did not understand was the American union situation and the fact that the soundman was one of the electrical staff. Apparently, my request to play with the sound system constituted a call for the entire electrical staff and as I checked the microphones and listened to the loudspeakers, it was somewhat intimidating to have a group of men standing on stage watching me. How much, I wondered, was this costing?

The foot-mikes and the three wireless microphones used by the lead performers all worked well. The problem seemed to be inadequate coverage of the auditorium by the main loudspeakers and the lack of a sensible cue-sheet. Some additional loudspeakers were shipped in and we plotted microphone levels throughout the show to obtain a better overall balance. Improvements were indeed made before I left. As things often turn out in the rough and tumble of a pre-Broadway tour, the director was replaced before the next date and, quite sensibly, a sound company from New York was brought in. Meanwhile, I was back in London designing the sound on Lionel Bart's MAGGIE MAY.

Continued resistance to sound operators in the UK

OF THE FOUR UK musicals I worked on in 1964, only MAGGIE MAY had a sound operator and a control position out front. Producers were still resisting the loss of seats in the auditorium and the payment of an extra salary. As there were no other freelance sound designers, mine was a lone voice fighting the cause. On June 11, an article appeared in The Stage (the newspaper of the British theatre) in which I tried to justify the existence of sound designers and proposed that they should become part of the creative team on every large production. I highlighted the fact that the sound designer's work could be hampered by the inadequacies of the person at the controls: *... the operation of the sound equipment often presents problems because it falls to the already busy assistant stage manager. As a result, one often hesitates to give too many cues or try out new ideas. The answer is a separate job – a "Sound Operator".*

Despite my efforts, many musicals I worked on over the next three or four years, including FIDDLER ON THE ROOF and CABARET had simple amplification systems operated from the prompt corner. These were installed by Stagesound who were effectively the only company now providing equipment in the West End. Typically, they used five Shure 545 microphones on short stands along the front edge of the stage, and four or six of their large column loudspeakers on the proscenium.

Stagesound did supply a sound operator in 1965 to cope with two wireless microphones for the original London production of HELLO DOLLY, and for Barbra Streisand in FUNNY GIRL the following year. Wireless microphones were not very stable in those days and the problems experienced on these two shows are discussed in Chapter 15.

Theatre Projects goes into the equipment rental business

IN 1965, BILL WALTON having so tragically died the previous year, a new managing director for Stagesound, Bernard Bibby, was appointed. It seems that his background was in accountancy, and Judy Walton thinks that his previous employment was in television. Without someone with Bill's charisma and knowledge of the theatre at the helm, the company went rapidly into decline. By

1968, the design and manufacturing department in Dansey Place and the equipment rental department based at the Coliseum Theatre had moved into new premises at 14 Langley Street in Covent Garden. Within another few years, the studios in King Street would close and the managing director along with the remnants of the recording business also squeezed into Langley Street. Meanwhile, many key staff left the sinking ship, some to set up in opposition.

Bernard Bibby did not see the point of continuing the discount arrangement Theatre Projects had for sub-hiring from Stagesound, so we began to build up our own hire stock by purchasing equipment for each new production. The bulky Cue Tape machines were no longer required as the German Studer company had brought out their semi-professional Revox tape recorder with a built-in photocell stop mechanism. Rather than splicing in clear leader between cues to trigger the photo-cell, we now created a window in the show tape by wiping off a section of emulsion with a cotton bud dipped in acetone (nail varnish remover).

More producers were seeing the advantage of having a sound designer and we were being offered more shows than Stagesound. One musical, however, we turned down. There was a phone call during 1968 from a gentleman asking if we would care to provide a whole lot of hand microphones for a new musical opening at the Shaftesbury Theatre. This would have been a large investment for us and my colleague, Antony Horder, declined the offer when he discovered that the show featured rock music (horror!) and was all about American hippies (even worse!). It was obviously far too dodgy to contemplate. The show, of course, turned out to be the mega-successful HAIR. In subsequent years, I was sound designer for two West End revivals – both most enjoyable experiences. The original system was put together by a gentleman involved in the recording industry who used a stack of 4-channel Shure mixers for a combination of foot, overhead and hand mikes (the musicians were not amplified in the original production). The show opened the day after the abolition of theatre censorship in the UK. Prior to this, the nude scene and much of the colourful language would certainly have been banned. Some weeks later, Dick Lock, now freelancing, took over as sound operator.

For the national tour five years later, one of Dick's ex-colleagues at Stagesound built him a mixing desk. This had rotary faders and sub-group masters for the long-distance mikes, the hand mikes and the band mikes (new addition), allowing a different mix of these to be sent to the stalls, circle and upper circle auditorium loudspeakers, plus stage monitor loudspeakers (also a new addition).

Condenser microphones and a crude time-delay system

IN 1969, HAVING designed SWEET CHARITY for producer Harold Fielding, he asked us to work on MAME at the Theatre Royal, Drury Lane, starring Ginger Rogers. The system was purchased from Philips following an approach by one of their salesmen who thought, quite mistakenly, that their standard 25 watt mixer/amplifiers developed for paging systems would be suitable for theatre use. The control for the show consisted of a stack of seven of these units. Each had four small plastic slider faders, adequate for pre-setting microphone levels but not suitable for constant operation with any kind of precision. On the plus side, the six Philips column loudspeakers were smaller than the big Stagesound 'coffins' and, although totally lacking in bass, they did have a better high frequency response. But the major revelation was the microphones they offered. For the past five years, we had been using the Shure 545 dynamic microphone for the floats, but Philips was now offering a slim pencil-like condenser microphone with a much better stage pick-up (we discovered later that it was, in fact, the AKG C451 painted black with a Philips logo added). Seven of these were installed on short stands, pointing upwards in the approved manner, and were found to be a vast improvement both in looks (less obtrusive) and performance.

Two years previously, we had installed a sound system at Drury Lane for a musical starring Harry Secombe and, when 'dead spots' were found at the sides of the first and second balconies, additional loudspeakers were added in these locations. The result was not satisfactory because of the garbled pre-echo effect caused by the electrically transmitted signals at these loudspeakers arriving a few milliseconds before the natural air-borne sound from the stage.

The concept of delaying sound was entirely new to us, but the man from Philips suggested that their new 'ambiophonic' unit, developed for recording studios, might correct this pre-echo problem. It was based upon a revolving drum (like a solid loop of tape) with a fixed record head and several playback heads that could be repositioned around the drum to adjust the echo timing. Unfortunately, the price of this machine was prohibitive and we had to seek a different solution. The first digital time delay unit had yet to come on to the market so, in the meantime, we needed to think of something else. The Philips man then came up with a crude but cost effective scheme which just might work. He placed two very directional 'column' microphones (never seen before or since) on the front of the first balcony, pointing at loudspeakers left and right on the proscenium. The signal from these was fed through separate amplifiers to loudspeakers at the sides of the auditorium. This meant that the microphones were 'hearing' sound from the stage at roughly the same time as the audience at the front of the balconies. The quality of sound from the side-fill loudspeakers was not very good, but they were only there to provide a slight boost. The important result was that speech intelligibility was markedly improved. Similar equipment was installed for the next two musicals at the Palace Theatre for which my colleague, Antony Horder, was responsible.

By now, with fifteen major musicals under our belt and numerous straight plays with complicated sound tracks, we found ourselves with a team of sound operators. Our star at the controls, Claire Laver, would set up each show and remain with it until another production came along, at which point it was handed over to someone new. By and large, producers of musicals had come to accept that control equipment in the auditorium was necessary – so long as it was located in a side box or tucked away in a far corner.

Microphones pointing at the floor

BY THE TIME WE came to do the next show at Drury Lane, THE GREAT WALTZ (1970), I had been told by Richard Pilbrow about the soundman (Jack Mann) on Broadway who had his foot-mikes on little stands pointing at the floor. Apparently, the theory was that when a microphone is raised in the air, the direct sound from the actor combined with reflections from the stage floor makes for a less clean sound. The short time-lag will mean that certain frequencies will arrive at the microphone out of phase with the original. This produces a cancelling effect with those frequencies. If the microphone head is near the floor, the direct and reflected sound waves will arrive at almost the same instant, producing a tighter sound with no audible cancellation effect.

We did not really believe all this. Logic had always dictated that the microphones should be as high as possible and pointed up at the actors. Many an argument about the ugly microphones sticking up along the front of the stage ended with the producer saying: *"Surely it would make no difference if you dropped them a few inches".* The usual compromise was a 6-inch (15cm) stand on a foam rubber pad. Notwithstanding our scepticism, we decided to carry out a test. Some of the microphones were installed on stands in the traditional way, and others were mounted on just the stand bases pointing down at the floor. We then retired to the auditorium whilst a colleague walked around the stage reading a newspaper and the operator switched from one set to the other. There was no question – it worked. Even the footsteps were not a problem once we had insulated the stand bases from the floor with foam rubber. So we used them like that for the production and never went back to our bad old ways.

To make these new float-mikes even less obtrusive, we commissioned some foam rubber mounts, long enough to take the body of an AKG C451 microphone, with the capsule protruding from one end on a swivel adaptor pointing down at 45°. As these were long and thin and grey, someone remarked that they looked like mice – and that is what they came to be called.

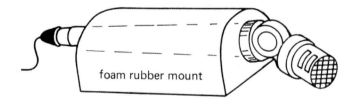

Our "mouse" float mount for AKG C451 microphone.

foam rubber mount

By pure chance, Electrovoice subsequently brought out a similar foot-mike housing for one of their microphones and these were also called mice. They were larger and wider than ours and when I eventually saw one, I thought it looked more like a rat!

For once, the theatre was ahead of the audio industry. It was not until 1980 that Crown introduced a small microphone mounted on a metal plate especially designed to sit on a flat surface and collect direct and reflected sound waves coherently. This was the Boundary or Pressure Zone Microphone (PZM).

12 PERMANENT INSTALLATIONS

Under the leadership of Bill Walton during the early 1960s, Stagesound with their tape machines had gone from strength to strength. Not only were they the major players in the UK rental market but they had a burgeoning business designing and selling permanent installations – something Jack Bishop had always refused to do. A typical example from the period was for the Chichester Festival theatre which opened in 1962. Here, they installed a sound console incorporating two disc turntables, two tape machines, loudspeaker switching and a few basic microphone channels. The theatre design was unusual for those days, having the audience on three sides of a thrust stage and, since there were no wings, the control room for lighting, sound and stage management was at the back of the auditorium. The sound equipment was placed so that the operator worked with his or her back to the stage. Very convenient. Moreover, the booth had no opening window and the only monitoring of the live performance was via a small show-relay speaker provided for the stage manager.

The artistic director of the theatre was Sir Laurence Olivier, deemed by many to be the greatest stage actor of the age, and he was using the Summer seasons at Chichester as a rehearsal for taking over the National Theatre of Great Britain, then in the design stage. Bill Walton told me how Sir Laurence was concerned about getting the audience into the theatre when many of them would be sauntering around the lawns on a summer's evening enjoying the fresh air. The usual warning bells placed in the bars and foyer would not be adequate. Bill suggested a voice paging system, to include outdoor speakers, operated by the stage manager. Sir Laurence was intrigued, but concerned about the dubious enunciation and vocal quality of some of his backstage staff. When Bill suggested the possibility of recording the announcements, he became really excited.
"We could have an actor record the announcements."
"Certainly, Sir Laurence."
A pause.
"Do you think that I should record the announcements?"
"That would be splendid, sir."
A pause.
"Could we have fanfares?"

This new way of calling an audience into the auditorium turned into a full theatrical production. It started with a grand fanfare followed by the mellifluous tones of the great knight himself: *"Ladies and gentlemen, the performance will commence in just three minutes".* The fanfare at two minutes is slightly more upbeat and the audience is warned with a growing sense of urgency that only two minutes remains. Then comes a strident fanfare and Sir Laurence, now with clipped tones, urges the audience to enter the auditorium at once because there is but one minute before the commencement of the performance. Finally, followed by an abrupt horn call, comes an almost sorrowful voice pleading with anyone who has not entered the auditorium to do so immediately because the performance is about to commence and he is sure that they would not wish to incommode other members of the audience as they take their seats.

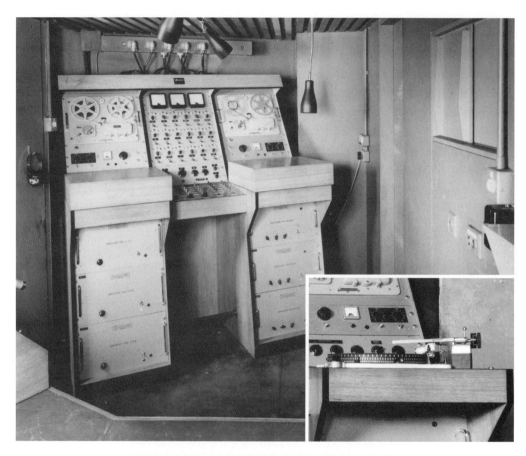

Sound Console at the Chichester Festival Theatre, 1962. Three amplifiers for the stage are in the right hand leg and three amplifiers for paging systems are in the left hand leg. The turntables are housed beneath the tape decks (see inset).

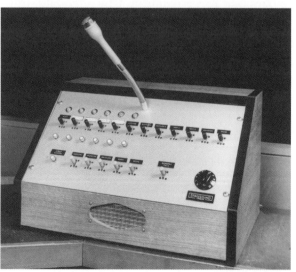

Chichester Festival Theatre. Stage manager's communication system with twelve talkback circuits, six of which have call lights and call light cancel buttons so that the stage manager can switch to listen mode when convenient. Bottom row is paging to five circuits, including dressing rooms, plus a general call switch.

Another prestigious system was installed the following year in London's Royal Opera House, Covent Garden. Phil Leaver had started his career as a 16 year old apprentice at Stagesound and spent several years in their workshops before being offered the job as the first ever sound engineer to be employed by the Opera House. As this was a permanent job as a technician, he became part of the electrical department working for chief electrician, Bill McGee. The big shock came when Bill showed him where they proposed to locate the "sound room". Phil was horrified. It was situated under stage where there was no chance of seeing the performance or hearing what anything sounded like in the auditorium. Nevertheless, this is where the system for sound effects and amplifying off-stage choruses was installed. During the next three years, the use of sound at the Opera House gradually increased and the job became more onerous. Phil was not allowed an assistant and could not persuade his bosses of the necessity to relocate the sound control. Eventually, the frustration caused him to hand in his notice. He was replaced by another Stagesound engineer and another Phil, Phil Clifford, who was to work there for nearly six years before masterminding a new audio system with a mixing position in the auditorium.

In 1971, Phil Clifford and his assistant, Andrew Bruce, decided to set up their own company, Autograph Sound Recording, initially aimed at recording opera sound and music concerts. When they landed a contract to install a sound system in a London church, Phil left the Opera House to run the business and Andrew stayed on as head of sound. More contracts materialized for Autograph and three months later Andrew left Covent Garden, to be replaced by Phil Leaver returning to his old job. Five years after that, Phil Leaver joined the, by now, very successful company to become a director in charge of sales and administration. But more of this later.

For the opening of the National Theatre Company in 1963, the Old Vic was to have a major lighting and sound re-fit and Theatre Projects was engaged to carry out this work. Sir Laurence Olivier told me that for his first production, HAMLET starring Peter O'Toole, one of the effects he required was for the ghostly voice of Hamlet's father to move rapidly around the stage from speaker to speaker. This was not feasible with the standard equipment available. I described the BLITZ! mixing console and we agreed that something along these lines was required. He also hoped that we could provide the wonderful sound quality he had experienced in New York from large loudspeakers high up over the proscenium. I pointed out that these were almost certainly manufactured by Altec or JBL and they were very expensive by British standards. I knew of nothing equivalent in this country, so could we afford to ship some over? Not wishing to be concerned with details of finance, he directed me towards his general manager – which is where reality set in. Although the entire theatre was to be given a face-lift, the stage was being rebuilt to include a revolve and traps, and there was to be an expensive new lighting switchboard with many new lanterns, the total budget for the sound system was a pitiful £2,000.

Nothing daunted, I was determined that the National Theatre Company should have a control room out front with an opening window. The general manager did not wish to lose any seats in the auditorium and my argument for seeing and hearing the performance was weakened when I was unable to cite a single theatre in the country that had this facility. Fortunately, there was absolutely no room backstage, but the best offer was a space in the follow-spot booth at the rear of the upper tier of the auditorium. This was a large echoey space with thick concrete walls and tiny windows with two layers of thick glass. I refused to even consider this option and, after a great deal of negotiation, was finally allotted just three seats to one side at the rear of the stalls, partially obscured by a pillar.

For this incredibly narrow space, I planned a slim console based upon the Blitz! mixer. Built and installed by Stagesound, it had the addition of six microphone channels, loudspeaker and microphone patching, and stage manager intercom. At the far end of the 'room', three tape machines were mounted in a rack. The amplifiers were installed in a cupboard which happened to be nearby. The window opened and, leaning forward, one was actually in the auditorium. The Stagesound invoice for all of this totalled £1,758.14. With very little left in the budget for loudspeakers, I bought some 15-inch (38cm) Goodmans monitor loudspeakers and commissioned a carpenter to construct cabinets. Not exactly what Sir Laurence Olivier had in mind, but superior to the loudspeakers found in most theatres.

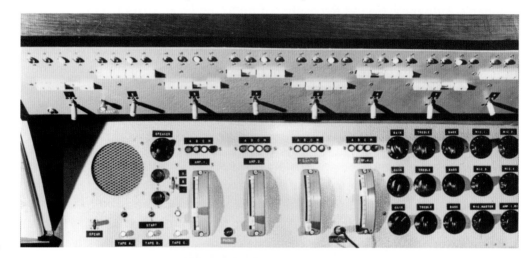

Sound effects console built for the National Theatre Company at the Old Vic – 1963.

The author at the controls.

Having created a control room with what looked like complicated equipment, the need for a permanent sound operator was evident and, similar to the Royal Shakespeare Company, the post was filled by a female assistant stage manager. As the sound for Hamlet was quite complicated, I was at the controls for the opening and handed it over after a week or so. The first performance of the National Theatre Company at the Old Vic was in October 1963, and they were to perform there for more than ten years before the National Theatre building was finally completed.

Sound consultants in the UK

THE ECONOMY OF THE UK had recovered during the twenty years or so since the end of the Second World War, and a wave of civic and university theatre building was sweeping Great Britain. Richard Pilbrow had become renowned as a lighting designer and I had received credits on many West End shows for sound. Because of this, in 1965, Theatre Projects began to be asked to advise on lighting, sound and communications for new theatres. It soon became evident that a separate company was needed to cope with this work. Theatre Projects Consultants Limited was appointed by the National Theatre and, later, the Barbican Arts Centre (new London home for the Royal Shakespeare Company) as consultants for stage planning, stage machinery, lighting, sound and communications. By this time, we had a team of specialists including mechanical and electrical engineers. Having met a sound consultant in Las Vegas and not been impressed, I now found that I was one. Fortunately, having no training in electronics, I could specify what was required from a theatrical point of view and this was translated into a technical format by someone qualified to do so.

Control Room at rear
of the auditorium in
the Stadttheater
Ingolstadt circa 1960.

As a learning exercise, I visited the Philips base in Eindhoven, Holland with two colleagues interested in stage machinery, and went on to tour round Germany. I was surprised to discover that the German civic theatres all had spacious sound control rooms at the rear of the auditorium with studio-quality equipment supplied by companies like Studer, Telefunken, AEG, Siemens and Philips. We were told by the 'Tonmeister' (Head of Sound) at one of the theatres how, at the end of the Second World War, the German government had decided to re-establish their cultural organisations as a matter of priority. Theatres, concert halls and opera houses throughout the country were rebuilt and refurbished and allotted very substantial operating subsidies. Consequently, they had sophisticated mixing desks long before they appeared in the UK and America.

Although things have changed since, being a Tonmeister was a prestigious, well-paid post on a par with the Lichtungmeister (Head of Lighting) and the Buhnenmeister (in charge of the stage) and, like the other department heads, he was a director of operations controlling his own staff. His responsibilities included liaising with the artistic director of a production, specifying the equipment and organizing any recording sessions. Normally, he was at the controls during a performance. To qualify as a Tonmeister, one had to obtain a university degree encompassing both electronics and music. Quite sensibly, an ability to read a musical score was thought to be necessary.

By the 1990s, the generous subsidies to civic theatres and opera houses had been drastically reduced. With a decrease in funding and an increase in the sophistication of theatre technology, theatre staff had to become more flexible and more efficient. The strict demarcation between departments broke down. A new qualification of 'Event Technician' was introduced to cover all aspects of lighting, sound and stagecraft for theatre, film, radio and television. With this grounding, students were free to specialise in the discipline to which they felt most suited. Since the acceptance of the event technician, retiring Tonmeisters have been replaced by this new breed of technician. They are cheaper to employ and more productive, since they are willing to pick up cables and get their hands dirty.

To specify equipment to anything approaching the standard of the heavily subsidized German theatres was out of the question, but it might be possible to introduce control rooms into the British theatre and, unlike the ones we saw in Germany, ours would have large opening windows. The spin-off from this decision, which I did not immediately appreciate, was that with the audio equipment installed in a separate working area, the theatre would have to employ someone to run it. So here were two major breakthroughs: properly equipped sound control rooms with opening windows (the next best thing to actually being within the acoustic of the auditorium) and theatres advertising the post of Head of Sound. With a kit of microphones, tape recorders and gram decks, theatres began to create their own sound tracks in-house. This was slightly shooting ourselves in the foot, as our studio at Theatre Projects was doing a brisk trade in supplying tailor-made sound effects to theatres all around the country.

Affordable mixing desks would not come on the market until 1972, so for the first seven years working as consultants, we specified what we wanted and could afford, then invited audio equipment manufacturers to tender for the contracts. The tendency was to invent a different console for each project, endeavouring to improve on the last one and tailor the facilities for the particular theatre. Consequently, a succession of bulky prototype mixing consoles appeared in new theatres all around Great Britain.

One of the first of these to be completed was the Thorndyke Theatre in Leatherhead (1969), just outside London. The budget for the whole building was around £400,000 including £20,000 for the lighting equipment, but only £5,000 for sound and communications. This included a purpose-built mixing console and stage manager control desk, plus tape and gram decks, amplifiers, loudspeakers, dressing room system, wiring and installation.

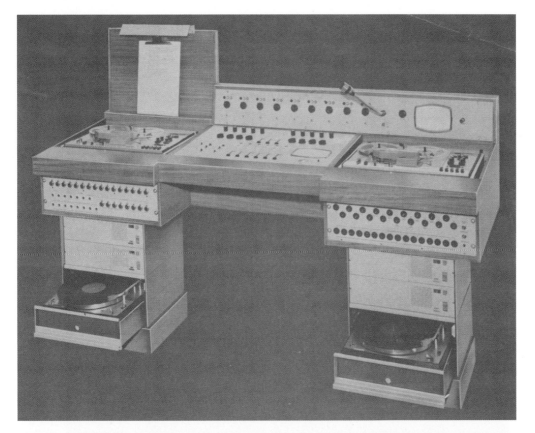

Purpose-built console for the Thorndyke Theatre, Leatherhead built by Philips (1969).

Purpose-built sound desk for the Crucible Theatre, Sheffield (1970). Tape starts and input faders bottom left. Faders for amplifiers are in the centre, the four on the left control installed loudspeakers above and around the thrust stage and the three on the right with loudspeaker switching above are for effects loudspeakers.
Also included is a microphone mixer (right), stage manager intercom and a PA microphone to talk to stage in rehearsals.
Photo: Theatre Projects Consultants

Mixing console for
the Birmingham
Repertory Theatre
built by Philips (1971).
Microphone mixing
far left, input and
output section in the
centre, loudspeaker
switching
and 'panorama'
wheel on the right.
High level and low
level patchfields
below left and right.
*Photo: Theatre
Projects Consultants*

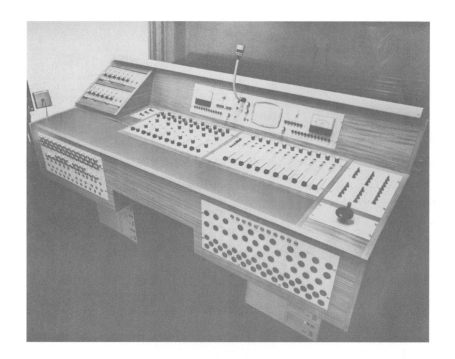

Console at the
Sherman Theatre,
Cardiff built by
Electrosonic, 1975.
*Photo: Theatre
Projects Consultants*

Console for the
rebuilt Lyric Theatre
Hammersmith by
Cambridge
Electronic Workshop
(1980).
*Photo: Theatre
Projects Consultants*

Matrix mixers in the USA

IN 1968, DAN DUGAN designed a revolutionary sound effects console for the Geary Theatre at the American Conservatory Theater (ACT) in San Francisco, subsequently reported at an AES (Audio Engineering Society) convention. Using plug-in modules from a company called Langevin who manufactured radio broadcast mixers, it was a line level mixer for three stereo tape decks with matrix routing to ten loudspeaker channels. Each tape deck had left/right channel and master level controls with ten left/off/right toggle switches to select tracks to loudspeaker channels (each channel having a pre-set level fader). The output panel had ten sets of controls for ten amplifier/loudspeaker combinations. Each set including rotary sensitivity, bass and treble controls plus a linear gain control.

Dan Dugan,
circa 2005.

Sound operator
Bill Freeman at the
world's first three-
deck preset sound
console designed and
built by Dan Dugan
for the American
Conservatory
Theater in 1968.

Charlie Richmond, who was later to set up a company manufacturing mixers on a similar principle, said that this was the first true matrix console. As a young theatre enthusiast, Charlie was a regular visitor to the Conservatory Theater in San Francisco where the astonishing use of sound on some of the productions made him want to discover how it was achieved. He met the innovative soundman, Dan Dugan, who showed him the equipment he had built, explaining that he was lucky enough to have an artistic director who actively encouraged his audio experiments. Unusually for that time, it was decided to give Dan Dugan a programme credit and the production stage manager, Dorothy Fowler, thought up the title of sound designer. This was possibly the first such credit because, although I had been calling myself a sound designer for a number of years, I was usually on the poster as "Sound by..."

Charlie Richmond
– 2002.

When Charlie was offered a job as sound operator at ACT, he quit university and began his theatrical career. Ten years later, Dan Dugan's console was replaced by a matrix mixer from Richmond Sound Design. A demonstration model was brought by Charlie to the UK and I remember thinking that with twelve inputs routing to any combination of twenty-four loudspeaker outputs, all with level controls, this provided the kind of flexibility we had been looking for. There were two problems: the price was high for the UK market and there were so many faders and controls and possibilities of error that it might be beyond the average technician to operate. What was needed was a computer. But when at last Richmond Sound Design brought out their computerized version in the mid 1980s, a number of major manufacturers were beginning to go this route and the competition became too great. Around a hundred Richmond memory mixers were sold into the theatre, but they were much more successful in the burgeoning theme park business. Disney, among others, bought a lot of systems for running pre-recorded shows. Meanwhile, the company diversified into manufacturing standard 8/2 portable mixers, similar to the early Allen and Heath models in the UK, for sale in music stores.

Matrix mixers in the UK

IN 1977, BRITISH SOUNDMAN, John Leonard, was designing a matrix mixer, very similar in concept to the one produced by Richmond Sound Design. John Leonard's interest in sound began as a student at the Bristol Old Vic Theatre School and led to a job as technical assistant stage manager and then head of sound in the Bristol Old Vic theatre itself. But it was not until he had become the theatre's production manager that ideas for a new form of mixing desk began to germinate. His successor as head of sound had some thoughts and together they drew up plans for a 10 x 10 'matrix' mixer with each input module routing to any combination of ten outputs, and the ten outputs, each with a level control, connected to an amplifier and loudspeaker. This provided the flexibility to route sound effects proportionately to any combination of ten loudspeakers.

Helios Electronics, a forward-looking mixer manufacturer, was asked for a price to build the unit, but the costs involved in creating such a prototype were prohibitive. They did, however, provide suitable cards and components for self build. So, during the summer of 1977, a new theatre sound effects mixer evolved in the workshops at the Bristol Old Vic. The final design included a patchable 'quad pot' and on-board communications and cuelights.

The engineers from Helios Electronics were so impressed with the unit that they proposed building their own version based upon the design – for which they would pay a small royalty. Called the Libra mixing desk, it won the "Hook-clamp Award" given each year by the Association of British Theatre Technicians for the best technical contribution to the theatre.

The mixer was priced at around £3,000 which in recording studio and broadcasting terms was not expensive. However, the standard mixers (Alice Stancoil, Allen and Heath, etc.) being used in the British theatre at that time were selling for around £1,000. Consequently, sales were slow. After only some twenty units had been sold, Helios Electronics, suffering from a colossal bad debt, were forced to go into liquidation. Thus ended the short life of the Libra mixer. The rights to the mixer were sold and a cheaper version was produced. Unfortunately, apart from the matrix, most of the features which made the desk so special were omitted.

John Leonard – 2002.

In 1980, John became head of sound for the Royal Shakespeare Company, and it was here that he devised his memory routing system with 4 inputs into 10 outputs controlled by a simple home computer. With only 256K of memory, it could store five separate shows each with up to 99 cues. DAISY (Digital Analogue Interface System), complete with on-screen display and mimic, was plugged into the outputs of a standard Alice 10/4 mixer. Simple and effective, and costing just a few hundred pounds, it was the first successful memory routing system designed for theatre sound in the UK.

Cueing and communication systems in the UK

IN 1969, I CHAIRED a public meeting of the Association of British Theatre Technicians Sound Committee to introduce the publication of a document we had prepared specifying basic requirements for permanent sound installations in new theatres and recommending standards for wiring and connectors. It also included proposals for the layout and colour-coding of controls for stage manager cueing systems.

There was also mention of the fact that we had finally persuaded the GPO (General Post Office) to allot three frequencies for radio-microphones in addition to the ones already in use.

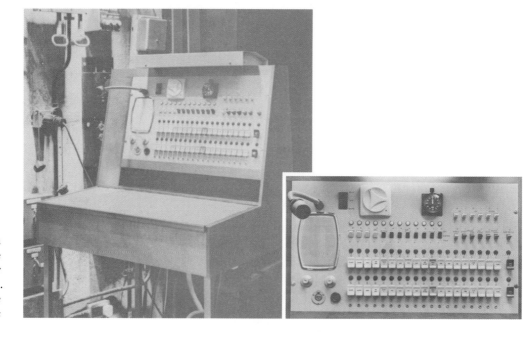

Birmingham
Repertory Theatre
stage manager
desk (1971).
*Photo: Theatre
Projects Consultants*

As theatre consultants, we at Theatre Projects were in a position to implement these ABTT standards and as rival consultancy practices came into being, the recommendations became generally accepted in the industry.

Stage manager desk
for Aberystwyth
Arts Centre (1972).
*Photo: Theatre
Projects Consultants*

One of the innovations in the Thorndyke Theatre Leatherhead came about because lighting designers were always complaining that their talkback units (basically office intercoms) were not hands-free. They wanted to converse with the switchboard, follow-spots and stage manager without having to push buttons. Bill Walton of Stagesound developed several systems for his lighting designer friend, Joe Davis, but with an open microphone near a live loudspeaker, the volume level was never sufficient before it squealed with feedback. The answer, of course, was to use headsets. Joe Davis refused point blank and my colleague Richard Pilbrow, equally adamant, complained that one could not possibly wear headsets for lighting sessions that often went on all through the night – and, anyhow, the cable would be too annoying. This was also the opinion of the team of young lighting designers that Richard had assembled within Theatre Projects. Except for one. Born in New York, David Hersey had worked in the American theatre where technicians used headsets as a matter of course. The Clear-Com company, founded in San Francisco, claim to have invented the first ever belt pack for headset communications in 1968. David did not see the problem. So, at his request, we purchased some cheap telephone operator single-earpiece headphones. Joined together by twin flex and powered by a battery, the system worked perfectly and, gradually, became accepted by the other lighting designers.

When we specified the cueing and communications for the Thorndyke Theatre, I suggested the inclusion of a similar headset intercom. Both the artistic director and the technical director of the theatre declared this to be a waste of money as it would never be used. *"Shows were controlled by cuelights and the traditional talk-back was sufficient for technical communications during rehearsals. It would be chaos if everyone was able to chat away on an open system during a show. The stage manager had to be in absolute control."* This argument did not make sense to the new managing director of Theatre Projects Consultants, Richard Brett, who had come from the Installation and Planning Department of BBC Television. In a television studio, all the technical staff wore headsets and, because they were disciplined, it worked perfectly. He put it to the client that a power supply and the installation of a few jack sockets around the stage and in the control rooms would cost peanuts. They need not use it, but it might possibly be useful in the future. To identify it from the standard two-way talkback, Richard Brett coined the phrase 'Ring Intercom' (the system comprised a number of jack sockets around the building connected by a ring of cable). The satisfying end to the story is that when we returned to the theatre several months later to evaluate the success or otherwise of our endeavours, the stage management had taken to the ring intercom and it was in constant use.

In the mid 1970s, I worked with our manufacturing department to develop a robust intercom, not dissimilar to the Clear-Com system, for temporary and permanent installations. We came up with a dual-channel version of the ring intercom. In 1986, the design was acquired by the British company, Canford Audio Plc, and at the time of writing is still distributed under the name of Techpro in the UK and Tecpro in the USA.

For the National Theatre of Great Britain, the ring intercom we specified allowed substations to listen, via volume controls, to a mix of the stage manager channel and any one of three other technical channels selected by a rotary switch. Each substation had a two-position switch to connect the microphone either to the stage manager or to the technical channel. The stage manager and the production desk (placed in the auditorium for rehearsals) were able to monitor all the channels should they so wish and, for cueing purposes or emergencies, the stage manager had a master button to 'crash call' the entire system. There was also a provision for connecting a radio transmitter to any of the channels for roving technicians to receive instructions via portable receivers.

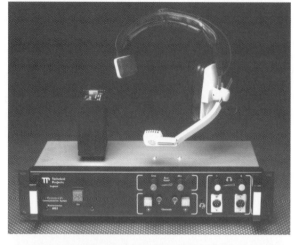

Dual-channel Ring Intercom master and belt-pack manufactured by Theatre Projects, circa 1976.

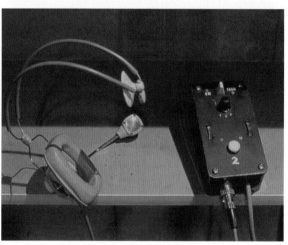

Ring Intercom belt-pack for the National Theatre of Great Britain.

The other innovation that Richard Brett brought from the BBC studios was what he called the General Facilities Panels (GFPs). Having been appalled by the hotchpotch of electrical boxes of all shapes and sizes attached to conduits and trunking (cableways) cluttering the walls of the prompt corner and running around the stages of existing theatres, he wanted to do something about it. First attempts at rationalization met with resistance because while electrical contractors installed the general lighting and power requirements, the specialist equipment suppliers liked to be in charge of their own wiring installations. It would not be unusual for the backstage domestic lighting, the general power points and the safety lighting to be installed by more than one contractor. Wiring for the stage lighting would be specified by the specialist lighting company and often installed by their own contractor. Similarly, the microphone and loudspeaker wiring was a separate installation specified by the sound contractor; and if the communications or cuelight systems came from different companies, yet more electrical installers could be involved. It was a minefield – but with an electrical consultant within the company, it proved possible to specify all the electrical work and put it out to bid for a single contract. It was then feasible to install General Facilities Panels which brought together what could be six or eight services into one box. The GFP contained three electrically screened compartments for mains power, high level signals and low level signals and were placed at strategic points around the stage and technical areas. Limited Facilities Panels (LFPs) were sited where only some of the services, e.g. cuelights or loudspeaker outlets, were required.

General Facilities Panel with protective cable rail and three colour-coded compartments:

1. Mains power.

2. Microphones, CCTV cameras and monitors.

3. Loudspeakers, cuelights, and communications.

National Theatre of Great Britain – 1976

The mixing consoles for the two main auditoria of the National Theatre had to be specified and budgeted, as often happens with large public building projects, some eight years before the equipment was installed. One could only guess what technical developments might occur in the meantime and make assumptions. When the National Theatre Building Committee saw our original budget for mixing consoles, they were horrified. We pointed out that these were based on recording studio mixers (hand-wired in those days) with the addition of complicated loudspeaker switching for theatre use. One incensed committee member demanded to know why it was necessary to have a studio quality mixer with hundreds of knobs in order to play a baby crying effect. Would the audience be able to tell? The argument was only won after they were shown pictures of current installations in the German theatres and reminded that it was our job to ensure that the flagship theatre of Great Britain was equipped with the latest technology.

The Lyttleton Theatre
sound control room
– National Theatre
of Great Britain.

My request for large control rooms with motorized windows was accepted by the architect and technical committee, but my proposal for a recording studio within the complex was turned down because recorded music in a theatrical production was prohibited by the Musicians' Union. I pointed out that the sound department (for there would have to be one) would need a sound-proof space to record voices and special effects and music could be used in a theatrical production if musicians, playing live, were piped through to the stage via the control room. Eventually, the architect agreed to include about half the space requested as an unfinished storage area, possibly to be converted into a studio at some future date. Twenty seven years after the theatre opened, the technical manager of sound, Rob Barnard, was finally given a budget to convert the store room into a studio. At last, the cableways to the theatre control rooms we had specified all those years before came into their own.

The author and
National Theatre
Head of Sound,
Rob Barnard, in the
new studio control
room, 2003.

In the case of the Barbican Theatre, which was to become the London home of the Royal Shakespeare Company, the time-lapse between specifications and manufacture was far worse than the National Theatre because the building was severely delayed. It did not open until some thirteen years after we started work on the specifications. Imagine the advances in audio technology during that period and the frustration of not being able to scrap the original concept altogether and start afresh.

Two years before the opening, John Leonard was appointed head of sound for the Royal Shakespeare Company where he developed his DAISY memory routing system and successfully ran complicated shows with a standard mixing desk and a home computer. Not surprisingly, he had strong opinions regarding the proposed installation at the Barbican and thought, quite rightly, that certain elements were out of date. Unfortunately, budgets and designs had all been approved by John's predecessors and contracts placed. Any changes required prior client approval, which was not usually forthcoming. The client for the building was the City of London and they were resistant to incurring additional costs for the preparation of new designs and quotations. Despite this restriction, we were able to increase the size of the mixing desk and add a memory routing system to cope with the 30 inputs, 10 sub-masters and two 26-output presets – nearly a thousand switch functions.

The contracts for both lighting and sound at the Barbican Theatre were awarded to Rank Strand Electric, the largest theatre lighting company in the world. In 1980, they had set up a company, Strand Sound, having acquired the designs for modular mixers originally developed by the Theatre Projects Research and Development team. The memory routing system for the Barbican console was based on the one used in their 'Duette' lighting board; and although the concept was good, the failure rate during operation was a cause for concern. It became a really serious problem when, after a few months, Rank Strand Electric decided to close their sound company leaving the Barbican sound staff without any maintenance back-up.

Sound control room
at the Barbican
Theatre, 1982.

When the Barbican Theatre finally opened in 1982, it had the last of the megalithic one-off sound control boards built into large pieces of immovable furniture. With the standard mixing desks now available, it had become quite normal to operate heavy sound shows from the auditorium, but there was no way that the Barbican console could be moved. John Leonard began to think about the possibility of having a digital remote control unit with faders which could be assigned to channels, groups of channels, or other control functions in the main mixer. Unfortunately, no money was available from the Royal Shakespeare Company for development, so he tried to raise interest in the industry. At a meeting of the Association of British Theatre Technicians in 1984, he read a paper putting forward his ideas for a digitally controlled mixer. His proposals were met with general scepticism and even laughter. It was, he said, a most embarrassing and unpleasant experience. Only two years later, the British company, Trident, produced their DIAN (digital/analogue) fully assignable desk.

The original Barbican mixing desk was replaced in 1987, by a standard mixer from Cadac.

Architectural mapping and speech intelligibility

DESIGNING AND INSTALLING a sound system became less hit and miss when, during the early 1980s, processes became available for drawing a plan of the auditorium as seen from the chosen position for a loudspeaker.

According to the excellent book, "Sound System Engineering" by Don and Carolyn Davis, the idea of architectural mapping for audio use was first given an airing in a paper by American sound consultant Edward Seeley in 1977. The process was to convert the ground plan dimensions of an audience area into an equivalent set of parameters describing the same area as viewed from a chosen location for a loudspeaker array. The calculations are then transposed to a suitably calibrated grid showing angles (in degrees) and distances (in dB) from the array to all points of the auditorium floor. Tom McCarthy delivered a paper to the AES in 1978 describing how he had used this architectural mapping on real projects. Having estimated the coverage patterns for loudspeakers he regularly used, he overlaid drawings of these patterns on to calibrated grids in order to discover the right combination of loudspeakers to cover an auditorium.

The Bose corporation was the first manufacturer to publish loudspeaker overlays in their catalogue and Altec went into the process seriously in 1982, providing specifications and coverage patterns for all their loudspeakers. One of my first experiences using mapping and overlays was for the Calgary Center for the Performing Arts in Canada where the concert hall had a massive loudspeaker array built into a moving piece of architecture. It was normally suspended above the motorized acoustic canopy but, when required, could drop through the canopy to its operating position. Initially, it was quite complicated working out the formulae for angles, distances and sound pressure levels, but companies like Altec and JBL soon brought out computer programmes to make life easier.

Around the same time, a great deal of work was carried out into measuring the acoustic properties of an auditorium with any anomalies that might be present. The ambient noise level in a room, the relationship of direct to reverberant sound levels, and the reverberation time all affect the intelligibility of speech. In particular, once the measurements could show where there were losses of consonants in speech, vital to comprehension, the sound engineer was able to choose loudspeakers and provide equalizers and other processing equipment to counteract this effect. The audio design process was fast becoming more professional and more predictable.

13 THE MIXING CONSOLE

In the early 1970s, the British companies Alice, Soundcraft and Midas started manufacturing professional mixing desks that were suitable for the theatre. Based on printed circuit boards with extensive use of integrated circuits, they were substantially cheaper than the hand-wired mixing consoles manufactured for broadcast and recording studios. Another British company, Allen and Heath, introduced a cheaper range of mixers for the music shops. About the same time, a similar low budget mixer, the Japanese Tascam M-10, was introduced in New York. In 1973, aimed at the growing market in pop concert tours, the Soundcraft Series 1 was the first mixing console to come in a flightcase.

The first professional mixing desk to be used for a West End musical was in 1972 for Stephen Sondheim's COMPANY. The 14 input stereo desk was manufactured by a British company called Alice Stancoil.

Broadway did not really embrace the mixing desk until the Yamaha consoles became established. Introduced in 1972, the PM200 had 8 inputs and 2 outputs. Altec launched their Model 1220 control console in 1974, but it was the YAMAHA PM1000 (16 inputs, 4 outputs with a 4 x 8 matrix) in the same year that became the most popular reinforcement console in the American theatre. This was followed by the bigger PM2000-24 in 1978 and the PM2000-32 in 1981.

The first fully modular mixing desks for the theatre were designed and built back in 1973 for the Theatre Projects rental department by the in-house design team under Sam Wise. At the time, the only other cost-effective consoles available had the controls on a solid top plate with all the circuit boards underneath. They were modular inside, but not fully modular like our "Theatre" mixer. This had input modules with mic/line input sensitivity, treble, mid and bass equalization, two auxiliary sends, output routing buttons, pan control, PFL and channel fader. The mixer frames could be constructed for any number of inputs and outputs.

Modular 8-4 'Theatre' mixer with 4-8 loudspeaker matrix designed and manufactured by Theatre Projects, 1973.

Soon the Theatre Projects hire department required something more sophisticated for the larger musicals and trade shows, and the 'Concert' console was designed. A number were sold to theatres for permanent installations, including the Talk of the Town in London, the O'Keefe Centre in Toronto, the Ciudad de Mexico and the Teatro San Rafael in Mexico City, and two more for theatres in Edmonton, Ontario.

In order to exploit the potential of these mixers, a deal was struck in 1980 with Rank Strand Electric. The intention was for Theatre Projects to carry on designing and Rank Strand Electric would manufacture and market a range of audio equipment to be sold worldwide alongside their lighting systems. Unfortunately, the setting up and launching of the new company, Strand Sound, took so long that before they were ready to take orders, modular consoles were already being produced by established audio specialists.

Although Strand Sound failed, the Theatre Projects team did design and build a one-off special for the film studios at Pinewood, just outside London. This had 60 input channels, 32 output groups and 6 auxiliary sends and was one of the first ever fully-automated film dubbing consoles. It was also the first in the world with an automated panning device for moving the audio signal around any loudspeaker arrangement. The console stayed at Pinewood until 1999 and was used for dubbing many major films, including all the SUPERMAN and several JAMES BOND movies.

The original London production of CATS (1981) designed by Abe Jacob used a 40-channel mixing console made by the British company, Trident. Masque Sound provided the equipment for the Broadway production in 1982, and Jack Shearing recalls that the Trident mixer they shipped over was the first really big studio console that Masque Sound ever used on a musical.

In 1983 the British manufacturer of studio consoles, Cadac, was persuaded to build a mixer for the theatre. When recording engineer Martin Levan was asked to design the sound for LITTLE SHOP OF HORRORS, he specified a studio console which, he insisted, should be installed in a central position in the auditorium. Following the usual argument with the producer about the loss of revenue, it was finally agreed that just five seats could be removed from the rear of the circle. Cadac then set about designing a very narrow mixer to fit into this space.

This was Cadec's first theatre mixing desk. Their second custom-built console was for STARLIGHT EXPRESS in 1984. Martin Levan specified a much more ambitious fifty-four input console to control twenty one wireless microphones, the orchestral amplification and some complicated effects. It was the first desk to have level control of the input channels and a matrix output run by a computer activating VCAs (voltage controlled amplifiers). Each of the orchestra input channels was routed by means of a variable matrix of sixteen rotary gain controls connected to sixteen main outputs feeding a multiple loudspeaker rig. All of the vocal input channels were routed to two sub groups having variable matrix routing to the same sixteen outputs. In addition, there were twelve outputs for surround effects, four quad effects outputs and six auxiliary outputs.

First Cadac theatre
mixing console built
for LITTLE SHOP
OF HORRORS – 1983.
Photograph taken in
the workshop of
Autograph Sound
Limited in 2003.

Martin said that the sub-group VCAs worked well, but computer control of the input level was eventually discarded as it was not accurate enough. Apart from the accuracy problem, it was difficult to see what was happening on the desk because the faders did not move when the computer adjusted the levels. They remained where they were. Manual adjustment could be achieved by pushing the fader up or down, but a line of static faders proved very confusing to operate under live show conditions. Once the inevitable problems with such a new concept had been ironed out, the system worked very successfully.

With the success of these two shows, Cadac was prompted to go into production with their A-Type mixers which became very popular for musicals and live concerts.

With computers and digitization, consoles are now being developed with all the necessary manual controls to hand, but taking up much less space than the colossal analogue mixers. This will please the producers. The difficulty is providing the facility to instantly select and grab the fader or facility you need. In a live theatre situation, you cannot afford to look up menus to find the Equalization page or the Echo Send page.

First mixing desk in a West End musical

HAL PRINCE'S ORIGINAL production of Stephen Sondheim's musical COMPANY opened on Broadway in 1970. At the end of its run in 1972, it became the first American musical to be airlifted across the Atlantic – cast, sets, costumes, *et al* – for a London run. Only the lighting and sound equipment were British.

The cast were scheduled to arrive only three days before the first public preview at Her Majesty's theatre, and this posed problems for the technical team. There would be too little time to get to know the show and sort out any problems.

So with Robert Ornbo, the English lighting designer of the Broadway show, and Tommy Elliot, our production manager, I flew to America on a fact finding mission. Having closed in New York, we caught up with COMPANY in Philadelphia during a short tour.

This was my first meeting with the famous sound designer Jack Mann who, most generously, went out of his way to explain the rigging and running of this complicated show. We also discussed the Bozak column loudspeakers that were an essential part of the 'Jack Mann sound'. I had never before experienced anything sounding so natural and unobtrusive. There was nothing to approach the performance of the Bozak columns in the UK, so I arranged to have eight of them flown over. But having brilliant tools is no good if you do not know how to use them. Jack then gave me a lesson on the placement of these very directional loudspeakers to ensure the right height and the correct angle to spray the audience with sound. By directing the maximum output at the rear of the house, he achieved a remarkably even coverage of the auditorium. The trick was to open some channels on the mixer to get some hiss, then sit at the back of the auditorium with an assistant adjusting the angle and tilt of each column. One could easily hear when the high frequencies were at their strongest. By the same method, the strength of signal across the auditorium could be evened out. It seems ludicrous now but, up until then, we had been placing loudspeakers around the proscenium wherever seemed convenient and pointing them – by eye – in the general direction of the audience.

I used to find it a great help to cup both hands behind the ears when concentrating on hiss levels. It turned out that my colleagues were amused by this and I only discovered that they had a pet name for it when a friend came to meet me in a theatre one day. She was puzzled to see me, hands behind the ears, sidling along the rows of seats, now standing, now crouching, and generally bobbing about from side to side with an intense expression on my face. She asked one of my colleagues what on earth was going on. He replied nonchalantly: "Oh, it's nothing. He is just *doing rabbits*".

The lyrics of COMPANY are very important but are often difficult to get across because of the complexity of the vocal arrangements and the orchestration. Even on the cast album, one has to concentrate to discern some of the words. As personal radio-microphones were not technically reliable enough to use in those days, the main pick-up was from the traditional row of float-microphones (foot mikes) but, because there was a large skeletal set with platforms on several levels, Jack used a set of five suspended EV 644 'shotgun' microphones (developed for the theatre by Electrovoice for long range pick-up).

Although it was not the custom to amplify the orchestra, Stephen Sondheim requested microphones on three instruments so that, for example, in a particular number he could give a slight lift to the clarinet or the flute for a few bars. The other unusual feature of the orchestration was an off-stage vocal chorus. There were two microphones for the four singers who, for some reason, Sondheim called 'The Unseen Singing Minority'. This was the start of studio recording techniques being brought into the theatre.

Electrovoice 644
"Sound Spot".
Photo: Stan Coutant

There was one other microphone placed off-stage for a joke tap dance effect. In one number, every member of the cast had a short tap solo but the actual sound came from a dancer performing in a tray of resin off-stage. The amplified tapping and sliding sound from every performer was really impressive – until it came to the turn of Elaine Stritch. At this point, we turned off all the microphones and she performed the same steps in utter silence – but with the most wonderful look of disbelief on her face.

Jack Mann was mixing the show with a stack of small mixers and, with limited facilities for equalization, it was difficult to obtain a seamless transition from the float-mikes to the very different sounding shotguns. One would also have wished for more control over the frequency response of the orchestra and chorus microphones. Fortunately for us, it so happened that a British company called Alice Stancoil had just started producing affordable stereo mixing desks with slider faders, bass, treble, and mid-frequency controls and input sensitivity adjustment on each channel. COMPANY, therefore, became the first West End musical to have a standard professional mixing desk.

The Americans had always been ahead of the British in loudspeaker technology but, for some reason, they lagged behind in the development of audio mixers. A studio console was used on the show PROMISES PROMISES in New York's Schubert Theatre as far back as 1968, but this was because the composer was Burt Bacharach. Used to creating his music with recording equipment, he arranged for the Regent Sound Studio to install a mixing desk and an EMT echo plate (standard in all the best studios at the time). Otts Munderloh, before he became a sound designer, mixed the show and told me that the plate was too large and difficult to remove at the end of the show, so they left it there. It was used on A CHORUS LINE and is probably still sitting in the theatre basement.

The year before COMPANY opened in London, there was a mixing desk of sorts on the Broadway production of JESUS CHRIST SUPERSTAR, but it was very basic. Imported from Philips in Holland, it had sixteen input channels with faders and bass and treble controls. These were selectable to two outputs, one of which was used for the auditorium loudspeakers and the other for stage monitors. For PIPPIN in the same year, Broadway sound designer, Abe Jacob, had Masque Sound construct a special console made up of little Altec 1604 mixers with a combining network to give him one overall master. When I did the London version of that show the following year, it was our fourth show to be run with an Alice console.

Apart from the mixing desk, COMPANY also became the first West End show to have a studio-quality reverberation unit. The reverberation plates, used extensively in recording studios, were far too large and far too expensive to contemplate, but AKG had brought out their much cheaper BX20 'spring' reverberation system (introduced in 1970). This came in a cabinet measuring about 36 inches (90cm) high and 18 inches (45cm) square. The introduction of a touch of echo on the chorus and the amplified instruments served to soften the unnatural hardness inevitable with close microphones.

The American cast arrived in London and we went straight into three days of technical rehearsals and run-throughs. On the final day, I was astonished to see Jack Mann and his wife, Jean, walking down the stalls towards our control position in a side box. He said that they were on a trip to Europe and thought that they would just pop in and see how things were going. I found out later that the producer/director, Hal Prince, was so concerned about the tricky amplification for his show that he had paid for Jack and his wife to visit London. Jack only had two comments: one, that the stalls speakers needed lifting by a few inches so that the entire cabinet could be seen by every person seated in the back row; and two, that the bass performance of the Bozaks would by improved by increasing the size of the cables.

After the first public preview that night, he said in his typically laid back manner that I was not to worry. He was sure it would be fine by the opening. Jean laughed and said: *"Come on, Jack. You just told me that it sounded as sweet as a nut!"* He laughed and we shook hands. Much to my regret, I did not see him again until I was researching for this book nearly thirty years later.

As a postscript to the show, I was there at one of those incidents during a long and tedious technical rehearsal that find their way into theatre folklore. It was about 2 o'clock in the morning and yet another hold-up because some lights had to be fixed. Everyone was flagging, and Elaine Stritch, who had been stopped in mid number for the umpteenth time, suddenly barked out in that wonderful gravelly voice of hers: *"Will someone tell me who the hell you have to sleep with to get out of this mess?"* Immediately, from the darkness of the auditorium the voice of Stephen Sondheim replied: *"The same person you slept with to get into it!"*

I imagined that COMPANY was a one-off and that there would be very few shows with the budget for American loudspeakers, mixing desks and echo machines. The Bozaks cost around £200 each as opposed to £60 for the Stagesound columns. The investment, and the subsequent hire charge to the producer, was many times more than on any other musical. I was wrong. The improved sound quality was recognized and producers seemed willing to pay for it. All our subsequent shows had mixing desks and we had to acquire several sets of Bozak loudspeakers.

Jesus Christ Superstar

IN THE SAME YEAR that we installed the first mixing desk for COMPANY (1972), I was asked to be sound designer for JESUS CHRIST SUPERSTAR and our second mixing desk was to handle eighty microphones – the largest sound system ever for a musical in Britain. This first big success for composer Andrew Lloyd-Webber and lyricist Tim Rice had a chequered career before arriving in London. Beginning life as a record album, the stage version opened at the Mark Hellinger Theatre on Broadway in October 1971. Abe Jacob, who was finally responsible for the sound, told me that the original designer had a background in concert sound and was engaged because the producer, Robert Stigwood, thought he would be right for his rock 'n' roll style production. The problem was that he had no experience in theatre.

The first big mistake was the choice of loudspeaker. Because the aim was to reproduce the sound of the successful album, they decided to use the biggest and best domestic hi-fi system they could find. This turned out to be the JBL 'Paragon'. It was rumoured that Frank Sinatra had a pair of them, so they must be good.

Benny Goodman
with a JBL Paragon
loudspeaker.
*Photo: Harman
International*

About the size of a large sofa, with a curved front and horns built in to the bass ports at either end, two were mounted at the sides of the proscenium with a third hung centrally overhead. Apparently, the sound quality was good, but if you were fifteen feet away from it, there was nothing there. The next mistake was trying to use wireless microphones supplied by the English company Audio Limited. They had problems with frequency, they had problems with stability, and they had problems with overloading.

They dug themselves into an even deeper hole by covering the orchestra pit with sheets of perspex in an attempt to recreate the sound of the recording studio. The first time they tried it, the musicians could not play because there was no air and the heat was unbearable, so they had to install an air-conditioning system. But such a restricted space with no acoustic treatment does not sound like a recording studio. Consequently, apertures were cut in the perspex to let out some of the natural sound.

The musical director had to be above the sheeting in order to see the stage, so he was encased in a special perspex dome. It must have been a wonderful sight at the beginning of each show to see the conductor, once he had taken his bow, pull a plastic fish bowl over his head. I was told by someone involved with the show that the conductor was so isolated in his bubble that, during rehearsals, he had no idea what was going on. In order to stop the orchestra, the stage manager was forced to stomp across the stage and rap firmly on the plastic bubble to get his attention.

The sound designer left after the second preview and the third preview was cancelled. It was at this point that Abe Jacob was brought in to rescue a potential fiasco.

Abe had originally worked for McCune Sound, an equipment rental company where he met John Meyer, who later set up his own company producing loudspeakers. During the early 1960s, Abe was working on concerts for McCune mainly using Altec mixers and "Voice of the Theatre" loudspeakers. He became involved in the theatre when the famous singing trio, Peter, Paul and Mary, introduced him to the producer of HAIR. The Broadway show was running, but they wanted someone to help with the touring versions. Between setting up tours of HAIR, he continued working for McCune handling concerts for such artists as The Mamas and Papas and Jimmi Hendrix.

Abe Jacob – 2002.

In 1971, he was offered a position to run the Hendrix recording studio facility in New York, Electric Lady Studios. This provided a regular salary for a year or so until he took over the sound design of JESUS CHRIST SUPERSTAR and went on to become a freelance designer.

The first thing Abe Jacob did on SUPERSTAR was to remove the plastic dome so that the musical director could hear what was going on. The orchestra pit covering stayed for a while, but eventually he removed that as well. The JBL 'coffins' were replaced by some smaller three-way loudspeakers which had been developed for McCune by John Meyer. Called the JM3, this was the precursor of the famous Meyer line of speakers.

There was discussion about replacing the British wireless microphones with the American Vega or Swintec, but Abe convinced everyone that, in the three days available before opening night, there was insufficient time to get them built and working. It was therefore agreed to go with wired hand-mikes. The Shure SM58 was the popular hand-held microphone of the time, but Abe opted for a new Neumann microphone with a large windscreen which he described as being something like a hand-grenade. The set designer, Robin Wagner, decided to wrap cord around all the cables so that they looked like vines. The only piece of equipment kept from the original system was the simple Philips mixer with treble and bass on each channel. This was located on a small perch tucked away at the rear of the upper balcony.

The show received mixed reviews and only ran for eighteen months. However, JESUS CHRIST SUPERSTAR was the first Broadway show to have a proper credit for a sound designer on the posters and the title page of the programme along with scenery, costumes and lighting.

John Shearing of Masque Sound recalls an earlier sound designer credit on Broadway, but is not sure if it was on the posters. Apparently, John became friendly with a studio engineer handling the live mix at one of the TONI award ceremonies for which Masque was providing the equipment. Robert Lifton from Regent Sound Studios in New York became interested in the theatre and mixed three shows for Masque. As he did not come from a theatre background, he considered sound to be as important as any other part of the production and he asked for a credit as sound designer. That was in the mid 1960s. John Shearing thinks that Robert Lifton could well have been the first.

Subsequent productions of SUPERSTAR in Australia and Germany suffered from inadequate sound systems, and it was not until a static concert performance in Paris, using close microphones for the entire cast and orchestra, that the writers and producers experienced the kind of sound they were seeking. This made them determined that the London stage production should use wired hand-mikes throughout and have a set designed to restrict the movement of the chorus. The two engineers from a French recording studio who had organized and mixed the concert in Paris agreed to handle the London production but, to the concern of the producers, failed to respond to requests for their technical requirements and failed to appear at scheduled meetings. With only three weeks to go before the first public preview, I was invited to become involved.

Before accepting, I telephone Ted Fletcher at Alice Stancoil to see if he could build us a 100-input mixing desk incorporating sixteen sub-mixers for delivery in under three weeks. There was a gulp – and he went away to think. A few hours later, he called back to say that we were on. Not knowing of any British loudspeakers with sufficient power or performance to handle a large orchestra with electric instruments, I next contacted Altec who promised to have eight "Voice of the Theatre" 1208 systems flown over. A call to the UK agent for AKG confirmed that they were more than happy to provide the range of microphones required totalling, with spares, more than seventy.

In order to contain the action, there was a relatively small central stage with nine microphones available to be picked up by the principles. Behind this main acting area, there was a high rear platform connected to steep ramps running down either side where eighteen microphones were located. These were for the chorus who often appeared up there to comment on the action below. With some off-stage chorus microphones and a few 'specials', we had a total of thirty-two vocal microphones. Another thirty-seven were used for the musicians and there was a direct input from the synthesizer. The main orchestra filled the pit, so the electric guitars and drums were located on one side of the stage and the electric keyboards on the other side. Even so, there was no room for the percussion section and this had to be accommodated on a separate platform off-stage.

Setting for JESUS CHRIST SUPERSTAR at the Palace Theatre in London – 1972. The keyboards were located at the base of the ramp to the left, to the right were the guitars and drums with the percussion section further back beside the ramp. Eight Altec 1208 loudspeakers were mounted either side of the proscenium.

Because of the impossibility of individually controlling all these microphones during a show, I arranged to have sixteen sub-mixers built into the console for groups of chorus microphones and sections of the orchestra; e.g. woodwind, strings, etc. The twenty-six main operating channels were divided into vocals and instruments with separate stereo masters to allow for two operators. The AKG BX20 reverberation unit produced a reverberation time of up to 2.5 seconds, adding depth and sparkle to the overall sound. There were no auxiliary sends or fold-back facilities on the desk because stage monitors were not used in the theatre at this time. The only monitoring consisted of separate amplifiers with microphones and loudspeakers to allow the two sections of the rock group on stage to hear each other. The off-stage percussion also had a speaker and a video monitor to see the conductor.

The author at the vocal end of the SUPERSTAR mixing console. The sub-mix section can be seen at the back.

I was pleased when the musical director insisted that the audience for SUPERSTAR should not be subjected to what he described as *"an aural assault course"* because I wanted to save the power in the system for those moments when the action and the score actually warranted a big sound. For example, when Jesus was singing the final number in Act One, the orchestration ranged from piano and voice with hardly any amplification at all, swelling to a highly amplified voice with the thirty-piece orchestra plus rock group playing full out. The effect was spine-tingling. It is this kind of dynamic range that makes a truly exciting aural experience. If everything is loud from the outset, there is nowhere to go. It soon becomes boring.

The whole idea of amplifying an orchestra was totally new to most of the musicians and I had a surreal exchange with the leader of the violin section. During the first long music rehearsal, every section of the orchestra was asked to play separately so that we could adjust the microphones and set a general balance. We then began to go through the score, stopping occasionally and going back to make improvements to the mix. The microphones for the violins were fixed to metal bars spanning the pit above the musicians and, during the break, I asked the leader if any of the microphones were in the way of their bowing. He said that they were fine, but then rather surprisingly said: *"But they won't be there for the performance, will they?"* I am still not sure what he thought we had been doing all morning.

Despite the competition of a Salvation Army band playing loudly outside the front of the theatre during the show on the first night, and protesters waving banners with slogans such as "Jesus is not Superstar", everything worked brilliantly. We had a slight concern when, at the end of Act One, I noticed the imposing figure of a Bishop wearing dog collar and purple vest making a beeline for our control position at the rear of the circle. Not knowing how he might be reacting to what many thought a blasphemous show, my colleague and I decided to run for it. Unfortunately, we were completely hemmed in by the crush heading for the bar, so all we could do was sit tight and wait. When His Grace finally arrived, he placed one hand firmly on my shoulder and, with the other, made a sweeping gesture at the console. *"You boys,"* he said, pausing for effect, *"are doing a fine job".* With that, he continued his way towards the bar – and we felt blessed. The production was well received by the critics and ran for eight years, becoming the world's longest-running musical at the time.

In this one year, with the introduction of the mixing desk and the use of more expensive loudspeakers, the average investment in a typical sound system had risen from £1,400 to £5,500 – about 400%. SUPERSTAR, being an exception, had cost in the region of £20,000. Six years later, the sound system specified by Abe Jacob and supplied by Autograph Sound for the London production of EVITA was to cost nearly £60,000.

Naturalistic sound

AS I HAVE MENTIONED before, with the exception of a rock show like SUPERSTAR, the aim of the soundman at that time was to amplify the performance *without the public being conscious of microphones.* Even with the uncoloured sound of the Bozak column loudspeakers, this took a great deal of skill, but it also relied heavily upon the cooperation of the musical director. One of my favourite conductors, Gareth Davis, used to say that he would control the orchestra so that all the lyrics from the stage were audible to him. What happened back in the auditorium was entirely my responsibility. Nothing could be fairer than that.

One of the problems of succeeding with a naturalistic reinforcement was that nobody was aware of what you were doing. Directors soon forgot about the shrieks of feedback and audibility problems experienced during early rehearsals, and the producers would come to the dress rehearsal and wonder why they were paying for all that expensive equipment. In order to justify my very modest fee (£100 if one was extremely lucky), I sometimes thought it necessary to employ the ruse of closing the master faders in the middle of a technical rehearsal. When the voices suddenly disappeared behind the orchestra, all eyes would turn to the mixing desk. The surprised expressions confirmed that everyone had forgotten about the sound department. *"Sorry, just a little technical problem."* I would gaily call out. Then, push the faders up again.

Two other examples of the transparent sound of the Bozak loudspeakers comes to mind. Before APPLAUSE opened in London in 1972, I had to demonstrate that the wireless microphone to be used by the star, Lauren Bacall, was reliable. We had only employed radios on two previous shows – with varying success – so Audio Limited had manufactured a special transmitter pack for us that they promised would be more stable. So vital was this to the show that, some weeks before the start of rehearsals, Miss Bacall made a special trip from America to see for herself. The microphone was duly fixed in place and members of her entourage descended into the auditorium to listen. As she began talking, one of the American producers came up to me and complained that the sound system was not switched on. At that very moment, she happened to turn her back and walk upstage. To the gentleman's great surprise, there was no lessening in sound level or clarity. The demonstration was deemed a success.

During the run of APPLAUSE, the wireless system turned out to be 'reasonably' reliable. The only real drama was on the first night. The first half seemed to go very well but when I caught up with the sound operator towards the end of the interval, he said that he thought – but was not sure – that the radio-mike was beginning to break up towards the end of the act. On such an important performance we could not take risks, so I grabbed the spare transmitter-pack and rushed backstage. Realising that the star would almost certainly be in her second act costume by now, and would have to completely undress in order to replace the transmitter, I tactfully suggested that the stage manager should take it to her dressing room. *"You must be joking."* he said. *"You do it".* I did not make it to the dressing room. Processing down a flight of stairs to the stage, was the star with her dresser holding up the train of her ball gown. With many apologies, I explained that the sound operator thought that there *might* have been a problem with the microphone and, *as* it was the first night, I would be *extremely* grateful if she would *consider* using the spare. There was a slight pause while she regarded me with an icy stare; then she turned on her heels and returned to the dressing room. The only remark she made was: *"Tell your soundman he will have to do better in future."* which I thought was perfectly reasonable under the circumstances.

Six years later, when a revival of KISMET had falling box office receipts and the producers hoped to nurse it through a hot summer by reducing the running costs, one of the first things they looked at, of course, was the rental bill for the audio equipment. The musical director disliked microphones on principle and, despite the fact that I had spent many hours of rehearsal time fine-tuning the orchestral balance with the authors, he queried their necessity. It was even suggested that the strong voices we had in the cast probably did not require amplifying at all. It was decided to carry out a test. At the next matinee performance, the musical director, the musical arranger, and co-producer Richard Pilbrow gathered at the rear of the circle. With the sound system switched off, the overture began and the musical director pronounced himself totally happy. The arranger, however, was far from content. *"Can you hear the oboe? Can you hear the harp? We might just as well send them home."* I was asked to have the mikes faded in and, reluctantly, the MD had to concede that, although subtle, it was a much better balance. When the show was under way and the two leads were singing a duet, neither the MD nor Richard could detect any amplification. When I confirmed that the float-mikes were indeed working, they asked for them to be faded out. Richard then turned to me with a look of astonishment as the voices slowly disappeared and said *"My dear chap, I have been working with you for nearly twenty years and, do you know, this is the first time I have really understood what you do!"* I am still not sure how much of a compliment that really was.

14 – EQUALIZERS AND TIME DELAY

Room equalization

Two VERY USEFUL weapons in the armoury of the soundman are the graphic equalizer and the time delay line. Altec developed a graphic equalizer and introduced what they called "Acousta-Voicing" in 1968. This was the forerunner of what later became generally known as 'room equalization'.

Early Altec
Third Octave
Graphic Equalizer.
*Klaus Blasquiz
Collection, Paris*

Every 'room' or auditorium has its own acoustic identity. Within the overall spectrum certain frequencies will be accentuated by reflecting off different types of hard surface and other frequencies will be absorbed. No auditorium is acoustically perfect. Similarly, no audio system has a completely flat frequency response. With pink noise (a broad band 'hiss' containing equal energy per octave) played through the loudspeakers, Acousta-Voicing initially used a sound and vibration analyzer to separately measure each third octave and record the results by hand on to a graph. The peaks were then attenuated at the equalizer and the process repeated until the overall response became relatively flat. The ironing out of any booming and pinging sounds produced by reflections and absorptions within the room, not only improved the sound quality but with the spikes removed, the flatter frequency response allowed for more gain in the system before feedback. The original Altec graphic equalizer was a passive unit which attenuated third octave frequency bands. It did not boost. The aim was to provide subtle corrections without creating phasing problems between the frequency bands.

Before long, the first Real Time Analyzers became available and room equalization was made easier when the result of any adjustments of the equalizer was immediately displayed. A favourite with sound engineers was the Ivie IE-30A, a compact hand-held unit with two memories allowing a reading in one area of the auditorium to be compared with that of another.

As Jack Shearing commented, Acousta-Voicing was the first real tool that could analyze what the sound system was actually doing in an auditorium. Before that, you had to have golden ears.

An example of someone with golden ears was the famous British acoustic consultant, Sandy Brown. He became interested in the subject when, as a musician, he found that the acoustic conditions in the halls and theatres where he was playing varied so incredibly. Many venues were so bad that he decided to set up a company to do something about it. I was told by one of his young assistants that even when the sophisticated analyzing equipment became available, Sandy Brown would first go into a performance space and play his clarinet. He would then report on the deficiencies and tell them where the trouble spots were. Only then were the technicians permitted to go in with their analyzers and confirm his findings.

Another case of ears over technology occurred in 1976 when I was working on a permanent audio system for the O'Keefe Centre in Toronto. Having completed the installation and adjusted the equalizers so that the frequency response from the system was as flat as possible throughout the auditorium, we put the analyzer away and carried out some subjective listening tests with amplified speech and recorded music. By reducing some mid frequencies and adding a little to the high end (all very gentle adjustments), we created what we thought to be a warm and natural sound. The following day, when carrying out an equipment check before the first public performance, we were puzzled to find that the taped music used in our tests was no longer pleasant to the ear. Did this mean that our hearing had been dulled by the end of the previous day and we had got it wrong? All was explained when a well-meaning Canadian sound engineer admitted that he had come in early to experience handling the analyzer and had discovered that the response in the auditorium was not flat. So he thought he would improve it. He was given a slap on the wrist and told that it was important to listen rather than rely entirely upon a piece of test equipment.

I once attended an Altec Acousta-Voicing seminar where the audio consultant, John Eargle, stressed that: *"He who equalizes least, equalizes best!".* The truth of this advice came home to me a few months before the O'Keefe Centre episode during a season at London's Palladium, featuring Julie Andrews and then Bing Crosby. At that time, we were using graphic equalizers but could not afford the exorbitant price of a spectrum analyzer. As had always been the case, it was all done by listening. That is, until the third star in the season, Andy Williams, came along. He had his own soundman and rather than fly in a quantity of large wooden boxes, it was agreed that he could use our mixing desk and rig of Altec loudspeakers. When the soundman arrived, the first thing he did was to produce his analyzer. With great interest, and even greater envy, we watched him change all our equalizer settings, ending up with some dramatic peaks and troughs which were far removed from our gentle curves. To our ears, the result was very hard and strident, but he seemed happy so we left him to it.

Unfortunately, the newspapers the following day were extremely critical of the amplification system at the Palladium. One critic wrote a half page open letter to the producer about the appalling treatment of one of America's finest singing stars. I received outraged telephone calls from the producer's office and the manager of the theatre demanding to know what I was going to do about it. The theatre manager did not seem to comprehend that the solution was not in my hands. He admitted that everyone had been entirely happy with the sound quality for Julie Andrews and Bing Crosby, so I went on to explain how the person in control of the mixing desk had the ability to change the sound quality. It was the same as the man in charge of a lighting board who was able to make the stage look bright or dim and change the colour from warm pink to cold blue. I suggested that he talked to Mr Williams's sound designer. He said that he would certainly do this and concluded the conversation by saying: *"Never do this to me again!"* Sometimes, you just cannot win.

The original Altec equalizers did not boost the frequency bands; they were only designed to attenuate. It was not long, however, before other manufacturers came out with boost and cut devices where the changes to the original sound could be more extreme. These often produced unpleasant phasing effects and, in the hands of an insensitive engineer, the results could be disastrous.

Time delay

As SOON AS DIGITAL technology facilitated the variable delay of audio signals, the soundman could place loudspeakers within the auditorium to enhance those tricky under-balcony areas, while the source still seemed to remain at the stage. Without a time delay, loudspeakers within the auditorium will have a disturbing pre-echo. This is caused by the fact that electrical signals travel much faster than natural air-borne sound. With a time delay set so that the signal arrives at the loudspeaker a few milliseconds *after* the air-borne sound, the effect will be the same as hearing a natural reflection from a surface in the auditorium.

Before the digital devices, there were various experiments using tape. In the early 1970s, Abe Jacob used a continuous loop of tape on a machine with a moveable playback head to adjust the time interval. Sound designer Jack Mann had a special machine made up with four playback heads on sliders that could be moved an inch either way. The American firm of acoustical consultants, Bolt Beranek and Newman, according to an article in the "Theatre Arts Magazine", installed a tape loop device in the Plenary Hall of the United Nations building in 1961. Manufactured by the Audio Instrument Company, it added a short delay to loudspeakers mounted close to the delegates seated under the balcony and out of sight of the main loudspeakers.

By 1969, as previously mentioned, Philips had their 'ambiophonic' unit based upon a revolving drum with a fixed record head and several moveable playback heads, but the first digital delay line, the 'Delta-T 101', was introduced in 1970 by the Lexicon company in America. Other versions soon followed from companies like Eventide and, in the UK, Klark Tecnik.

Abe Jacob first used digital time delay from a company called Gotham for the New York production of A CHORUS LINE in 1975, but when the show came to London, Lexicon units were used. Otts Munderloh mixed the show in New York and recalls how one producer complained that the auditorium in-fill loudspeakers were not on. He was told that they were on, but the time delay was carefully set so that they sounded like natural reflections. The producer's reply was: *"I have paid for the loudspeakers and I want to <u>hear</u> them!"*. Otts suggested that a worthwhile ploy is to install a delay speaker or two at the back of the auditorium pointing behind the seats where the production team stand during previews. If it is not loud there, then you are in trouble. The speakers can be removed, of course, once the show has opened.

My first experience with time delay in a large auditorium was in 1970 when I designed a permanent system for the 3,212-seat O'Keefe Centre in Toronto. To enhance the main proscenium arrays, we installed two rows of loudspeakers set flush into the ceiling above the rear of the balcony and another two rows in the ceiling of the balcony-overhang for the rear orchestra (stalls). The distance from the centre front of the stage to the rear corner of the balcony is approximately 155 feet (47 metres), so we were dealing with a considerable time delay. The settings for the two rows of loudspeakers downstairs were 70 m/s and 96 m/s, and in the balcony they were 90 m/s and 108 m/s. When the system was set correctly, we achieved a gain of 16dB without being aware of the speakers at all. The effect of switching them off was dramatic. It was as though the ceiling had been lowered and the sound source had moved back 20 feet. More importantly, with the distances involved, there was a lack of the higher frequencies from the main speaker system, resulting in a loss of clarity and 'presence'.

In addition to delaying sound to loudspeakers within in the auditorium, digital delay began to be used for the main loudspeakers where there were multiple arrays above and to the sides of the proscenium. However, to accurately synchronize when a sound reaches a section of the auditorium from a number of loudspeakers requires sophisticated measuring equipment.

In the mid to late 1980s, when entire casts began to be wired up with radio systems, another use was found for time delay. Jack Mann recalled a production in 1986 in which each microphone could be switched to any one of three different delay times. If the artiste was right at the back of the stage, the microphone was switched to the longest delay. Right down front, it was switched to the shortest delay. It was simple to tell how effective the delay units were because if you switched them off, the voices immediately seemed to be coming more from the loudspeakers than the performers. With traditional foot-microphones, the natural air-borne sound compensated for the time difference of being upstage or downstage. With the advent of digital memory consoles, the switching of time delays on multi-microphones systems became easier. But with the incredible cost involved, I asked a few sound designers if they thought this level of sophistication was really necessary. The answer came back that it is only necessary if it sounds better.

My first experience as an audience member of computer consoles and radio-mikes on delay was on the Hal Prince production of KISS OF THE SPIDERWOMAN (1991). The sound design by Martin Levan was the best I had ever heard in a theatre. Proof of the pudding, I suppose.

Sadly, since then, I have experienced less than satisfactory results from immensely expensive installations. However, wonderful the equipment, the key to success will always rely upon the skill of the sound designer.

15 WIRELESS MICROPHONES

It is generally accepted that wireless microphones were not successfully employed in the theatre until the 1960s, so I was not entirely convinced when a friend of mine claimed to have seen one working as far back as 1949. This was in a production of ALADDIN ON ICE in the south coast resort town of Brighton. After a little research, we managed to track down the skater, now long retired, who confirmed that he had, indeed, been wired for sound. He said that it tended to crackle a bit, but had generally worked extremely well. Moreover, he thought that the person responsible for the device was still living in Brighton.

In June 2002, I visited Reginald Moores, the man who probably invented the first personal wireless microphone. Eighty-one years old and bright as a button, his two-room flat was more like an electronics workshop than a living space. Every surface was covered with files, paper and electronic equipment. There was not even room on the dining table for my small recording machine without moving all manner of junk on to the floor. On a series of cup-hooks screwed around the edge of the table were hanging connecting leads, headsets, soldering irons, tools and meters. Shelves overflowed with video cassettes and CDs and, in one corner, a video camera was mounted above two large television sets. There was a cupboard for the domestic hot water tank and it was in this cramped space that he had installed his computer.

Reginald Moores
at his computer in
the boiler cupboard,
2002.

I was offered a cup of tea but this took a little time because access to the sink was hampered by another table piled with equipment which occupied most of the kitchen. The sink itself was full of unwashed crockery and the draining board was covered with tools and pieces of electronics. Even when we went into his bedroom to look for a box containing the original radio-mike, shelves overflowed with files, technical manuals and tapes, with leads, headsets and tools hanging all around the walls. The bed, too, was piled with papers and pieces of electronics in various stages of assembly. One side of the bed was relatively clear and one imagined that he could just slide beneath the sheets without having to move anything.

Reg told me how, as a very young man during the war, he had been in the Royal Air Force as a wireless operator in Bomber Command, flying in "Liberators". When the war ended in 1945, he became a sound engineer for Tom Arnold, producer of ice shows at London's Wembley Arena. In his spare time, he decided to use his knowledge of radio to develop a microphone without wires. In 1947, he presented his first wireless microphone to the BBC for evaluation. It was a hand-held device with built-in transmitter working in the 70-80 megacycle band. It was rejected by the BBC on the grounds that it had no practical use. The original is now in the Science Museum in London.

First Reginald Moores wireless microphone – 1947. The wire around the box is the antenna.

Tom Arnold heard about the invention and enquired if it could be adapted for his next ice show, ALADDIN, rather than having the skaters mime to unseen actors talking into microphones. Reg rose to the challenge. Using components from old Air Force wireless systems, he constructed a transmitter with a separate battery pack small enough to be concealed in the flowing costume of the evil wizard, Abanazar. An earpiece from an airman's headset was used for a microphone and the antenna was sewn into the belt strap that went around the waist of the wearer. All was ready for the Christmas show in 1949, ALADDIN ON ICE. The programme credit read *"Telephonic microphone invented by Reginald Moores".*

Right: Microphone, transmitter and battery pack used in 1949 for Ababazer in ALADDIN ON ICE in Brighton.

Far right: Inside the transmitter.

During the performance, Reg sat at the side of the rink with the receiver and a separate aerial that had to be pointed at the performer as he skated around the ice. It all worked perfectly, but he soon tired of sitting there night after night brandishing the aerial. He had the idea that a cable running around the entire rink might act as a giant antenna. To his great satisfaction, the experiment was entirely successful (was this the first ever loop aerial?).

When he showed me the actual transmitter and battery pack, I marveled at how compact they were and was completely stunned when he said: *"But the other one was smaller"*. Apparently, there was not one, but two radio-mikes in that show. The second one was for a female skater playing the Slave of the Ring and as she wore a tight costume, he constructed a single transmitter pack incorporating the batteries. The microphone could not be mounted on her chest, so he put it in her hat. He even had a head microphone many years before anyone else thought of it.

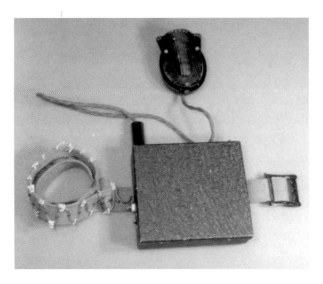

Far left:
Microphone and transmitter for the Slave of the Ring. The antenna is sewn on the belt.

Left:
Reginald Moores in 2002 with his 1949 Slave of the Ring transmitter.

Two years later, the comedian and film star, Norman Wisdom, wanted to use Reg's microphone for Tom Arnold's production of LONDON MELODY. But by 1951, a broadcasting licence from the General Post Office was required and they would only issue one in a band above 400 megacycles. It was not technically possible to adapt Reg Moores' units to this high frequency, so they resorted to a Japanese system with bulky battery pack and a receiver that required a visible antenna. It is quite likely that this was provided by Stagesound, because when engineer Roger Westgate joined the company in 1955, one of his first jobs was to check the Japanese radio-mike used on BABES IN THE WOOD ON ICE. Staged by rival producer, Claude Langdon, at the Empress Hall, Earls Court, the production starred a famous comedy duo of the time, Jimmy Jewel and Ben Warriss. Roger Westgate recalls that it was a single valve (tube) transmitter in a square bakerlite box measuring approximately 4" (10cm) x 3" (8cm) x 1" (2.5cm) with the valve sticking out of the top. It was powered by a large battery pack strapped to the waist. You could tell which one of the duo wore the microphone because there was a 10" (25cm) high "H" antenna (like an old television aerial) protruding from his hat. The other member of the duo could only talk if he was standing very close to his partner. The programme credit read: *Special "Personal Speech" sound effects for Messrs. Jewel and Warriss by Stagesound Ltd.*

Another member of the Stagesound staff, Phil Leaver, recalls a horror story when they tried to use this microphone at the Royal Opera House, Covent Garden. A new ballet had been created by Frederick Ashton requiring Prima Ballerina, Svetlana Beriosova, to talk between dancing. It turned out that the Japanese microphone was not sufficiently reliable, so Bill Walton managed to borrow a more powerful device from the BBC. The transmitter, of a similar size, was strapped to her stomach under the costume with a cable going round to a separate battery pack strapped to her back. Being a valve system, it required a serious chunk of batteries.

Unfortunately, during one of the performances a 'short' developed causing frying noises to issue from the PA system and the battery pack to overheat. The ballerina was obviously in distress, but dancers are used to pain and she completed the performance with the hot battery pack searing into her waist. After curtain down, the technical director demanded to know why the microphone had been crackling during the show, so they decided to see if it was still making noises by listening to the monitor. What they heard was not radio interference but the Prima Ballerina sobbing her heart out in the dressing room.

In America, as far back as 1952, Sam Saltzman, partner of John Shearing at Masque Sound, had devised a pocket radio transmitter. Unfortunately, because of the valves (tubes) and large batteries, he had the same problem with size. Being more than nine inches (23cm) long and four inches (10cm) wide, it was too large to conceal in most costumes. In the same year, the Shure Microphone Company claims to be the first company to go into production with a commercial system. Called the "Vagabond", it was powered by two hearing aid batteries, but it could only transmit within an area of 700 square feet (200 square metres) so its theatrical use would have been restricted.

According to an article by Guy Harris in "Theatre Crafts" magazine (1978 No.1), the first practical radio microphone developed for theatrical use in the USA was the Port-O-Vox. Jack Shearing remembers that they were hand-wired and quite bulky. Only one microphone could be used at a time and they were terribly unreliable, constantly getting out of tune. The last time he used one was in 1961 for Rudy Vallee (the famous crooner who was used to singing into a microphone) in How To Succeed In Business Without Really Trying.

There was an incident when Bob Maybaum was working on Carnival. Apparently, the bulky transmitter worn by the star, Anna Maria Alberghetti, and another transmitter were both sent for repair. The second transmitter was from How To Succeed In Business Without Really Trying, playing in the theatre next door. Due to an error, the wrong crystal was replaced in one of them. That night when Bob turned on Miss Alberghetti's microphone, the audience was surprised to hear the voice of Rudy Vallee.

Even as late as 1973, I had a similar problem on the original production of Joseph And The Amazing Technicolor Dreamcoat at the Albery Theatre in London. This was the first show we dared to use as many as six radio-mikes, squeezing them into the narrow high frequency band then allotted to the theatre. During the first sound rehearsal, I was surprised by a breathless and ashen-faced gentleman appearing beside our mixing desk at the side of the upper circle. It turned out that he was the stage manager from the next door theatre currently in the middle of a performance of GODSPELL. He begged me to switch off our transmitters as, apparently, our Joseph was broadcasting loud and clear onto their system. I suggested that a touch of the Old Testament might add a little piquancy to their show, but he failed to see the humour of the situation. The following day, the manufacturers, Audio Limited, changed the operating frequency of the offending microphone.

As soon as solid state technology came in, the transmitter packs became smaller. In 1962, the German company, Beyer, went into production with a wireless microphone called the "Transistophone". A few years later, Vega brought out a hand-held unit with a tuneable receiver in the FM band that was later to become the Citizen's Band. Masque Sound initially used one from Edcor, but none of these tuneable microphones was very stable. It was not unusual for a transmitter to drift during a performance on to the frequency of a powerful hotel paging system or a passing taxi cab. When Carol Channing played HELLO DOLLY on Broadway in 1964, she used an Edcor microphone and Otts Munderloh, who mixed the show for part of the run, recalls that it had to be tuned every night to find a clean frequency. Even so, one sat through the show, just sweating, because anything could suddenly break through. In a quote from the June 1974 edition of "Playbill", Gwen Verdon says that during a performance of SWEET CHARITY, she was surprised to find that her singing was replaced by a male voice saying: *"Calling Doctor Klein. Calling Doctor Klein".*

The reverse situation occurred in London when Ethel Merman used her American FM system, quite illegally, for a cabaret performance at the Talk of the Town. Seemingly unaware of breaking the law by using a broadcasting device without a licence, she amazed the audience by walking around the stage singing into a microphone without wires. Unfortunately, she was operating in the same frequency band as the London police force – who were totally baffled to hear a brassy American voice singing *"It ain't so surprisin', you don't need analyzin'..."* issuing from their car radios. Apparently, it took them some days to track down the source of the problem, by which time she had nearly completed her engagement.

The later wireless systems had crystal controlled transmitters and receivers operating on a legal frequency fixed by the manufacturer. These had little chance of interference unless another system was operating close by on an identical frequency. By the late 1970s, American manufacturers included Swintek and Electrovoice. There was also Thomas SCF in France, Sennheiser in Germany and Sony in Japan. In the UK, the first company in the theatrical field was Audio Limited who began producing their hand-wired crystal controlled systems in 1963.

Before setting up Audio Limited to produce the first British wireless microphones, Geoffrey Blundell had a company manufacturing Jason radio tuners and amplifiers for the domestic market. As a young design engineer, he had worked for John Logie Baird in the development of the first television pictures in 1926.

Stagesound used two Audio Limited systems for HELLO DOLLY at the Theatre Royal, Drury Lane in 1965. They were not totally reliable, often tending to drift off frequency and produce loud crackling noises. Fortunately, the performers were able to rely on their vocal power aided by the foot-mikes when this happened. This was not the case, however, when Barbra Streisand came to London the following year to star in FUNNY GIRL. She did not possess a powerful stage voice. On Broadway, she had relied entirely upon her radio-mike supplied by Masque Sound, but the low band American system could not be licensed for operation in the UK. There was no alternative but to use the less stable high band microphone from Audio, since it was the only legal system available.

Following a disastrous preview, Dick Lock from the Stagesound hire department was summoned to a meeting on stage. He admitted that there had been problems with the wireless system, but protested that the orchestra was so loud that the microphone was picking up more orchestra than singer. Julie Stein was conducting the orchestra and he did not agree. The producers, Bernard Delfont and Richard Mills, sided with the composer and demanded to know what action would be taken. Tempers became frayed. Much to Dick's relief, the situation was diffused when Barbra Streisand swept on stage, put her arm around his shoulder and said *"When everyone realizes that I am a recording artist and not a stage performer, we will all be happier and Dick can go home and get some rest. It is not his fault."* Sanity restored, it was proposed that Bernard Delfont should approach the BBC to borrow one of their radio-mikes which were licenced for low band frequencies. This was done and at the preview the following night, the BBC microphone worked perfectly. The only problem was that the star could still not be heard. Conclusion? The orchestra was too loud.

We were using the occasional Audio Limited microphone for West End musicals in the early 1970s, but only if really pressed because they were still prone to intermittent failure. The main business of Audio Limited was in the film industry where, if there was a problem, they could always do another take. Most frustratingly, they often worked perfectly during rehearsals, and even public previews, but then on the opening night they would start spluttering and crackling and losing signal. It was incredibly nerve-racking. I had a theory that somehow the electricity caused by the actor's first-night nerves affected the radio waves, or perhaps it was just an excess of moisture from their sweat glands.

Among the many horror stories, one of the worst was suffered by my colleague, Antony Horder, when CAROL CHANNING & HER TEN STOUT-HEARTED MEN came to London's Theatre Royal, Drury Lane in 1970. During very stressful public previews the radio kept breaking up. Different frequencies were tried and aerials were repositioned until, at last, the system seemed to be working. The opening night went without too many clicks and crackles, but on a subsequent performance, the star's voice was completely eclipsed every ten minutes or so by a brief but very loud buzzing noise. Eventually, she stopped in mid routine and told the audience that she was going off-stage to change her microphone. This took a few minutes as she had to remove her tee-shirt. The audience and the Ten Stout-Hearted Men all waited patiently until she reappeared – to loud applause – and resumed the show. Unfortunately, at regular intervals, the same ghastly buzzing continued. Totally frustrated, she announced that she did not need this ******** microphone and demanded that it should be switched off. More wild applause from the audience. She then continued, and although the sound operator brought the foot-mikes up to feedback point.... nobody could hear a word. In the interval, many people complained and had their money refunded. Meanwhile, every electrical device in the building was switched off, the neon signs outside the theatre and even the stagehands' television set. All to no avail. The show was completed with the orchestra playing softly.

The cause of this debacle was explained by a chance remark from an acquaintance who happened to be in the audience that night. She had noticed, parked in the street just behind the theatre, a Mass Radiography Unit giving people free chest X-Rays. She wondered if the radio interference had occurred every time the machine was activated for a new client. This was obviously the case because, for the remainder of the run, there were no X-Ray units and no buzzes.

BILLY at the Theatre Royal, Drury Lane in 1974. The star, Michael Crawford holds an Audio Limited transmitter while sound operator, Claire Laver adjusts the electret microphone.

For BILLY at Drury Lane in 1974, Michael Crawford wore two transmitters so that the sound operator could switch over to a receiver on a different frequency if the one in use started breaking up (diversity systems had yet to be invented). There were three other radio-mikes in that show, so interference was quite likely. During the run of BILLY, when BBC television was recording an excerpt, I was amused by remarks made by the chief sound engineer that proved how we lived in two very different worlds. He congratulated me on the sound in the big dance routine from the special 'tap dancing' microphones we had installed along the front edge of the stage. When I pointed out that the main purpose of these 'tap dancing' mikes was for amplifying the cast, he was both amazed and horrified. The idea of a microphone being more than a few inches away from a performer's head was beyond his comprehension. We discussed the budgetary and technical reasons why we had only four of the cast on radio-mikes and he enquired how many of our sound crew were backstage looking after them. This, I explained patiently, is "theatre". See that young lady mixing the show from a box at the side of the upper circle? She is the sound crew.

The original body microphones (lavaliers) were dynamic or moving coil types. The miniature electret condenser microphone, coming into general use in the 1970s, had a much flatter and wider frequency response and could be more easily concealed in the costume. When even smaller versions became available, the fashion for taping the microphone to the performer's head was introduced.

A rival to Audio Limited with a confusingly similar name, Audio Engineering Limited, introduced their Micron system in 1972 which was better engineered but too expensive for general use in the theatre. However, budgets for sound equipment had increased significantly by 1980 when Audio Engineering became the first manufacturer to produce a modular rack system with individual diversity receivers. Wireless microphones used to suffer from mysterious dead spots on a stage, sometimes caused by the direct wave reaching the receiver being cancelled out by an equally strong reflection of the radio wave from a metal object. The two signals reach the receiver a few milliseconds out of step and cause 'phase cancellation'. This problem was not solved until 'diversity systems' were developed. With two antennas and two receivers for each transmitter in the diversity system automatically switching to the strongest signal, at last we had a reliable and superb quality device. But the narrow frequency band dictated by the British licensing laws still restricted the number that could safely be used on any one production.

An article in "Theatre Crafts" magazine describes the sound systems used in Las Vegas at the Tropicana and MGM Grand in 1974 where, despite vast budgets, the quality was not very good. Both shows were mixed from large consoles located in the middle of the auditorium. At the Tropicana, the stars sang live on hand held radio-mikes while the chorus was recorded and the band miked from a 'studio' off-stage. In the Ziegfeld Room at the MGM Grand, the orchestra was again miked from a sound-proofed room in the basement and fourteen hand held wireless microphones were used for the performers. Entertainment director, Bill de Angelis, admitted that the sound was one of the shows weakest points, but commented: *"Fortunately, we have a lot of people in the audience who don't know from good or bad soundwise..."*

Even in the USA, as late as 1981 when Otts Mundeloh designed DREAM GIRLS, the number of microphones in use was limited. They had five systems on that show, but it was not unusual for a major production to have only three or four microphones that were passed around the principle performers. This was partly due to the expense and partly because of the technical difficulties of running a lot of radio systems.

The musical STARLIGHT EXPRESS, opening in London in 1984, required the cast to spend a great deal of the show roller-skating on ramps around the auditorium. It was decided that the only way of hearing their voices was to build microphones into the elaborate headgear which formed part of the costumes. The exact location of these microphones was critical and British sound designer, Martin Levan, booked a studio in London to carry out some tests. Using a studio was ideal because, unlike in the theatre, one could listen to the microphone without hearing the natural voice. With microphones taped all round a singer's head, the best results were logged. If one imagines the face sticking through a cardboard cut-out in front of the ears, it was discovered that anywhere behind that was not good. Anywhere in front – up, down or sideways – produced a good pick-up. Following the successful use of microphones in this position for STARLIGHT EXPRESS, Martin employed the technique on subsequent shows, setting a trend. He told me that he favours hiding the microphone in the hair above the forehead and we agreed that microphones stuck to the forehead or up on the cheek bone in full view of the public look ghastly and are unnecessary.

The twenty-one radios used in STARLIGHT were substantially more than had ever been attempted in a British musical before and, having run out of the official frequencies allotted for theatre use, a number of the microphones were operating within a frequency band used by BBC television. This was not strictly allowed, but the nearest studio was some miles away, so there should not have been a problem. Everything went without a hitch during the two weeks of previews, but on the first night, Martin Levan experienced the kind of scenario that is every soundman's worst nightmare.

After the first few numbers, most of the microphones started picking up serious interference. When a fader was opened, all that could be heard was a colossal buzzing sound. Andrew Bruce, who was backstage monitoring the microphones on an early RF analyzer, saw a huge spike appear right in the middle of their frequencies. Only six of the microphones remained unaffected. The others had to be switched off. There was one hand-held radio that happened to be working and this was passed around a harassed cast so that at least some of the vocals could be heard.

In an attempt to discover the source of the interference, Andrew dashed outside the theatre and there, parked in the street, was a BBC outside broadcast van, preparing for live interviews with the celebrity audience at the end of the show. Unfortunately, they were using a very powerful transmitter in the same frequency band to relay the interviews back to the studio. The engineer had his system up and running and refused to switch it off. By the time Andrew managed to contact someone in authority at the BBC who could instruct the engineer to cease broadcasting, it was too late. The audience was totally aware that there was a technical disaster and when one of the characters sang a verse from a song at the end of the show that began: *"When the power goes dead...",* they burst into sympathetic laughter and applause.

At this time, Andrew Bruce was involved with a pressure group set up to persuade the government that the current restrictions on radio frequencies for the theatre were untenable. The press coverage of the debacle on Starlight Express, combined with the outraged comments by Andrew Lloyd-Webber and director Trevor Nunn, went a long way to strengthen the case for change. A committee was set up and a major campaign was launched involving the National Theatre, the Royal Shakespeare Company, and several leading West End producers. They were invited to the Department of Trade and Industry for a private interview with the Minister, Paul Channon. When they arrived at the Radio Regulatory Department, the officials welcomed them with enthusiasm. The committee had apparently been given Category A status. Perhaps the reason for this was the fact that Andrew Lloyd-Webber knew Paul Channon and could well have exerted a little pressure. The result of the meeting was the allocation of twenty-four new frequencies for indoor use only.

It was not long before more frequencies were allotted and the entire cast of a musical could be wired. Legally and, for the most part, reliably. Theoretically, the blanket use of wireless microphones has solved all problems of inaudibility. This is only true, of course, if the actor is aware that communication in the theatre still requires projection and diction. An amplified voice without decent vowel sounds and enunciation, is just a louder voice that cannot be understood. Reliance on the radio-mike brings with it a concern that vocal prowess and – most importantly – energy is no longer perceived by some to be necessary. Consequently, performances become flatter, less theatrical and less exciting.

The artificial processing of voices can have the effect of dehumanizing the theatrical experience. It is easy, and tempting, to turn up the volume and blast the audience with glorious sound but, hopefully, producers and directors will always keep in mind that theatre, as opposed to films and television, is all about communication and interaction between real people in a live situation. Any form of artificial barrier between the actors and the audience must have a negative effect.

16 COMINGS AND GOINGS
IN THE WEST END

Theatre Projects had more than its fair share of designing and renting equipment to shows from the mid 1960s into the early 1970s, but we were not to have it all our own way for long. Stagesound had become less of a force since the death of Bill Walton, but one of London's theatre owners had built up a stock of equipment and decided to go into the hire business. Sir Donald Albery owned the Donmar group of theatres and his son, Ian, was the technical manager who spearheaded this new development. Consequently, it became difficult for us to get equipment into any of the Donmar theatres or on any of their productions.

More seriously, a new organization, Theatre Sound and Lighting Services (TSL), was quietly launched in 1968 and was to become a major competitor. The two founders, Joe Davis (lighting designer for H M Tennent) and Cyril Griffiths (chief engineer and later managing director of the Stoll Moss Group), had co-opted a formidable team of partners. There was Ian Dow (production manager for H M Tennent), Anthony Chardet (freelance company manager), Arthur Watson (businessman formerly involved with ENSA, the armed services entertainment group) and Dick Lock who had resigned from Stagesound. TSL therefore had access to all the H M Tennent productions and was on the inside track for any productions going into the thirteen West End theatres owned by the Stoll Moss Group including two of the largest, the Palladium and the Theatre Royal, Drury Lane. Stoll Moss also owned a string of major touring theatres around the UK.

Joe Davis liked to remain in the background, so it was Cyril Griffiths who really ran the company. Cyril had gained a knowledge of electronics in the Royal Navy during the Second World War working on the submarine locating system, SONAR. Afterwards, he found employment as an electrician at the Phoenix Theatre in London and, in the early 1960s, began his theatrical career with Stoll Moss when he became chief electrician at the Queen's Theatre.

Cyril Griffiths.

Stocky, slightly less than average height, full of energy, Cyril Griffiths had an open friendly face topped by a shock of light wavy hair. He would greet you with a ready smile, but his beady eye would be summing you up. He did not suffer fools gladly – or at all, if he could help it. Much of his business was conducted in one or other of the theatre bars or in clubs frequented by theatre people.

He particularly loved the company of lighting designers and electricians but, sadly, did not have the same kind of rapport with members of the audio fraternity, sometimes referring to them as "noise boys". Basically, he did not understand sound. Like many people involved in theatre management, he completely accepted the necessity for an assortment of tin cans placed higgledy-piggledy all around the proscenium to light the show, but was irritated at the very thought of seeing loudspeaker boxes. Even worse was the idea of a soundman wanting to install a mixing desk in the auditorium. This would be greeted by a pained expression and a speech about how unsightly it would be for the audience and the amount of lost revenue at the box office if he had to remove.... "_how many seats?_" But this was his negotiating stance and, once a compromise was reached, he would efficiently arrange all the technicalities.

Although he had strong opinions and would argue his case, he was always fair and scrupulously honest. In fact, much to the annoyance of some of his colleagues, he would try to ensure that TSL did not appear to have any advantage over rental contracts for shows coming in to the Stoll Moss theatres. If TSL did win a contract, he worried that the rivals would think he had not been playing fair.

Cyril's son, Matthew, who later joined the company to head up the Conference Division, kindly lent me the minutes of their board meetings in which I was fascinated to discover how concerned the rival companies were about the formation of TSL. Within six months, Ian Albery made an approach to investigate the possibilities of a merger between TSL and his Donmar hire company. This was rejected because of Cyril's distaste of the clause in Donmar's contract for hiring their theatres where the producer was obliged to rent Donmar lighting and sound equipment. The following month there was an approach from Jack Bishop (just before he retired) suggesting "mutual cooperation" and offering the Bishop Sound effects library and contacts. This was also rejected. Within weeks, a letter came from the general manager of the Theatre Projects Group suggesting a meeting to discuss "one or two propositions which could be of mutual interest". There was a meeting, but nothing came of it.

Because of the conflict of interests when theatre owners and producers were involved in providing technical services, Anthony Chardet felt that his position as a freelance company manager was prejudiced, so he resigned. For the same reason and also because of Cyril's attitude to soundmen, Dick Lock followed suit. Shortly afterwards, Eric Turner (ex director of Stagesound) joined as hire manager and Jim Douglas became technical manager.

By 1970, TSL had sound equipment in four West End plays, with three more in the pipeline. Their first big musical, PROMISES PROMISES, produced by H M Tennent was running at the Prince of Wales Theatre with sound design by Jim Douglas.

TSL had offices in the Queen's Theatre with a very favourable rental deal from Stoll Moss, but they now required workshop space. The former prop room in the Theatre Royal, Drury Lane was made available as a lighting and sound equipment hire store, with a dubbing suite for creating effects. A voice booth was added later. The token rental charged by Stoll Moss was just £15.00 per week. By May 1970, TSL was in profit. The weekly outgoings were £300.60 with the rental income totalling £473.22 (£258.70 lighting and £214.52 sound).

To give an idea of equipment costs in those days, £150.00 would purchase a new Ferrograph tape machine, a 60 watt amplifier was £60.00 and one of the big Stagesound column loudspeakers was also priced at £60.00. The weekly rental charge for a sound effects playback system ranged between £12.00 and £25.00. The weekly hire charge for the sound reinforcement system for PROMISES PROMISES was £70.00 which meant that the show had to run for eighteen months to recoup the £1,260.00 investment in equipment. The sound operator, paid £21.00 per week, was charged out at £30.00.

In 1973, TSL introduced American Spotmaster cartridge machines to the West End on the play HABEUS CORPUS. Popular with radio stations for playing jingles and commercials, they used quarter inch tape enclosed in a plastic shell running around a central spool – taking it from the inside and returning it to the outside. For each show, individual effects were recorded on separate cartridges. To play back a cue, one simply inserted a cartridge into the letter box opening of the playback machine and pressed the button.

Theatre Projects was slow to follow suit because of our large stock of tape machines (shades of Jack Bishop and his panatropes), but the cartridge machines took off, mainly because they had an almost instantaneous start mechanism and they were mechanically silent. Although we modified the Revox tape machines, they still made a significant 'click' when starting and stopping, which made them difficult to use within an auditorium. The downside of the cart machine was in rehearsals when the director wanted to stop and hear the effect again. The only way of setting up the beginning of a cue was by running forward at double speed. This took much longer than rewinding on a reel-to-reel tape deck. The other problem that sometimes occurred was when the person in charge forgot to set a cartridge back to the beginning before the show. Thus, when the button was pressed, there was either a deafening silence or the sound of the tail end of an effect.

Over the next few years TSL expanded. The optical lighting effects department was acquired from Strand Electric Limited, they set up a separate division for the lucrative conference and trade show market, and they took a 48% interest in Green Ginger, a design/manufacturing company set up by technical manager Jim Douglas and an ex-Strand Electric electronics expert. A number of audio installations were carried out for Stoll Moss theatres in London, and their touring theatres throughout the country had new stage manager and dressing room systems.

But, as the minutes of a board meeting in 1974 showed, TSL began to suffer from the usual problems of a growing business. There was a major concern about large bank loans. They had a serious cash flow situation. More space and more secretarial staff were needed, but could not be afforded. Existing staff were demanding increased salaries and the setting up of a pension scheme. Internal communications within the company seemed to be poor. To top it all, the telephone switchboard was hopelessly inadequate and the GPO had quoted a delivery time for a replacement of eighteen months (the telephone industry had yet to be privatized). With the sound division losing money, partly because TSL had been unsuccessful in challenging the Theatre Projects grip on the West End musical, staff cuts were implemented.

1974 was, in fact, a landmark year for the Theatre Projects sound business, in that we had designed and supplied equipment for every musical in the West End bar one (it would just not come off to let us sweep the board). In that year, we also acquired Stagesound. After Bill Walton's death in 1964, the new managing director's strategy was to reduce overheads and cease all capital expenditure. The result was disaster. Where Bill Walton's investment in tape machines and a new range of well designed equipment had virtually put Bishop Sound out of business, our purchase of American loudspeakers, solid state amplifiers and mixing desks, had a similar effect on the Stagesound hire business. Without Bill Walton running the recording studio complex, this too faltered. Their main area of activity, with many new theatres being built in the UK, became systems sales and installation. Phil Leaver, who had been head of sound at the Royal Opera House before working for a major recording studio, was enticed back to Stagesound to manage the design and manufacture department. But without leadership and investment, the business could not be sustained and, after another few dismal years, the remnants of the company were sold to Theatre Projects.

Aside from the manufacturing expertise and a store full of audio equipment, we acquired two large buildings in Covent Garden. One of these became a base for the lighting hire department and a theatre shop, the other housed the expanding sound hire business and our Special Projects Group which was developing high quality modular sound mixing consoles and communications equipment. We were riding high, but there was more competition to come.

In 1974, a new company called Autograph Sound Recording provided equipment, including cartridge machines from ITC, for a play at the Comedy Theatre called ABSURD PERSON SINGULAR. Autograph had been founded the previous year by Phil Clifford, an ex-Stagesound engineer who had become head of sound at the Royal Opera House, and Andrew Bruce who briefly succeeded him in this post. Jonathan Deans, who went on to become a renowned sound designer in America, was given his first West End job as sound operator on that show.

It was not long before Cyril Griffiths of TSL approached Autograph Sound with a proposal of joining forces, but they knew that Cyril's dealings with his own sound department were not always harmonious and, anyhow, they wanted to be their own bosses. More crucially, Autograph's first really big contract was on the horizon. Abe Jacob, sound designer for the Broadway production of A CHORUS LINE, came over to Great Britain in 1975 to meet possible equipment suppliers for the London production. He was impressed by the enthusiasm and technical ideas of Messrs. Clifford and Bruce and decided (much to my chagrin – but I forgive him!), to go with the new boys on the block.

Far left:
Phil Clifford

Left:
Andrew Bruce.

A Chorus Line opened at the Theatre Royal, Drury Lane in 1976 and was Autograph's first credit in a theatre programme. The show was extremely successful, as was the sound system. The control console was the 'Fleximix' built by the British company Trident, and Abe Jacob specified Altec loudspeakers which Autograph had to purchase from Theatre Projects because we were the UK agents. Somehow Abe persuaded the theatre management to let him hang four of these above the orchestra pit in front of the beautiful proscenium. I had been trying to do this for years, but was always informed that the splendour of the architecture was never to be sullied by a group of unsightly black wooden boxes hanging from chains. I suppose I did not argue too strongly because I rather agreed. However, Abe would not have been hampered by my English reserve and, according to his assistant at the time, Otts Munderloh, he had a tremendous row about it and almost stormed out of the theatre. Otts also recalls that Abe very nearly came to blows with the lighting designer, Tharon Musser, over locating the cluster where she wanted her lights. Abe Jacob denies all this. His memory of the event is that he told Andrew Bruce where he wanted to hang the loudspeakers and Andrew went ahead and organized it. Simple as that. Whatever the truth, this became the first 'central cluster' for a musical in the West End.

The next few years saw the emergence of Autograph as the leading audio company in the British theatre. They worked with Abe Jacob in 1978 when he returned to the UK to design Evita. The bi-amped loudspeakers on this show, specially flown over from the United States, were McCune type JM-1 and JM-3 designed by John Meyer who was still working for McCune.

Autograph also handled the installation when Jack Mann, the second American sound designer to work in the West End, came to Drury Lane with Sweeney Todd (1980). Of course, he specified Bozak column loudspeakers. Andrew Bruce thought these were heavy and rather expensive, but he admitted that he was impressed by the coverage of the auditorium and their uncoloured sound.

The following year, Abe Jacob returned to Drury Lane with another American show, THE BEST LITTLE WHOREHOUSE IN TEXAS, bringing with him a new loudspeaker. Designed by John Meyer, who had just set up his own company, this was the iconic Meyer UPA-1. Built into the two-way enclosure was a 12-inch (30cm) cone low frequency driver, and a 3-inch (76mm) diaphragm compression unit driving into a 45° symmetrical high frequency horn.

I was told by John Meyer that it was Abe who suggested the successful UM-1 wedge monitor could be developed into a PA product. Because of its small size, directivity and high power output, the UPA-1 was to become widely used in the theatre for a number of years. In fact, Autograph bought so many of them that they were offered the European agency. The drawback for some would-be users was the need for a two channel 550 watt output amplifier which made each system very expensive.

Meyer UPA-1.

Another small speaker that sacrificed efficiency for size and required a large amplifier, was manufactured by Bose from the early 1980s. The Bose 802, developed for the theatre, did not have the directivity, frequency range or power of the Meyer, but with the addition of a separate woofer, it was used with some success on a few shows. Being small and portable they were, however, in great demand for one-off product launches, fashion shows and conferences.

A pair of Bose 802
Series 2 loudspeakers.

A few months after first trying out the UPA-1s, Abe specified them for the blockbuster musical, CATS, at the Royalty Theatre, London and, once again, Autograph handled the installation.

With the continuing patronage of the producer of CATS, Cameron Mackintosh, and the composer Andrew Lloyd-Webber, Autograph Sound was soon to take over as the leading sound company in the UK and have a major influence on Broadway.

By the end of the seventies, Theatre Projects still had a few musicals running, but our main audio business was now directed towards multi-media systems for product launches and conferences, making good use of our recording studio and video suite. For my part, I was busy specifying sound and communications for new theatres and concert halls rather than designing shows. The Theatre Projects consultancy company had, during twenty years of operation, completed more than a hundred projects in twenty-five different countries and new commissions kept rolling in.

Things were not going so well at TSL. The November figures for 1980 were "not favourable" and a series of economies were implemented. Eric Turner retired as hire manager and then Green Ginger parted company with TSL and began manufacturing low cost lighting control systems.

Cyril Griffiths became even more frustrated with the sound department because the rapid advances in technology meant a continuing investment in equipment in order to keep up – and the company did not have the resources. Consequently, the next two or three years saw the departure of a number of key members of staff. Sound designer Rick Clarke left to join the National Theatre, Terry Saunders moved to Autograph to run their equipment store and Tony Robinson joined Autograph to head up engineering and manufacture. TSL also lost sound engineer Terry Hewitt with his important link to a major producer and theatre owner; Terry was married to the daughter of Maurice Fournier, production manager for Bernard Delfont.

The heart totally went out of the company when, in 1984, Joe Davis died during a break in a lighting rehearsal at the Theatre Royal, Drury Lane. Shortly after this sad event, Cyril Griffiths, now aged sixty six, retired from the business. With the charismatic and influential founders of TSL no longer around and the company relying on conferences and other non-theatre work for survival, a deal had to be done. John Simpson from White Light Limited had previously bought the lighting optical department from TSL (originally acquired from Strand Electric) and, in 1991, he bought the rest of the company.

The Theatre Projects Group had also hit financial problems. There were massive losses from a subsidiary in Holland where most of the lighting and sound equipment in the rental store went missing (!), and a commercial lighting company within the group suffered from bad debts in Nigeria and the Far East. A number of companies had been acquired over the previous years and the high bank borrowings became unsustainable. In 1984, the lighting and sound rental business was sold to the Samuelson Group, a major equipment supplier to the film industry. Other companies, such as the audio-visual and video operation, and sound design and manufacturing were sold off. Within two years, Theatre Projects was paired down to the very successful consultancy companies in London and New York. Richard Pilbrow moved to America where there was a boom in the building of theatres and arts centres, and he continued to light shows. After being managing director of the group during a very trying four year period, I decided to set up my own company designing historical themed visitor attractions, using my knowledge of technical theatre and audio-visual production.

For me, it was the end of an exciting era. I had known one of the first theatre sound pioneers, R G Jones, and had been involved with Jack Bishop whose company seemed untouchable until Bill Walton came along with a more friendly approach to the customer and a new range of equipment. I was fortunate during the 1960s and 1970s to be at the forefront of theatre sound in the UK during a period of vast changes in technology. Now it was the turn of a younger generation to take the art of sound design into a new digital world.

17 BIG SOUND AND BIG BUCKS

Once the role of the sound designer had been recognized, collaboration between the director and the sound designer, who both wanted the best for the show, led to the possibility of sound controls front of house, bigger budgets for more sophisticated equipment, and expert operators. It took off in the 1980s. This was an era when spectacle became paramount. Hal Prince produced and directed large scale shows such as SWEENEY TODD and FOLLIES, and the Cameron Mackintosh productions included EVITA, PHANTOM OF THE OPERA (both directed by Hal Prince), MISS SAIGON and SUNSET BOULEVARD. Composers like Stephen Sondheim and Andrew Lloyd-Webber became as powerful as the directors – perhaps, even more so.

The staging of these productions was lavish, relying on large casts, mammoth sets (often motorized and computerized), enormous lighting rigs and enough musicians to fill the orchestra pits. In contrast to the natural reinforcement strived for in the 1970s, these larger than life productions called for a larger than life sound. And with the availability of wireless microphones, small powerful loudspeakers, time delay and computer-controlled mixing desks, high levels of amplification became possible.

Andrew Lloyd-Webber was largely responsible for this trend. He was determined to have what he considered the best sound possible for his musicals – and he had the power and resources to insist upon it. From the days of JESUS CHRIST SUPERSTAR when he tentatively approached our mixing console and was impressed when I showed him how we could change the balance of the woodwind section with "that row of knobs", he progressed to actually sitting alongside the sound operator, sometimes even on the first night, directing the mix like a producer in a recording studio. Only, in the theatre, of course, you cannot go back and do another take if you get it wrong.

When the wave of successful musicals hit Broadway, American producers demanded the same big sound for their productions. But whereas British producer Cameron Mackintosh, and later Andrew Lloyd-Webber with his own production company, were willing to invest in the most expensive equipment and sacrifice seats in the house for large consoles, many Broadway producers were not. During the 1980s, the old style of creative producer was giving way to production conglomerates in the hands of accountants. The purse strings were tightened. With the gradual loss of the legendary Broadway directors who could dictate artistic requirements, like Michael Bennett, Bob Fosse, Gower Champion, Michael Kidd and Jerry Robins, the money-people became the source of power.

When Richard Fitzgerald designed the sound for BEAUTY AND THE BEAST in 1992, the mega-rich Disney Corporation (run by accountants) refused to contemplate losing a single seat for the large and complicated sound control. After protestations, a consultant was brought in who managed to find space for nine extra seats at the side of the orchestra stalls. Eight seats at the rear of the orchestra were then removed for the console. The producers were happy. They had gained one seat. But Richard has a very pragmatic attitude: *"Ideally one wants to be in the centre of the auditorium, but I am a realist. Those are the most expensive seats, so I try to be flexible. As long as the control position is in the listening area and the system is all properly tuned, the sound operator can make adjustments. I believe in saving the seats because I know that the producer has to make money in order to pay me. Ten or twelve $100 seats taken out of every performance is a lot of money on a run."*

Widespread criticism of over-amplification

I WAS SURPRISED to find that not a single one of the American practitioners I interviewed said they were in favour of a style of amplification which is out of scale with the human voice. Unless, of course, it is for a rock musical. Abe Jacob cited EVITA as the first non-rock show where he was asked by Hal Prince to make many moments larger than life because the character of Evita was larger than life. A sound designer, says Abe, is always at the mercy of the director, the composer or the producer. Quite often, he receives comments from all kinds of other people who happen to be working on the show. He echoes the sentiments of all soundmen, including me, when he says: *"Every person connected with the theatre knows two jobs: their own... and sound! Everybody is a sound expert."*

Producers sometimes equate loudness with excitement, not understanding that the impact of loud sound is only effective if contrasted with quieter sound. Often if a show is failing, they cast around for reasons and quite often fool themselves into thinking that a lot of noise will somehow disguise the fact that there is a turkey on the stage. An example of this was on the rock musical TIME, starring Cliff Richard with sound design by Julian Beech of Autograph in 1986. I sat through one of the previews and although it was the most ill-conceived and poorly directed show I had ever had the misfortune to endure, Julian's contribution was excellent. Far better than the show deserved. The voices were clear and the variation in dynamics within the score was perfect. Quieter moments were contrasted by a full exciting rock sound, but at no time was the audience blasted out of their seats. A couple of days later, I telephoned Julian to say how much I had appreciated his work, but I found him in a state of depression. Apparently, after the performance I attended, he was instructed to raise the levels all through the show by two hundred percent. Julian tried to argue his case, but the producer, one Dave Clark who had headed a rock band in the sixties, said that he knew more about rock music than Julian ever would, and he was to do as he was told. The audience was deafened. The show failed.

In 1982, there was a piece by Harold Schonberg in the "New York Times" complaining that the electronic amplification of Broadway shows was generally awful. He claimed that critics and the general public leaving the theatre could often be heard voicing comments such as: *It sounds canned. I couldn't hear him at all – his microphone must have gone off. What's that crackling and buzzing? The voices didn't seem to come from the stage. It was too LOUD!* The article caused a stir in the profession and in response, "Theatre Crafts" magazine (February 1982) contacted a number of sound designers who, by and large, agreed that the primary problem with the large Broadway musical was over amplification. Reasons given varied from arrangers not scoring for a live performance, producers and directors being influenced by the sound of television, films and recordings, the inherent limitations of the equipment to produce a natural sound, and the escalation in the size of the theatres being built. To a greater or lesser extent, all the sound designers seemed to feel that they were middle men carrying out the wishes of the producers and directors, and having to live with a certain amount of compromise.

In the article, Jack Shearing of Masque Sound complained: *"These days doing a Broadway show is like doing a TV spectacular. There is not one musical that isn't too loud. The use of amplification was originally to enhance intelligibility and to balance the various musical and vocal elements. It has now become primarily a device for stimulating excitement. A few years back, if you could not hear a singer's voice in the back row, the conductor or arranger would take out whatever was interfering with that vocal line. Nowadays, the orchestrations are so cluttered that there is no way you can hear the voices without heavy miking.*

Jack Shearing,
1982.

The audiences have been conditioned by rock, disco, or whatever, and they are losing the ability to listen, to strive to hear. They want to lay back and have it all happen for them." He went on to say that while he could understand that producers demanded this kind of sound for good commercial reasons, he did not enjoy creating it. *"It is not really fun any more."* As a result, Jack Shearing had virtually abandoned his role as a designer in favour of the contracting side of the business.

Otts Munderloh, an up and coming sound designer in 1982, had similar worries: *"I agree that Broadway sound is currently suffering from a severe case of excessive amplification, but I do not put this down to the soundman. I feel the source of the trouble is not artistic or technological, so much as having to fulfill the wishes of the producers who are the ultimate bosses. The trick is to work with the smarter people who make you look good, or at least let you do your job well."*

Otts Munderloh,
1982.

Richard Fitzgerald of Sound Associates was concerned that the theatre bosses, through lack of understanding, sometimes make it impossible to produce a good sound. *"As an example of what we are up against, we have just installed a sound system for 42ND STREET in the Winter Garden theatre. When the owner, David Merrick, walked in and saw the JBL speakers stacked against the walls on either side of the stage, he commanded that they should be removed from view. This required moving them far out to the right and left of the stage and camouflaging them with 'duvetyne'. Consequently, they were too widely spaced to allow for the customary mono mix. It had to be mixed in stereo, otherwise singers on one side of the stage are going to be jumping out of the wall on the opposite side. We also added some time delay to help compensate for this problem."*

Richard Fitzgerald,
1982.

In my contribution to the article, headed "A View from London", I suggested that Harold C Schonberg's piece in the New York Times might perhaps be overstating the case. How many shows, I wondered, had he sat through and not given the sound system a second thought? Bad sound is obvious whereas good sound will go unnoticed.

Even plays are being amplified

IN MAY 1988, there was an article in "New York Newsday" by Linda Winer (apt name!) in which she was very critical about the increasing use of amplification for straight plays. *"Already, sound designers have slipped from the back of the book to major title-page credits on most programmes. They have their own unions. They have their own superstars. They have agents and lawyers. Most of all, they have power. Anyone who doubts their mega-volt impact need only go to Broadway these days and try to remember the sound of the human voice. Not only the musicals, even the distinctive timbres of Glenda Jackson and Christopher Plummer in* MACBETH *have been flattened into sounds of undetermined origin."*

She goes on to blame the British musical and, in particular, Martin Levan, whose involvement with most of Andrew Lloyd-Webber shows meant that he, perhaps more than anyone, had been responsible for the fundamental change in the use of sound equipment. She then added the rider that the last time she checked Levan's sound for CATS, it did sound remarkably real.

On September 3 1988 in the "New York Times", there was another piece decrying the fact that voice amplification had now become commonplace in the world of drama. Peter Fitzgerald, brother of Richard, supervising the miking of several Broadway plays was quoted as saying: *"People don't want to work at hearing an actor anymore."* Jason Robarts, starring in LONG DAY'S JOURNEY INTO NIGHT, one of the plays currently being amplified, utterly condemned the use of microphones: *"It is part of an actor's equipment to project his voice. We are not playing in theatres that require amplification. It is like putting a piece of glass between the audience and the stage. It cheats the listener and the play."* There is also a quote from playwright, David Mamet: *"If you are an actor and you cannot make yourself heard in a 1,000-seat theatre, you are doing something wrong. You should get off the stage and go home."*

I have to admit to being responsible for providing a speech reinforcement system for an American production of the play THE LITTLE FOXES in 1982. It was a limited run and the producers knew that with Elizabeth Taylor in the starring role, it would be a sell-out. They therefore booked one of London's larger theatres, the Victoria Palace, which is more suited to staging musicals. We installed a Bozak loudspeaker system and, knowing that there would be adverse criticism if it was thought that Miss Taylor could not perform without microphones, I tried to make it as unobtrusive as possible. It was not the star, however, who was the problem. Her projection and diction were more than adequate. The difficulty was with some of the other American actors, one or two of whom were more used to working in television and did not have the technique for playing out to a large audience. Everything was directed towards the stalls (orchestra) so that the people seated in the two balconies only ever saw the tops of their heads. When the director kept asking for the microphone levels to be increased, I warned that the London critics might be unkind if it became too obvious. Could the actors not speak up – and perhaps look up? The director passed these comments on to the cast, but the worst offender declared that there was nothing he personally could do about it because his voice was in the baritone range and everybody knew that *"deep voices do not carry".* After that extraordinary statement, we increased the level of amplification – and still nobody in the balconies could understand what he was saying.

Back in 1968, I was once asked by the actor/manager, Sir Bernard Miles, to install a reinforcement system for a play at his Mermaid Theatre in Puddle Dock in the City of London. I went along to a rehearsal and, although I was doing myself out of business, I queried whether it should be necessary to amplify the voices in such a small theatre with excellent acoustics. Standing at the back of the auditorium, it was only the younger members of the cast who could not be heard. Complaining about drama schools no longer teaching the art of enunciation and projection, he agreed to go down and have a word with them. I was then given an extraordinary demonstration of the vocal technique of an actor of the old school. He gathered the cast around him and gently suggested that they should be constantly aware of the people at the back of the auditorium. Some of these actors had been inaudible during the rehearsal but, with his back to me and speaking in a conversational tone, every syllable of what Bernard Miles was saying came across as clear as a bell.

At the time of writing, plays are not generally amplified in the West End (long may it last!), as they are normally produced in one of a number of intimate and well-designed 19th century theatres where the acoustics are excellent.

Surprisingly, a voice enhancement system was actually installed in the Olivier Theatre, one of the National Theatre's two main stages, during the mid 1990s. The acoustics of this auditorium are notoriously poor, for which a great deal of the blame has to be laid at the door of the architect, Denys Lasdun. During the design process for the building, Richard Pilbrow complained that the ceiling was too high for angling the spotlights from the lighting bridges. He was told that it could not be changed because the height was stipulated by the acoustic consultant. After the auditorium had been built, Richard met the acoustician who said that his ceiling reflectors were far too high to be effective, but he had been told by the architect that Richard required this height for his lighting. When the theatre had been open for a few weeks, the artistic director Peter Hall, concerned about complaints of inaudibility, told me of a letter he had been shown which was written by a female member of the company in which she said *"The only way to be heard in the Olivier is to move down stage centre and shout. The only problem is that Dame Peggy Ashcroft or Sir Ralph Richardson have always got there before you."*

As it would have been very costly to close the Olivier theatre and virtually rebuild the auditorium, the then artistic director, Richard Eyre, decided around 1995 to install a complex American acoustic enhancement system employing a number of distributed microphones relaying the actors' voices to banks of small loudspeakers sited within the auditorium. The basic idea was that these banks of loudspeakers would perform the same function as correctly placed acoustic reflectors. According to sound designer Paul Groothuis, it did not work because the distant microphones picked up indistinct voices plus all manner of background sounds. It was a case of garbage-in-garbage-out.

Two years later, the next artistic director, Trevor Nunn, asked Paul if he could solve the problem. The answer was yes, but only if he was given the funds to install a completely separate system with three proscenium arrays and distributed loudspeakers on time delay and – big question mark – if the actors could be persuaded to wear radiomikes. It was put to the company and once leading actor Sir Ian McKellan declared that he would agree if it meant that he could be understood in the far corners of the auditorium, then the rest fell in line. Naturally, not everyone was comfortable with the situation, but there was no comment from the public until, two years later, someone informed the press. An outcry ensued at the very thought of the finest actors in the country resorting to microphones, and critics began to write about the unnatural sound at the National Theatre. Paul Groothuis was invited to appear on the BBC's 'Today' programme to justify the perpetration of such a calumny. Initially, he was given a tough time, but his detractors had the wind completely taken out of their sails when he reminded them how the critics used to regularly mention the audibility problem in the Olivier, but that all comment had ceased since introducing the enhancement system – and that was two years before. They only noticed the microphones now (or thought they did) because they had been told about them. The National Theatre continued with the vocal reinforcement and soon everybody forgot about it.

Return to natural sound

As DEMONSTRATED in the Olivier Theatre, with so many different types of processors and electronic aids available, it became possible to achieve a natural sound for the amplified voice and distribute it equally to every seat in the house. For example, the Meyer SIM (Source Independent Measurement) system, first introduced in 1984, can make an acoustic analysis of the sound system at different points in the auditorium and display the frequency and phase responses on a screen at the mixing console. Corrective adjustments can then be made to equalizers and time delays, even during a performance when the presence of the audience will change the natural reverberation time and often soak up some of the higher frequencies. Decisions about loudness, of course, will always remain with the sound designers or whoever is employing them. Similarly, the balance between music and vocals will continue to be a matter of cooperation (sometimes battle) between the musical director and the soundman. Of course, the best audio system will still be disastrous in the wrong hands.

18 SOUND DESIGN IS
HERE TO STAY

From the early days of electric sound right up to the end of the 1970s, people specialising in theatre sound were a rare breed. Even during the 1980s, despite significant technical advances, it was still a small number of inspired and dedicated individuals, mostly self taught, who dominated the West End and Broadway. In New York, the groundwork for the many people who have a career as sound designers today was quietly being laid out by a handful of innovators such as Jack Mann, Robert Maybaum, Jack Mitnick, John Shearing and his son Jack, Saki Oura and Tommy Fitzgerald. These people operated almost in secret, because the very idea of sound reinforcement was seen as a deficiency in the abilities of the performers.

As we have seen, the first proper acknowledgement that someone was actually responsible for the sound on a Broadway show did not occur until Abe Jacob negotiated a credit for Jesus Christ Superstar in 1971. The obvious amplification of the rock musical, beginning with Hair three years previously, meant that producers could no longer pretend that the sound system did not exist. Nor could they ignore the fact that it was vital to the success of the show. They capitulated and sound design credits became generally accepted. Sound designers were not, however, recognized by the union IATSE until 2004, and there was still no category for sound in the TONY awards.

During the early days in Great Britain, R G Jones, Jack Bishop or his son-in law Bill Spragg would oversee the installation and, once satisfied that it was working, hand it over to the stage management. It was then up to the director to decide playback volumes for the effects or the level of the microphones if they were being used. Installations from Stagesound were handled in the same way until the introduction of the wireless microphone. Dick Lock or Roger Westgate from Stagesound's hire department would often be in attendance during rehearsals to sort out technical problems and advise on sound levels, but they were not given proper sound design credits. For ten years or so from 1959, I enjoyed a solo run in the West End as sound designer except, of course for my colleague Antony Horder during the later years. Then, in 1970, a rock musical called Catch My Soul transferred from the Royal Exchange Theatre in Manchester to London. A local electronics enthusiast employed as the theatre's head of sound, Ian Gibson, received a sound design credit on that show. Paradoxically, the producer who brought the show into London was my colleague at Theatre Projects, Richard Pilbrow.

As budgets increased, equipment became more sophisticated and the contribution of the sound designer became accepted. More people were attracted into the profession and designers were able to demand worthwhile fees and even royalty

payments. Whereas the largest fee I ever received was £500 for designing
Jesus Christ Superstar in 1972, within five or six years the next generation
of designers was receiving, by comparison, remarkable rewards for working on
large scale musicals.

Although I designed revivals of West Side Story and A Funny Thing Happened
On The Way To The Forum in 1984 and 1986 respectively, I did very little work
in the live theatre after 1978. By then, I was heavily involved as a consultant working
on new buildings. It also has to be said that I was not comfortable with the
proliferation of wireless microphones and what I felt was an unnatural sound
being demanded by producers and directors.

Abe Jacob told me that he retired from sound design in 1999 because he was not
sure he could handle the constant advancements in technology with computers,
samplers and MIDI control. He decided to leave it to the younger guys who have
grown up with all this stuff; people like Tom Morse and Steve Kennedy. *"Andrew
Bruce and Martin Levan did major things in the era of musical spectacles by
making sound much more exciting for the theatre-goer, but there is now a whole
new group of talented young designers. For example, Jonathan Deans, now working
in Las Vegas, was our sound mixer on Evita in London. Steve Kennedy, who mixed
Evita in New York, is now designing shows like The Producers. Otts Mundeloh
was an engineer on A Chorus Line on Broadway and has now become an
important freelance designer. But remember, despite
all the technology, what it all comes down to in the end,
is that set of ears. You decide what sounds right and
what sounds wrong – and that is why people hire you."*

Richard and Peter Fitzgerald, through their company
Sound Associates, werevery active as designers
during the 1970s and 1980s. Peter Fitzgerald had
more Broadway credits than most during the 1990s,
continuing as a major player into the 21st century.

Peter Fitzgerald, 2007

One of the young designers making their mark during
the 1980s was Tom Morse, working on such original
Broadway productions as They're Playing Our
Song, Joseph And The Amazing Technicolor
Dreamcoat, Sunday In The Park With George
and Good Vibrations. Listed below are some of the
other leaders of this new wave of sound experts who,
by innovating and pushing the frontiers of technology,
changed the way that sound design became regarded
both in the West End and on Broadway.

Tom Morse, 2007

Otts Munderloh

Otts Munderloh,
2003.

OTTS MUNDERLOH IS ONE of the most successful of Broadway sound designers whose credits include BARNUM, DREAMGIRLS, MY ONE AND ONLY, BIG RIVER, GRAND HOTEL, THE SECRET GARDEN and CRAZY FOR YOU.

Otts always knew he wanted a career in the theatre, but it was a question of what. While at college in Baltimore, he knew David Merrick's electrician Joe Donahue, also from Baltimore, who advised him to choose between one of two up and coming departments in the theatre, winches and sound. It was true that electric winches were being used more and more to move scenery and trucks, but he knew nothing about engineering and the idea had little appeal. He had no electronics training either, but he did like fiddling with hi-fi equipment, so mixing audio looked like it could be more fun.

In 1969, Joe offered him a job mixing sound on a ten month national tour of I DO, I DO and he took time off from college to do it. The main loudspeakers were Altec bass cabinets, each with two 811 horns mounted one over and one under. A pair of these were rigged each side of the proscenium for the orchestra, another pair for the mezzanine, and there was just a pair of horns for the balcony. The show was mixed on two Altec 1567 mixers, one for foot-mikes and the other for two shot-guns, from a position in the auditorium. The big touring theatres did not mind losing a few seats for a sound control, but it was very different in New York.

The tour ended in September and he returned to college, but in the Christmas break, the electrician from I DO, I DO called from Florida to say that they had just fired the follow-spot operator on COMPANY and would he like to do it. Apparently, there was a point in the show when the follow spot had to pick up the star in a blackout and the operator had taken so long searching the stage that, when he eventually found her, the audience gave him a round of applause. Otts pointed out that he had no experience with follow-spots but the reply was: *"You've got to be better than what we had. Get yourself on a plane to Florida."*

After four months as a follow-spot man, he returned to college once more. But every now and then there would be requests to substitute on shows in New York. He ran the sound on PROMISES PROMISES for a while and then mixed HELLO DOLLY on an Altec 1567 from a control position located backstage way up on the fly floor! On that show there were five foot-mikes and Carol Channing wore one of the early wireless microphones. Apparently, stars could be very proprietary about their sound men. Carol Channing insisted on David Merrrick's man, Bob Nabaum, being there. She felt safe with him. Similarly, Mary Martin always wanted Joe Donahue to be around.

In 1974, a job on ULYSSES IN NIGHT TOWN starring Zero Mostel, led to mixing sound on a tour of SEE SAW where he first met Abe Jacob and director Michael

Bennett. *"There was one wireless microphone on that production to pick up an actor in a hospital bed that moved around the stage. It was fixed to the frame of the bed. That was in the days when if the bed moved upstage, you turned the level of the microphone down – because they were moving further away. You wanted it to sound natural, not in-your-face like they want it today. That is the style of theatre sound mixing I really prefer, but the producers and directors do not want this anymore. Just because you can have forty microphones on a show, it is not necessarily better. Theatrically, it is often worse."*

That same year, Otts was asked to take over the tour of MACK AND MABEL and bring it into New York, and then Abe Jacob asked him to mix CHICAGO. During the run, Abe and Michael Bennett came into the theatre one night and invited him to move to the theatre across the street to be sound operator for A CHORUS LINE. That was in 1975. The following year, when the show was produced in London, he went as Abe's assistant and taught Jonathan Deans how to mix the show. Soon after that, Otts started designing in his own right with AIN'T MISBEHAVIN' and BALLROOM in 1978 and THE 1940S RADIO HOUR in 1979 and BARNUM in 1980.

I was amused at his attitude to the producers who ask him to specify the best equipment for their shows, but have not made sufficient provision in their budgets. When presented with the rental cost, they ask him what reductions he can make. On these occasions he has been known to say: *"Well, you let me know how many principals you are going to cut and then I can omit some radio-mikes"* or he might ask: *"Exactly which part of the show do you not need to hear?"*

Tony Meola

FROM THE MID 1980S, Tony Meola has been one of New York's most in-demand sound designers, with credits on more than twenty-six Broadway productions including KISS ME KATE, GUYS AND DOLLS, FORUM, HIGH SOCIETY, SMOKEY JOE'S CAFÉ, ANYTHING GOES and WICKED in New York (2003) and London (2006).

Tony Meola, 2007

In common with many designers, he strives to have the sound appear to come from the performers and not from the loudspeakers. He spends a great deal of time trying to achieve a natural sound with the right balance between pianissimo and forte. *"Sound designers sometimes get blamed for ruining a show by making it too loud, but this is usually because some producer or director steps in and asks for the volume to be pumped up to generate more 'excitement.'"* Paradoxically, he won a Drama Desk award for one of his louder shows, THE LION KING (1997), whereas the subtle sound of, say, A SWEET SMELL OF SUCCESS (2002), which took an enormous amount of work and creativity, was completely ignored. Nevertheless, he remains hopeful that one day there will be a greater understanding and appreciation of what the soundman contributes to the art of theatre.

Steve C Kennedy

Steve C Kennedy,
2007

DURING THE 1980S, Steve Canyon Kennedy was the production engineer on such Broadway hits as CATS, STARLIGHT EXPRESS, SONG AND DANCE, CARRIE and PHANTOM OF THE OPERA before becoming a sound designer in his own right.

From the early 1990s, his New York credits include THE WHO'S TOMMY (Drama Desk Award), revivals of CAROUSEL and HOW TO SUCCEED IN BUSINESS WITHOUT REALLY TRYING, TITANIC, AIDA, THE PRODUCERS, HAIRSPRAY. JERSEY BOYS (Drama Desk Award) and MARY POPPINS (2006). He likes having the entire cast and members of the orchestra individually miked as it gives him complete control. It also provides the opportunity to produce a larger than life sound where a musical requires that extra impact. On the whole, he has not experienced any major conflicts with directors or producers on the style of sound for a show. They pretty much leave him alone. Although he does not favour digital mixing consoles at present, he feels that this is inevitably the way things are going.

Julian Beech

BRITISH DESIGNER, Julian Beech was in charge of sound for the Royal Shakespeare Company before joining Theatre Projects Consultants where he helped to oversee audio installations in the two main auditoria at the National Theatre. Some months prior to the opening of the National in 1976, he was appointed their first head of sound. Having spent more than two years there in a managerial role setting up a successful department of designers and operators, he left to join Autograph. Here, as a director of the company and a sound designer, he worked on many West End shows, included SONG AND DANCE and a popular revival of THE SOUND OF MUSIC in 1981. Because of ill health, Julian retired from Autograph in 2001.

Julian Beech at the controls of the Trident 'Fleximix' desk on THE SOUND OF MUSIC at the Palace Theatre, 1981. Note the cartridge machines on the right.

Andrew Bruce

JOINT FOUNDER-DIRECTOR of Autograph Sound, Andrew Bruce began his career at the Glyndebourne Festivale Opera in 1968. He was appointed head of sound at the Royal Opera House, Covent Garden in 1971 and a year later was co-founder of Autograph Sound. Andrew's specialist work in musicals began with involvement on technical installations in London for Abe Jacob on CATS and EVITA, Jack Mann on SWEENEY TODD and Martin Levan on SONG AND DANCE and STARLIGHT EXPRESS. In 1981, he was sound consultant for the original Paris version of LES MISERABLES and then designed the 1985 London production which, in October 2006, completed 8,500 performances to become the world's longest running musical. He was responsible for the Broadway production in 1987 and among his other London/New York shows are MISS SAIGON and MAMMA MIA. Andrew told me that working on Broadway was quite a shock at first, because of the precise way the union influenced the working day. This was very different from Britain whcrc you often work on into the early hours of the morning, or until you drop. Initially, he found the restrictions irritating but the advantages soon became apparent. *"You ordered your day, did not waste time, got your work done, and then went out to play."*

Andrew Bruce, 2005

Andrew admits that when his generation of sound designers was first given the tools to make things sound pretty good, many were guilty of creating a product that resembled a CD, paying little heed to the real sound of people's voices or the true energy of the performance. He soon learned that this was detrimental to the theatrical experience, and now ensures that his operators do not level everything out into one undynamic mix.

Although he has been a big fan of the Meyer UPA loudspeakers for many years, during the 1990s he came round to the principle of the line array that formed the basis of so many shows two or three decades earlier. They are not suitable for every occasion, but the modular versions with their ease of rigging and their control of directivity have become increasingly popular with designers.

Andrew uses the SIM system (Source Independent Measurement) for aligning and equalizing his speakers, but relies for a final judgement on his ears. Aware, however, that his hearing will have changed over the years, he likes his younger assistants to give their opinion – just to ensure that he has not made the system appallingly bright and sizzling.

Derrick Zieba

Derrick Zieba,
2003.

DERRICK ZIEBA ENJOYED a successful career in theatre sound for twenty-five years before making a name for himself handling large scale concerts and international award ceremonies.

Derrick's first job after leaving the technical/stage management course at the London Academy of Music and Dramatic Art was with Theatre Projects, where he worked in the equipment rental department and mixed shows at night. That was in 1974. He then moved on to be head of sound at the Crucible Theatre in Sheffield before joining the National Theatre in 1976 as assistant to Julian Beech, eventually taking over from him. For eight years, he ran the department and designed numerous shows including an award winning production of GUYS AND DOLLS.

His next move was to become the leading sound designer/engineer for TP Services Limited (an equipment rental company that had recently been acquired by the Samuelson Group from Theatre Projects) working on major corporate events, designing West End shows and managing installations for musicals such as PHANTOM OF THE OPERA. Having gained valuable experience in the burgeoning trade show market, he decided to strike out on his own. His company, Dimension Audio Limited formed in 1990, not only worked on large corporate events, but handled some prestigious theatre installations including the revival of JOSEPH AND THE AMAZING TECHNICOLOR DREAMCOAT at the Palladium. By 1999, his skills as a designer were so much in demand that he decided to part from the company to concentrate on this activity. One of his most prestigious projects was Live Event Sound Supervisor, coordinating all of the sound requirements for the Queen's Golden Jubilee Concerts in 2002, transmitted live around the world from the gardens of Buckingham Palace. These two concerts, one classical and one rock and pop, featured such musical legends as Kiri Te Kanawa, Rostropovich, Sir Paul McCartney, Eric Clapton & Brian Wilson. In 2006, he reprised this role at Buckingham Palace for the Queen's 80th Birthday Celebration, broadcast live on the BBC.

Rick Clarke

Rick Clarke,
2004.

FOR BRITISH SOUNDMAN Rick Clarke, the starting point of any design is to ensure that the audience will not be aware of the loudspeakers once the lights go out. A man after my own heart, he likes his systems to be imperceptible. Although he had no background or training in electronics, like many successful soundmen he has a love of music and, consequently, a good ear. After studying Art and Design at college, he became friendly with some young musicians who were forming a band called Medicine Head. Inevitably, he became their roadie and put together a PA system with WEM columns. That was in 1972. It was not until Jim Douglas, head of audio at TSL, offered him a job that he became interested in sound effects, the structure of sound and how it all worked in a theatrical setting. In 1980, he joined the National Theatre and worked there for four years with Rob Barnard and Derrick Zieba. Whilst at the National, he started exploring ideas for making the sound emanate from the lips of performers rather than from boxes on the side walls. These ideas were developed with colleagues Tony Oates and Mark Burgin and together they formed their company, The Sound Department. Their first opportunity to attempt 'natural imaging' was in 1985 when Rick secured the audio design for ME AND MY GIRL. The critics made no mention of the sound – but that was a compliment to Clarke. In those days, it was not unusual to read condemning reviews of disembodied voices emanating from the side walls of the theatre.

Clarke amicably parted company with the Sound Department in 1993 to become a freelance designer, since when he has designed the sound on many West End productions including the London production of CHIGAGO.

"I'm an egalitarian designer, I believe everyone should hear the same thing, whatever the seat. This has proved expensive because it requires more speakers, more delays, and more matrix outputs. But with the advent of digital control some of the problems of more complicated designs have been solved – you can be even more defined". He's not alone in using the physics of time delay and the Haas effect to pull the sound image into the heart of the action, but he was one of the pioneers.

Martin Levan

THE PERSON WHO PROBABLY had the most radical effect on the way sound design was perceived in the 1980s was not initially a theatre man at all. From the mid-1970s, Martin Levan worked as a recording engineer and producer at Morgan Studios in London, where he often handled sessions for Andrew Lloyd-Webber. At the end of 1981, Andrew telephoned him out of the blue to ask if he fancied getting involved in the theatre. His response was: *"What's that?"* – and he was only half joking, because most of the past ten years had been spent incarcerated in a basement studio with little time for theatre-going. Andrew explained that

Martin Levan,
2006.

his new show, SONG AND DANCE, was based on two albums recorded at the Morgan studio. One half was a ballet based on "Variations", composed by Julian Lloyd-Webber, which Martin had engineered. The other half was a dramatic story portrayed in a series of songs called TELL ME ON A SUNDAY. Martin knew the piece as he had been involved in some of the sessions. The question was, would he supervise and mix the opening of the show? It was agreed that he would attend rehearsals and operate the sound console for the first few weeks of the run. What Martin did not know was that producer Cameron Mackintosh had already asked Autograph to supply the equipment and contracted Andrew Bruce and Julian

Beech as sound designers. Andrew and Julian were somewhat surprised, not to say a little peeved, when the first production meeting was attended by a recording engineer who had opinions on the types of microphones to be used, and was going to be in charge of the mixing desk.

Fortunately, they managed to work well together and Martin was able to suggest the inclusion of some studio techniques while, at the same time, learning a lot about how live theatre worked. After SONG AND DANCE, their cooperation continued with Martin Levan designing and Andrew Bruce of Autograph handling all things technical on several major musicals.

Soon after SONG AND DANCE opened, Cameron Mackintosh mounted the Broadway version of CATS at the Winter Garden Theatre (October 1982) and Lloyd-Webber once again asked Martin to act as his audio consultant. Abe Jacob, who had designed the original London show was the official sound designer, and he and Martin struck up a good working relationship. Unfortunately, a few days before the first public preview, Abe had a disagreement with the producer and walked out. With so little time available, Martin was asked to take over. This was only Martin's second experience of working in the theatre and he was suddenly thrown in at the deep end with the responsibility for a major Broadway musical.

At the first sound rehearsal, Lloyd-Webber complained that it sounded too much like a recording. After significant alterations were made to the loudspeaker rig and a few changes to the microphones, everybody was happy and that is how it remained for its run of well over 7,000 performances.

The following year, 1983, Martin's second show as designer was the London version of the Broadway show, LITTLE SHOP OF HORRORS, where he used the first Cadac theatre mixing desk, as mentioned in a previous chapter. This was followed, in 1984, by STARLIGHT EXPRESS with a computer-controlled console from Cadec.

On his next show, PHANTOM OF THE OPERA at Her Majesty's Theatre in 1986, Martin was asked by Andrew Lloyd-Webber if it was possible to create a natural sound that appeared to come from the stage rather than from loudspeakers on the proscenium. To achieve this kind of naturalness and transparency combined with audibility was going to be a challenge. Tests with various loudspeakers and enclosures brought him to two conclusions; firstly that the raw frame loudspeaker always seemed to lose something when placed in a box and, secondly, that a speaker in a box tended to pinpoint the source of sound.

This led to experiments with a 15-inch (38cm) Tannoy dual-concentric loudspeaker, which has an excellent frequency response, working in free air. Naturally, there was a lack of bass response, but this could be handled with the addition of some standard bass cabinets. The concept was to create a uniform dispersal of energy in the environment, rather than pointing loudspeakers at the audience.

The final installation had Tannoy loudspeakers, strung up on brackets with bits of wire and string, mounted within the scenic décor around the proscenium, augmented by loudspeakers on time delay distributed throughout the auditorium. Many of these were unusual in that they consisted of flat panels of polystyrene with transducers on the back. Manufactured by BES, they had a non-coherent phase dispersion which spread the sound with very little focusing effect.

Feedback was not a problem because filling the air with sound proved, in this instance, no more troublesome than using directional loudspeakers that reflect sound from walls and balcony fronts, often creating hot-spots on stage. Most feedback is low frequency and traditional cabinets produce more side dispersion at low frequencies than speakers working in air. Rear dispersion was not a factor because the back of the cones tended not to be facing the stage. Of course, the extensive use of wireless microphones also helped.

To assist with focusing the sound on the performer, the microphones had three different time delay settings to mirror the natural air-born sound of the actor being upstage, downstage or somewhere in between. This was manually operated for the original London production but, in New York, it was automated for the first time.

Having designed ten musicals in Her Majesty's, I know that the acoustics are particularly fine. Nevertheless, it took someone with limited theatrical experience and no preconceived ideas about what is supposed to work, to come up with such an unconventional idea. Relying on a great deal of reflected sound to enhance the natural acoustics of the architecture, Martin Levan managed to amplify the stage and the orchestra without it seeming to come from the loudspeakers. The concept has been admired by other designers, but not many have been tempted to try it. This is probably because it is very tricky to pull off. The design was refined and similar systems were incorporated on subsequent shows such as SUNSET BOULEVARD (London and Broadway, 1983/84), and two musicals directed by Hal Prince, KISS OF THE SPIDERWOMAN (Broadhurst Theatre, 1993) and a revival of SHOWBOAT (George Gershwin Theatre, 1994).

In 1988 Martin developed and pioneered the 'A-B System' to minimize the distortion caused by phasing problems with multiple radio microphones. It was first used on the Andrew Lloyd-Webber musical, ASPECTS OF LOVE at the Prince of Wales Theatre. Up until then, the only way of handling this unfortunate effect, which occurs when two people are in close proximity, was to fade out one of the microphones and try to pick up both performers on the remaining one. The A-B system went a long way to solving this problem by having one of the microphones on a duplicate, but completely separate, set of loudspeakers. This only became possible with the advent of the computer mixer bringing with it the facility to programme the routing of the radio-mikes from one system to the other.

Although not a 100% cure, it does drastically reduce the effect, particularly in the high frequencies. Another benefit is that it can help with microphone spill from one instrument to another in the orchestra pit. The careful selection of microphones to one or other of the systems provides more harmonious blending between instruments and it has the added bonus of broadening the sound of the entire orchestra.

Martin Levan retired from theatre sound design in the late 1990s, built a studio in the picturesque Welsh countryside and returned to his first love, recording; although when I talked to him in November 2006, he was contemplating an offer from a theatre producer.

Jonathan Deans

Jonathan Deans,
2005.

As a child actor with an interest in electronics, Jonathan was for two years a member of the Royal Shakespeare Company at Stratford-upon-Avon. There he met head of sound Julian Beech, who taught him how to edit tape. While still a teenager, Jonathan decided to abandon acting to become a technical assistant stage manager concentrating on sound. His first job in the West End was as sound operator on Absurd Person Singular where he met the equipment suppliers, Andrew Bruce and Phil Clifford, founders of the newly formed Autograph Sound Limited. He recalls how an extra loudspeaker was needed for the show and they had to go out and get a loan to pay for it. It really was early days.

After a spell working at the Royal Opera House, he operated the mixing desk for Autograph on A Chorus Line and then went on to Evita. Recognising his obvious talents, Andrew Bruce invited him to join the company as a sound designer. He worked on several musicals before deciding to try his luck in America. Following the completion of projects in 1990 for Universal Studios in Los Angeles and for Siegfried And Roy in Las Vegas, he received the LDI award for Sound Designer of the Year at the Live Design International tradeshow. This led to an invitation from Cirque du Soleil to work on another large-scale spectacle in Las Vegas, since when he has designed the sound for several more of their productions. He also has a number of credits on Broadway. If Martin Levan changed the way people thought about sound in the 1980s, Jonathan Dean's work with Cirque du Soleil has pushed the frontiers of audio technology even further. For the 2006 production of Love, based on remixed Beatles recordings, he designed a massively complex system to produce an all-encompassing spatial sound. The automated console has 280 outputs driving a mind-boggling 6,341 speakers. This includes three loudspeakers built into every seat in the auditorium. What next, one wonders?

Full Circle

The National Theatre in London has, at any one time, productions going on in three performance spaces. In 2003, when I visited the theatre, the team of engineers and technician-operators necessary to run the sound department was headed by technical manager, Rob Barnard. Yet another ex-Theatre Projects person, his involvement with the National Theatre began as a casual sound operator before being offered permanent employment in 1978. In their newly opened recording studio, Rob introduced me to senior sound designer Paul Groothuis.

Paul began his career as a technical instrument maker in his native Holland, but a weekend job at the local theatre made him determined to use his technical skills in a more creative way. A move to London to take a course in sound and stage management at the Central School of Speech and Drama led to three years working in recording studios, first as a tape operator and eventually as an engineer. In 1983, he started working at the National Theatre. After ten years of operating sound in the three theatres and on tour, he was given the opportunity to become a sound designer. In addition to creating effects for numerous plays in the National Theatre's repertoire, he was responsible for the sound reinforcement on many of their major musical productions, including CAROUSEL and MY FAIR LADY which both transferred to the West End and OKLAHOMA which ran on Broadway. In 2003, he went freelance, but remained an associate designer to the National Theatre.

Paul Groothuis in the National Theatre recording studio, 2003.

One of the first things that struck me about the new recording studio at the National Theatre was the absence of tape recorders. Everything is run by computers. I was told that a digital sampler and keyboard was first used in a production way back in 1986 to play in a few effects. The experiment was not repeated because the limited memory capacity of the Akai S900 could only hold a few short cues. They continued using Sonifex cartridge machines and Revox reel-to-reel tape recorders until, in 1989, they were able to purchase a sampler with sufficient memory to make it worthwhile.

I was more than amused when Paul Groothuis explained how, with the sampler, modern technology was at last able to provide the flexibility that I used to enjoy in the 1950s with my 78 r.p.m. records; i.e. the ability to play a selection of effects in rehearsal in any order. As he said:

"In your day, you used to choose your sounds and put them on individual records so that, with several turntables, you could actually mix the effects in the theatre. In rehearsal, if the director wanted to hear a different noise, you could give it to him.

Some thirty or more years later, we were able to do that again. The technology has improved but the technique is exactly the same."

He then explained his working method:

"After talking to the director and watching rehearsals, I spend a lot of time selecting sound effects to transfer into the sampler. I do not assemble anything in the studio. All the ingredients I think might be needed are sampled and assigned to keys on the keyboard so that I have a whole palette of sounds. Then, in the theatre, I can press a key and play a gunshot to the director on the correct loudspeaker. Usually, he will want to hear several alternatives and I can play them to him immediately. Then, instead of what you used to do manually with a fader, I can programme the attack and decay time and the maximum level so that when the key is pressed the effect will fade up at the predetermined speed, and when the key is released it will fade out as programmed. Any key can have one or a number of sounds with fade in and fade out profiles. The keyboard is only used in rehearsals as all the effects will be sequentially memorized in the sampler. During the show, all the sound operator has to do is press the "Next" button at the appropriate moment.

The sampler has 256 megabytes of memory and the playing time depends upon the bandwidth – or quality – selected. At 20k the sampler will record around 20 minutes of sound and at 10k it will memorize up to 40 minutes. In the theatre where the effect often comes out of a loudspeaker sitting behind three layers of cloth, whether it is 20k or 10k is usually not important. The fact that I am using digital equipment is great, but I worry more about the content than the quality. With your old 78 r.p.m. discs, the quality could not have been very good but that did not matter. It is all to do with having the right sound and the way it fades in and out theatrically and dynamically that counts. I spend a lot of time looking for the right ingredients and if something has a bit of hiss or a low level of extraneous noise, that is irrelevant. By the time the level of the bird track has been adjusted so that it does not intrude into the dialogue, no one will hear the background.

Of course, if one is using stereo the sampler will only give you half the playing time, but I normally record all the effects in mono. To my mind, spending ages trying to record a special perspective for the stage is a waste of time. Theatrical stereo often involves the movement of sound from one location to another – which you must be able to control – or it is a combination of different sounds coming from a number of locations. Spatial effects can also be controlled. For example, if I have an identical wind on two keys and play them separately on loudspeakers either side of the stage, they will sound the same. But if I slightly increase the pitch of one of them – easy to do – suddenly it broadens out and has much more depth. The same technique can be applied to gunshots, thunder, etc. Another spatial effect is generated by having, say, two explosions on different loudspeakers and programme them a few milliseconds apart. In the theatre, this kind of spatial sound can be very exciting because it has enormous breadth and it appears to have movement.

When we started using samplers, the limited memory meant that we sometimes had to load the next sequence of cues on to the hard disc during a performance.

This could be nerve racking because the glass discs they used then were prone to failure. You would lose the whole sequence and have to start again. We always allowed enough time to have three attempts at loading. Now, we have sufficient memory for any show and the equipment is much more reliable. Moreover, the price has come right down so, just in case, we always run two samplers in tandem. That way you get to sleep at night!"

Since my days struggling with the panatrope at the Arts Theatre Club in the 1950s, the technique for creating sound effects seems to have come round full circle. What has changed is the method. Back then, digital technology would have been the stuff of science fiction.

But whether you were throwing rocks into copper jars in the ancient Greek theatre, rolling cannon balls around the roof of an auditorium in the 1800s, or a 21st century audio engineer producing a whole range of amazing noises from a little black box, we were all striving for the same thing – to assist the telling of the story, to heighten the drama, and to help create a world that is believable.

19 A FEW MORE ANECDOTES

Missing the show

ONE OF THE THINGS you should never do is be late for a show, especially if you are responsible for a complicated sound plot and there is no understudy. I was guilty of this crime during the run of the musical BLITZ! at the Adelphi Theatre in 1962. Having worked late recording sound effects for another production, I arrived back at my room in London's Bayswater in the early hours of the morning. For some reason, perhaps I did not set it properly, my alarm did not go off. I was roused by my landlady knocking on the door, saying that she had received a phone call from some gentleman who seemed to think that I should be in some theatre or other. She had informed him that she would let me know if she saw me.

I glanced at the clock and was horrified to see that it was nearly 2.15 p.m. and there was a matinee performance starting at 2.30. In panic, I leapt out of the bed, threw on some clothes and dashed out into the street to find a taxi. I had made the decision not to telephone the company manager as this would have wasted several vital minutes. Consequently, nobody knew that I was on my way. I begged the driver to get me to the theatre as fast as he could; but I had, of course, picked an elderly taxi driver who seemed to stop for every pedestrian and slow down at every traffic light. Whilst sympathizing with my predicament and appreciating the urgency of the situation, he was not prepared to do anything that might jeopardize his licence.

The journey was interminable. By curtain up time we were only half way there and in the thick of London traffic. It was nearly a quarter to three when we arrived at the stage door. I raced up the four flights of stairs to the stage management office where the three tapes were kept – but the door was locked. I could hear on the dressing room loudspeakers that they must have delayed the show for at least ten minutes, but it was now well under way. I had missed the air raid siren and some airplane and bomb effects that started the show and they were about to arrive at the point where a group of people in an air raid shelter turn on the radio to hear a news bulletin. Praying that someone had taken the tapes to the control position, I set off on the tortuous journey to where it was located at the side of the upper circle. The only way to get there was by running all the way down to the stage door again and then tackling several flights of another staircase right up to the top of the building where a passageway ran across the roof of the auditorium to more stairs leading down to the side of the upper circle.

By the time I arrived, hardly able to breathe, one of the stage management team, Antony Horder (who later became my friend and colleague despite this debacle), was groping around in the dark desperately trying to find the mains switch. At that moment, we were about to miss the first radio cue. The actor turned the switch and when nothing happened he complained that there must be something wrong with the set. With great presence of mind, one of the other actors pretended to read a piece from a newspaper, brilliantly paraphrasing what should have come from the tape. The next cue was seconds away, another radio sequence. This started with Vera Lynn singing a song which was gradually taken up by the cast until, after the first verse and chorus, the orchestra joined in. How were they going to get out of that one? The system was now switched on, but there were only seconds to spare. I grabbed one of the tapes, slapped it on the machine, threaded it with fumbling fingers and fast forwarded to what I hoped was the right cue just as one of the actors said: *"Murphy, try your wireless again and see if it is working now."* With my heart in my mouth, I pushed the button, half expecting to hear an explosion or a fire engine. The gods were with me. Never have I been so pleased or grateful to hear the voice of Vera Lynn, or anyone else for that matter. Somehow, I managed to pull myself together and get through the rest of the show without incident. Subsequently, the company manager suggested, quite forcibly, that one of the stage management should learn to operate the show.

The boot was on the other foot on the opening night of a revival of KISMET at the Shaftesbury Theatre in March 1978. It was mainly a float-mike show with some orchestral enhancement and, unusually for me, I did not personally check through the entire system before the audience was allowed in. We had been rehearsing earlier in the afternoon and everything was working well, so what could possibly have gone wrong since then? Around fifteen minutes before curtain up, I became concerned that the sound operator was not in evidence. Valuable time was wasted as I searched for him backstage and then in the front-of-house bars. With only minutes to go, I moved to the control desk, ready to mix the show if he failed to turn up. Perhaps he had had an accident. It was then that I noticed the five AKG float-microphones sitting in their boxes neatly stored beneath the mixing desk. The orchestra had been in the pit for some time and the show was about to begin. Grabbing the microphones I barged my way through the groups of late-comers milling around at the side of the stalls (orchestra) down to the pass door and on to the stage. I told the stage manager to hold the show, but the musical director was already on his way to the orchestra pit to begin the overture. An assistant stage manager was dispatched to try and stop him. It was at this point I experienced one of the more embarrassing episodes in my audial career. Dressed as I was for the first night in a DJ with black bow tie and frilly shirt (it was the seventies!), I must have been a peculiar sight emerging from the prompt corner on to the stage in front of the house curtain, clutching a handful of microphones. The hubbub in the auditorium subsided. They probably thought that I was about to make some important announcement. There was a puzzled silence as I knelt on the floor and connected the first microphone then, as the truth dawned, there was muttering mingled with some laughter. Eventually, the fifth microphone was put in place. I then had to walk the entire width of the stage, with as much dignity as I could muster, back to the prompt corner. The long walk was accompanied by a sympathetic round of applause.

It was then a quick sprint to the control position at the rear of the stalls to bring up the orchestra microphones for the overture. Five minutes into the show, the missing sound operator appeared at my side, gasping: "Sorry, sorry. I can take over now." He was in such a state that I told him to go and sit down until he had recovered. It turned out he had forgotten that curtain up on the first night was an hour earlier than normal to allow the critics time to write their pieces for the morning papers. Not until he was sauntering up the street towards the theatre and noticed that the foyer was devoid of people, did he realize his mistake. That is when his blood pressure shot up and breathing became difficult. I well recognized the symptoms from that little incident on BLITZ! sixteen years previously.

Taking over at the last moment

THERE HAVE BEEN a number of occasions when I was forced to take over a show at the last minute under difficult circumstances. The most nightmarish was FIRE ANGEL, produced at Her Majesty's Theatre in 1977. This was a rock musical based on Shakespeare's MERCHANT OF VENICE (probably not the best idea). It all started, as these things often do, with a phone call from the musical director, Anthony Bowles, with whom I had worked on JESUS CHRIST SUPERSTAR. He told me that they were in the middle of previews, with only four days to go before the opening, and the sound was disastrous. Was I prepared to help? With so little time, there was not much I could do, but I agreed to go along that night and see if I could make any helpful suggestions.

At a meeting following the performance with Anthony Bowles and the producer, Ray Cooney, I could think of little to say that might be helpful. I mentioned that the reliance on chest-mounted wireless microphones (the practice in those days) for some of the louder numbers was never going to produce a full-bodied rock sound, but introducing wired hand-microphones was not an option at this point as it would necessitate a great deal of re-staging. What I did not touch on was the fact that the whole loudspeaker rig needed replacing.

After talking generalities for some time, the question I was expecting finally arrived. Would I take over? Ray Cooney did not care how much it cost. I could have whatever I wanted. A producer has to be pretty desperate to utter those words! Money, I explained, was not the problem. The crucial factor was time. How could we possibly install an entire sound system, introduce hand-held microphones and rehearse the necessary changes with the cast when the premiere was only three nights away? But, I was asked, if we did make the attempt, could it possibly sound worse than it did now? This put me on the spot. The answer had to be that I sincerely hoped not. That was it. After another ten minutes of emotional blackmail, it was finally agreed that we would have a go.

The lads in our hire store spent the next day assembling all the equipment including more than thirty microphones: six hand-held, four personal radio-mikes, floats, general coverage, and a full rig for the orchestra. That night, there was the embarrassment of having to load our equipment into the theatre while the other company was getting theirs out. By lunchtime the following day, we had everything up and running in readiness for the rehearsal scheduled for the afternoon. My chief sound operator, Claire Laver, was at the controls, having arranged for a deputy to stand in for her on the vocal desk at JESUS CHRIST SUPERSTAR. The rehearsal got off to a bad start. Valuable time was lost with the orchestra wanting some of their microphones repositioned and when that was sorted, the director wasted more valuable time on every number discussing the re-staging for the new hand-microphones. It was obvious by the time the musicians stopped for their break, that we would never get through the show. I informed the director that he would have to let me take charge. From then on, we cut from number to number with me on stage instructing members of the cast what microphone to use, where to pick it up, when to put it back, even where to stand. Then, as soon as Claire confirmed that she had an acceptable balance, we moved swiftly to the next song. Even so, we reached the end of the orchestral session before several pieces had been heard and, of course, the musicians downed their instruments and departed. For the remainder of the show, it was a matter of plotting the use of microphones with the cast and hoping for the best.

Under the extremely fraught conditions, Claire had not had time to write down all the microphone levels, but this was not a worry because I knew she had an incredible memory. During rehearsals, one could discuss the mix on any item in a show and she would be able to tell you the exact levels of any fader. But then came the bombshell: a message at the stage door stated that the deputy operator for SUPERSTAR was ill and could not make it. This meant that the only person who could possibly mix FIRE ANGEL that night was me.

Before she had to leave for the Palace Theatre, Claire only had time to write down some very basic notes on which microphones were used in each number. I would have to follow the script to keep abreast of who was going to sing and when. It did not help my nerves to be told by the producer that this last preview before the first night was to be attended by radio disc jockeys and other important people from the music recording industry. The lighting designer later told me that he had caught sight of me sitting behind the mixing desks just before curtain up, looking so sickly white that he thought I might not survive the performance.

Somehow or other, the cast remembered to pick up the right microphones and I managed to open the faders on time. The overall balance could have been improved but, at least, the lyrics were now audible. Even the radio-mikes worked. Over a very large scotch, I was effusively thanked by the producer for "saving the day" and promised the sound design on every one of his shows in the future. I may have saved the day, but I did not save the show. It was savagely attacked by the critics and only survived a few performances. Some months later, I heard that Ray Cooney was producing another musical, so I rang his office to talk about equipment and sound design. Despite several attempts, he was never available. The contract was awarded to a rival company. I was never asked to do another show for Ray Cooney. But was I bitter…?

I should have learnt my lesson when, a few years later, the production manager for a new show at the Victoria Palace rang to say that his 'star' refused to do any more performances unless the theatre sound system was replaced. Once again, I had my arm twisted. Once again we installed a complete rig overnight ready for an orchestral rehearsal in the afternoon before launching blindly into a public performance. The star was Max Bygraves, a comedian who had transformed himself into a major recording artist with many gold discs to his name. As far as he was concerned, the sound was the most important element in the show.

All went well and the only request was for much more foldback. He liked to hear himself a lot. We agreed to install a pair of column loudspeakers each side of the proscenium pointing at the stage. At the next performance, I was invited to meet the star in the circle bar after his first thirty-minute spot in the first act when he had a long gap before closing the show in the second half. One of his assistants jokingly warned me that I was unlikely to be bought a drink. However, when I took my seat, he expressed himself pleased with the general sound quality and did indeed ask what I would like to drink. Thanking him, I opted for a gin and tonic. Without pausing to register my response, he went on to talk about the foldback system and how his performance was affected if he could not hear himself clearly and that just a little more level would really make everything perfect. The discussion went on for some time and, eventually, the production manager went to the bar and bought me my gin and tonic. At then end of the show, there were no further notes, but I said that I would attend one more show.

The following night, during Mr Bygrave's spot in the first half, one of his assistants warned me that there was going to be trouble. It was nothing personal, but he knew the star would be unhappy because his big entrance when the spotlight hit him at the top of a glittering staircase had not received sufficient applause. This was always a danger sign. Sure enough, I was summoned to the bar and told that he could not perform unless the foldback was much louder. The amount of level we were pumping through these speakers was already affecting the overall quality of sound and I cautioned that any further increase would be seriously detrimental to what was being heard by the audience. The response to this was: *"Turn it up. I sing for me."* To which there could be no answer.

Although I was far from happy with the result, we were given the thumbs up when he came off between songs during the second act, and I thought we had cracked it. Not so. At the end of the show, when the entire cast were on stage taking their bows, Mr Bygraves suddenly signalled for the orchestra to stop playing. Then, to sixteen hundred bemused people, not to mention the other performers and musicians, he made a speech about there being new sound equipment in the theatre and how the sound people sitting up there (pointing us out) always say it is impossible to tune the system without an audience. *"So I am going to sing another song, so that we can get it right."* There followed a discussion with the musical director and a rustling of musical parts in the orchestra pit until, finally, they struck up with one of his most popular songs, "Tulips from Amsterdam". It went something like this:

> When it's spring again I'll bring again
> More foldback *from Amsterdam*
> *With a heart that's true I'll give to you*
> *Tulips* and a bit more bass
> *I can't wait until the day you fill*
> That's better *arms of mine*

Like the windmill keeps on turning
Try some treble *keeps on yearning...*

And so on for several verses, until he was happy and brought the song to a conclusion with a flourish. There was wild applause from the audience, pleased to have witnessed something extra for their money. The cast, on the other hand, had been left standing there like lemons with some finding it difficult to maintain even a sickly grin. In his dressing room afterwards, Max Bygraves said that he hoped I had not minded sorting out the foldback problem in that way. I replied that we had actually found it rather embarrassing and would have preferred some prior warning; but he shrugged this aside, assuring me that it had all been worthwhile.

In 1976, we had to endure a third experience of replacing an entire system, but this time, it was less traumatic. SIDE BY SIDE BY SONDHEIM was previewing at London's Mermaid Theatre, and although each member of the small cast was using a hand-mike, there were audibility problems. The previous year, I had been sound designer for Sondheim's A LITTLE NIGHT MUSIC, and he now asked me to see what could be done at the Mermaid. The simple answer was that the installed equipment, barely adequate for playing interval music, was certainly not suitable for vocal reinforcement. Once again, the lads in the workshop went into action and a replacement system was ready just in time for the following evening's performance. There being no spare sound operator available at such short notice, I found myself in the hot seat. It was not a difficult show, but I had only seen a few minutes of it the night before and there had been no time for any rehearsal. Consequently, some of the voices came as a surprise.

At the end of the first half, I saw Stephen Sondheim heading towards the mixing desk. I was ready to explain that the mixing would become much smoother once I had completed a show and had a chance to make a proper cue sheet. Before I could proffer my excuses, he grasped me by the hand, saying: *"Thank you so much. I can hear my lyrics."* Not only a genius, Mr Sondheim, he is undoubtedly a gentleman. Incidentally, that musical was produced by a young Cameron Mackintosh, and turned out to be his first big success when it transferred to the Wyndhams Theatre and then to Broadway.

Jack Mann had one of these crazy last minute experiences, only he was called in to replace a complete system for the New York production of GREASE on the day of the opening night. That was in 1971. As he said: *"I had never seen the production, there was no time for a rehearsal, and I was supposed to mix the show. They told me not to worry because the girl who had been mixing on the old system would be sitting by my side giving me the cues. The only problem was that nobody thought to tell the girl she was supposed to be there. So I was on my own with a system which included fifteen hand-mikes. I was so hyped up that I managed to get the right fader up every time a cast member picked up a mike. I was brilliant. The following night... I did not get a single cue right. It was disaster."* I do not believe that Jack would ever have presided over a disaster, but I know what he means.

Fire the sound operator

THE BRITISH SIXTIES rock star turned actor/singer, Tommy Steele, appeared in his own show at the Adelphi in 1971. The popularity he enjoyed from a large following of fans did not, unfortunately, extend to most of his fellow artistes and stage crew. Rehearsals were fraught affairs with members of the cast and production team receiving unnecessarily acid comments. Although he did give me a lecture at our initial meeting about where the loudspeakers should be placed and how many microphones should be used, the sound department escaped major criticism and we thought ourselves lucky. After the first couple of uneventful previews, we left the sound operator in charge, but one morning there was a panic call from the producer. During a taped sequence in the previous night's show where Mr Steele danced around the stage miming to his recorded voice, the brand new Revox machine had decided to slow down. Most of the audience did not realize that they were hearing a recording, so were amazed when he began to sing out of key and even more surprised when the voice ran down like an old wind-up gramophone. It was entirely due to a technical defect and by no means the fault of the man in charge. Nevertheless, the producer's dilemma was: *"My star refuses to perform tonight with that sound operator in the building"*. There was nothing for it. I agreed to take control that night, as long as the person who knew the show sat alongside to give me the cues. I was told that Mr Steele would look through the curtain before the show and would not perform if he saw the man. Consequently, we went into the performance with me at the mixing desk and the erstwhile sound operator sitting on the floor with the cue sheet, hissing instructions. Fortunately, there were no hiccoughs, but to expect someone to take over a complex sound show without any form of rehearsal, demonstrates a breathtaking ignorance of what is involved.

I could hardly believe it when the same producer, Harold Fielding, rang me three years later with exactly the same message: *"My star refuses to perform tonight with your sound operator"*. This time it was a different star, Michael Crawford, and the show was BILLY at Drury Lane. One has to admit that Mr Crawford always gave the public their money's worth, but he was not the easiest person to get on with backstage. On the whole, however, the sound department had experienced very little trouble with the star. I did have a worrying moment at the first rehearsal when the very loud orchestra struck up and even when Michael Crawford was standing twenty feet from the front of the stage, his radio-mike was picking up more band than voice. The lyric writer, Don Black, rushed up to the sound console and shouted above the din that the star could not be heard. This was patently obvious and I yelled back that the only live microphone at the time was Crawford's radio which meant that the band was too loud. Not seeming to comprehend this simple concept, he screamed hysterically: *"Turn up the knob!"* Not quite knowing how to react, I asked: *"Which knob would you like? I have about two hundred here."* *"I don't care."* he cried, turning on his heels, *"Just turn up the bloody knob!"* Of course, we then sorted out the stage to orchestra balance with the musical director. That is what rehearsals are for. But that kind of exchange was one of the reasons I gave up being a sound designer.

Having a light voice, Michael Crawford relied entirely upon his radio-mike, and the sound operator, Claire Laver, did a brilliant job making him sound good, even to the extent of dropping the fader whenever he took a breath. Knowing that she got on well with him and he appreciated her skills, I could not believe that *"My star refuses to perform..."* had anything to do with her technical ability. Sure enough, the reason for the hiatus turned out to be a failure of the equipment. As mentioned in chapter fifteen, we had arranged that Michael Crawford should always wear a second radio transmitter operating on a different frequency as a safety back-up. Unfortunately, during the previous night's performance, when the first microphone began to break up and Claire switched over to the stand-by system - horror of horrors - that one failed as well. There was absolutely nothing she could do from her operating position in a side box in the second tier of the auditorium, but turn up the foot microphones. Not unreasonably, the star was not pleased and, later, when Claire visited his dressing room to explain and apologise, he gave vent to his feelings in no uncertain terms. As the failure of technical equipment was very regrettable, but in no way caused by negligence or incompetence, she was equally upset and made it clear that she no longer wished to have anything to do with the performer or his microphones. "So this actually turned out to be a case of the sound operator refusing to perform with the star."

Claire was not altogether unhappy to move on from Drury Lane because she claimed that the auditorium box housing the mixers was haunted by one of several ghosts inhabiting that theatre. The heavy door to the box would sometimes open or slam shut and, more annoyingly, spectral fingers sometimes tampered with the controls. Having checked everything before the audience came in, she would go away, making sure that the door was locked. Unlikely though it may seem, she insisted that various switches and settings would sometimes have altered on her return. She admitted talking sharply to the ghost, telling it to stop interfering as she had a job to do. Apparently, all would be well for a week or two, and then the meddlesome spirit would get up to its tricks again. When interrogated, two other sound operators who had worked in the same auditorium box, sheepishly admitted to having similar experiences.

Incidentally, the opening of BILLY on May 1 1974 was the last time I witnessed a first night audience in evening dress, as used to be the custom. To see the splendid auditorium at the Theatre Royal, Drury Lane entirely filled with gentlemen in black ties and ladies in their gowns and jewelry, was an unforgettable sight.

John Shearing told a good theatrical story about a Broadway musical starring Shelley Winters, who was obviously suffering at the time from a psychological problem about going on stage. The curtain was late going up every night because she would always find something or someone to complain about. *"I can't go on. Get me the producer."* or *"I can't go on. Get me the director."* The sound designer received an urgent call one day to get down to the theatre as the star wanted to sack the sound operator for some trivial reason that nobody could quite understand. He managed to sort out the problem and then came up with a scheme to protect the rest of the production team. He installed a set of coloured lights on the side of the stage to warn people that it was their turn to be in the firing line. The green light was for the producer, the yellow light was for the director, the blue was for the soundman, and so on. The were six or seven lights in all. If one of them walked into the theatre and saw their light on, they would turn right around and leave. There was also a button that flashed all the lights at once. If this happened, *everybody* went to the bar.

That story reminded me of an incident related by my colleague, Robert Ornbo, when he was lighting the original production of COMPANY in 1970. It involved Boris Aronson, the famous scene designer of such shows as FIDDLER ON THE ROOF, A LITTLE NIGHT MUSIC, CABARET and FOLLIES. Originally from Kiev, he moved to New York in his early twenties but never lost his thick Russian Jewish accent. One day during the technical rehearsals before the opening in Boston, there were some problems with the set and the head of the scenery construction team, a young man in charge of one of his first big shows, was given a hard time by the producer.

They broke for lunch and Boris and Robert left the theatre with the scenery man. Seeing that he was obviously upset by the experience, Boris stopped and took him by the arm. *"Listen"*, he said, *"I gotta tell you some advice about the American musical. There are two rules you got to know. The first rule is that there is always going to be a wictim. They will always find a wictim. They gotta have someone to blame when the show goes wrong. It could be the leading man, it could be the scenery man, it could be the lighting man. That is the first rule. Now the second rule is very important. The second rule is: NEVER BE THE WICTIM."*

When working on subsequent shows with Robert, we would often conjecture who was going to be the 'wictim' that particular day. One of us might say: *"I got it on Friday, you were in trouble yesterday. Who is it going to be the wictim today?" "How about Wigs!" "That's it! Wigs. It's got to be their turn to be the wictim."*

Trouble with the musicians union

DURING THE 1950s, recorded background music for drama productions in the British theatre was outlawed by the Musicians Union. Any music had to be played live by a minimum of six musicians. As this was not viable technically, artistically or financially, mood music could no longer be used. The National Theatre and the Royal Shakespeare Theatre had special arrangements with the union to use recorded music because they both had groups of musicians on their staff. Even this came to an end some time during the seventies, and it happened in the Theatre Projects recording studio. A session with the Royal Shakespeare Company was abandoned when one of the session musicians discovered that an actor was going to sing on stage to the recording. He objected on that grounds that, according to union rules, a singer had to be present when recording a backing-track. The union upheld the complaint and we never recorded music for a theatrical production again. The union had shot themselves in the foot, because it also put an end to any associated fees for composers, arrangers and session musicians, not to mention the income for studios.

Similar rules apply on Broadway; if any instrument is played on stage, the production is deemed to be a musical, and the minimum complement of union musicians has to be employed. This ruling came as a bit of a shock to the famous comedian, Victor Borge, whose one-man show in the 1960s consisted of telling jokes and playing the piano. Outraged at having to pay a number of expensive musicians for doing nothing, he was determined to stop them checking in at the theatre at the start of the show and then going off to earn another fee elsewhere. To ensure they stayed to the very end of the show, he made each one of them take a bow at the curtain call. After completing his final number, he would take a bow and walk off. The applause continued with the audience expecting his return. Instead, a completely unknown gentleman wearing a DJ would walk to the centre of the stage, solemnly take a bow, and walk off again. The audience was mystified, but when a another man appeared followed by another, and then another, they joined in on the joke – although not aware of the reasoning behind it. So successful was this ending to the show that when he came to London, where the union did not insist on employing musicians for no reason whatsoever, he recreated the event with several stagehands wearing an assortment of overalls, tweed jackets and caps. When I saw this show, we were all rolling in the aisles by the time the great man himself eventually emerged to take the final bow.

Theatre Projects fell foul of the Musicians Union on a production of A STREETCAR NAMED DESIRE starring Claire Bloom at London's Piccadilly Theatre in 1974. Mixed in with various street noises and sounds of life in a tenement block, the director, Ed Sherrin, wanted to hear some New Orleans jazz music as though coming from a distant radio. The union refused permission for this, suggesting that five musicians should be employed to create the effect. The union's representative had his bluff called when asked if he could produce an authentic New Orleans jazz band, and a compromise was reached. It was agreed that we could use the recording so long as we employed a live pianist to play along with it. A piano was installed in the wings but it was far too loud and sounded ridiculous. At my suggestion, it was moved to a dressing room where I could use a microphone to control the level and mix it in with the recording. This was more satisfactory. During one of the previews, Ed Sherrin asked for the level to be taken down a little. This, he thought, sounded better. But what if I took it down a bit more? Yes, even better. And what if I faded it out completely? Even better still!

The pianist turned up every night for the show, donned a headset to hear the jazz record, waited for the cuelight and then played the music that had been specially transcribed for him – and nobody ever heard a note.

SOURCES – PART ONE

1   "Acoustics and Acting in the Theatre of Dionysus Eleuthereus" – B Hunningher 1956

2   "A Study of the Use of Sound Effects in Elizabethan Drama" – James Wilson Brock 1950

3   Julian Rhodes Dream organs – www.ondamar.demon.co.uk/organs.htm

4   "A History of Theatre Sound Effects Devices" – Max Culver

5   "The Staging of Religious Drama in Europe in the Later Middle Ages", edited by Peter Meredith and John E Tailby, 1983

6   "Scenes and Machines on the English Stage during the Renaissance" – Lily B Campbell, 1923

7   "The Theatre, a Concise History – Phyllis Hartnoll, 1968

8   "Shakespeare's Use of Off-Stage Sounds" – Frances Ann Shirley, 1963

9   "The Elizabethan Player" – David Mann, 1991

10   "A Dictionary of Stage Directions in English Drama 1580-1642" – Alan C Dessen, 1999

11   "Trucs et Decors – La Machinerie Theatrale" – Georges Moynet, 1893

12   "Noise off" – Frank Napier, 1936

13   "Cambridge Guide to Theatre" – Martin Banham, 1988

14   "De Architectura, Book V" – Marcus Vitruvius Pollio (translated by Joseph Gwilt), 1874

15   "Signs and Wonders in the Imperial Cult: a new look at a Roman religious institution in the light of Rev 13:13-15. Journal of Biblical Literature 103/4 – Steven J Scherrer, 1984

16   "Ancient Greek Gadgets and Machines" – Robert S Brumbaugh, 1966

17   "Efficiency of 13th Century Acoustic Ceramic Pots in Two Swiss Churches" – Desarnaulds, Loerincik and Carrelho (paper presented at Noise-Con 2001)

18   A Brief History of American Theatre www.dgillan.screaming.net/stage/th-ushist.html

19   American Theatre History webhost.bridgew.edu/adirks/ald/courses/hist/hist_Amer.htm

20   Stage Lighting Design – Richard Pilbrow, 1997

SOURCES – PART TWO

1   "An International History of the Recording Industry" – Pekka Gronow and Ilpo Saunio.
Translated from the Finnish by Christopher Moseley.
Cassell ISBN 0-304-70590-X

2   "The Audible Past" by Jonathan Sterne, 2003

3   BBC Television programme

4   "The Golden Age of Radio" – Dennis Gifford, 1987
B T Batsford (London) ISBN 0-7134-4234-4

5   "America On Record" – Andre Millard
Cambridge University Press
ISBN 0-521-47544-9

6   Website – Western Electric

7   Website – Bell Telephone Company

8   Website – Altec history

9   Website – JBL
"A Brief History of James B. Lansing and James B. Lansing Sound, Incorporated"
– John M. Eargle

10 Website – AEG

11 Website – Siemens

12 Website – History of Public Address – www.historyofpa.co.uk

13 Website – Sony

14 Library of Congress – Motion Picture, Broadcasting and Recorded Sound Division.
Washington, D. C. 20540 USA

15 Website – Private Line's Telephone History – Tom Farley
www.phonewarehouse.com/HistoryTelephone

16 Website – The History of Microphones – www.inventors.about.com

17 "Sound Recording" by Copeland
BBC Publications

18 Website – EMI archives

19 "From Tin-foil to Stereo" – Oliver Read and Walter L. Welch, 1959
Publisher: Howard W Sams and Company, Inc.
ISBN 0-672-21206-4

20 Website – Phonautograph.com

21 Website. A Timeline of Audio/Video Technology

22 Klaus Blasquiz – museum of sound equipment in Paris

23 Website – Shure

24 Website – Texas Instruments

25 Website – Chronology of Personal Computers – Ken Polsson

26 Website – inventors.about.com

27 Website – BBC History

ACKNOWLEDGEMENTS

Thanks go to many people who assisted with this book
including special gratitude to:

Rob Barnard, Klaus Blasquiz, Jenny Brett, Andrew Bruce, Stan Coutant,
Max Culver, Jonathan Deans, Marion Dhaems, Professor Victor Dixon,
Dan Dugan, Randy Earle, Richard Fitzgerald. Bill Graham, Matthew Griffiths,
Pekka Gronow, Paul Groothuis, Catherine Hail at the London Theatre Museum,
Jennifer Hoare, Florian von Hoffen, Professor Peter Holland, Antony Horder,
Abe Jacob, Robin Jones, John Kilgore, John Leonard, Martin Levan, Phil Leaver,
Dick Lock, Iain Mackintosh, Jack Mann, John Meyer, John Moss, Reg Moores,
Otts Munderloh, Richard Pilbrow, Julian Rees, Tony Robinson, Geoff Shearing,
Jack Shearing, Dennis Short, Dennis Stripp, Professor Oliver Taplin, Professor
Peter Thomson, Richard D. Thompson, Judy Walton, Charlie Watkins,
RogerWestgate, Professor David Wiles, Derek Zieba, the staff at the Library
of the Performing Arts at the Lincoln Center and at the New York Public Library.

Every effort has been made to ensure that photographic and
other material reproduced in this book is properly credited.

Musicals designed by David Collison in London's West End

1961	The Pub Show	Comedy
1962	Blitz!	Adelphi
1963	A Funny Thing Happened on the Way to the Forum	Strand
	Pickwick	Saville
	Half a Sixpence	Cambridge
1964	Maggie May	Adelphi
	She Loves Me	Lyric
1966	On the Level	Saville
	Ad Lib (Larry Adler/Libby Morris)	Fortune
1967	Fiddler on the Roof	Her Majesty's
	The Four Musketeers	Drury Lane
1968	Sweet Charity	Prince of Wales
	Cabaret	Palace
1969	Mame (Led by Antony Horder)	Drury Lane
1970	Kiss Me Kate	Coliseum
	'Erb	Strand
	The Great Waltz	Drury Lane
	Tommy Steele at the Adelphi	Adelphi
1971	Tyger	Albery Theatre
	Oh Kay!	Vaudeville
1972	Company	Her Majesty's
	Applause	Her Majesty's
	Jesus Christ Superstar	Palace
	Trelawney	Prince of Wales
	I and Albert	Piccadilly
	Tom Brown's Schooldays	Cambridge
1973	Joseph and the Technicolor Dreamcoat	Albery
	Kingdom Coming	Roundhouse
	Pippin	Her Majesty's
	Grease	New London
1974	John Paul George Ringo & Bert	Apollo
	The Good Companions	Her Majesties

	Billy	Drury Lane
	Hair (Revival)	Queens
	Royalty Follies	Royalty
	Rocky Horror Show (Re-mix)	King's Road Theatre
1975	Jeeves	Her Majesty's
	Dad's Army	Shaftesbury
	A Little Night Music	Adelphi
	Pilgrim	Roundhouse
	Gulliver's Travels	Mermaid
1976	Side by Side by Sondheim	Mermaid
	Side by Side by Sondheim	Wyndhams
	Julie Andrews Show	Palladium
	Bing Crosby Show	Palladium
	Carte Blanche	Phoenix
1977	Fire Angel	Her Majesty's
	SwingalongaMax	Victoria Palace
	Hair (Revival)	Her Majesty's
1978	Kismet	Shaftesbury
1978	Travelling Music Show	Her Majesty's
1981	I'm Going to Get My Act Together And Take It On The Road	Queens
1984	West Side Story (Revival)	Her Majesty's
1986	A Funny Thing Happened on the Way to the Forum (Revival)	Piccadilly

Musicals designed by Antony Horder in London's West End

1969	Danny La Rue at the Palace	Palace
	Phil the Fluter	Palace
1970	Carol Channing and Her Ten Stout-Hearted Men	Drury Lane
	Jacques Brel is Alive and Well and Living in Paris	Duchess
1972	Behind the Fridge	Cambridge

INDEX

THE AUTHOR:

David Collison's career in the theatre started as an Assistant Stage Manager at the Arts Theatre Club in 1955. His career spanned the use of mechanical wind machines, thunder sheets and 78 r.p.m. records, through to LPs, reel-to-reel tape machines, tape cartridges and CDs, right up to digital recording and sampling. He was privileged to know and work with the pioneers of amplified sound in the UK. In 1962, he was the first person to receive a programme and poster credit for sound design.

During more than thirty years working in the theatre from the mid 1950s, the author knew and worked with the two people who formed the original British theatre sound companies, Jack Bishop in the 1930s and R G Jones in the 1940s. He was also involved with Bill Walton whose company, Stagesound, introduced tape machines and took over as the market leader in the 1960s.

As the leading sound designer in the UK for some fifteen years, David Collison was responsible for a number of innovations including the first mixing desk ever to be used in a West End musical. He designed the sound on more than fifty major musicals including FIDDLER ON THE ROOF, COMPANY, CABARET, and JESUS CHRIST SUPERSTAR. He also worked for Sir Peter Hall at the Royal Shakespeare Theatre and for Sir Laurence Olivier on the inaugural season of the National Theatre Company. As a sound consultant and director of the Theatre Projects Group, he designed audio systems for the Barbican Theatre, the National Theatre and numerous others in the UK and around the world.

In 2007, the USITT (United States Institute of Theatre Technology) honoured David Collison with the Harold Burris-Meyer Distinguished Career in Sound Design Award.

"As a young director, I was fortunate enough to encounter a technician of genius: David Collison. He could cue a sound to a tenth of a second – by hand on a pick-up. We did not have tape then. Surrounded by three or four turntables and a mass of records, he built up a sound track which was at one with the dialogue.... and although he has for many years been able to do the impossible with sound, he has the humility of every great theatre technician. He knows that sounds, lights, and elaborate effects are nothing if the words are not just, and the actor expressing them true. This book is like the man: modest, precise, and unexpectedly humorous. I believe it will prove invaluable."

SIR PETER HALL
From the foreword to STAGE SOUND